STANDARD GRADE | GENERAL | CREDIT

MODERN STUDIES
2007-2011

Publisher's Note

We are delighted to bring you the 2011 Past Papers and you will see that we have changed the format from previous editions. As part of our environmental awareness strategy, we have attempted to make these new editions as sustainable as possible.

To do this, we have printed on white paper and bound the answer sections into the book. This not only allows us to use significantly less paper but we are also, for the first time, able to source all the materials from sustainable sources.

We hope you like the new editions and by purchasing this product, you are not only supporting an independent Scottish publishing company but you are also, in the International Year of Forests, not contributing to the destruction of the world's forests.

Thank you for your support and please see the following websites for more information to support the above statement –

www.fsc-uk.org

www.loveforests.com

© Scottish Qualifications Authority
All rights reserved. Copying prohibited. No part of this publication may be reproduced, stored in a retrieval system, or transmitted in any form or by any means, electronic, mechanical, photocopying, recording or otherwise.

First exam published in 2007.
Published by Bright Red Publishing Ltd, 6 Stafford Street, Edinburgh EH3 7AU
tel: 0131 220 5804 fax: 0131 220 6710 info@brightredpublishing.co.uk www.brightredpublishing.co.uk

ISBN 978-1-84948-178-6

A CIP Catalogue record for this book is available from the British Library.

Bright Red Publishing is grateful to the copyright holders, as credited on the final page of the Question Section, for permission to use their material. Every effort has been made to trace the copyright holders and to obtain their permission for the use of copyright material. Bright Red Publishing will be happy to receive information allowing us to rectify any error or omission in future editions.

[BLANK PAGE]

G

2640/402

NATIONAL
QUALIFICATIONS
2007

TUESDAY, 22 MAY
10.20 AM – 11.50 AM

MODERN STUDIES
STANDARD GRADE
General Level

1   Read every question carefully.

2   Answer all questions as fully as you can.

3   If you cannot do a question, go on to the next one. Try again later.

4   In question 3, answer **one** section only; Section (A) The USA **or** Section (B) Russia **or** Section (C) China.

5   Write your answers in the answer book provided. Indicate clearly, in the left hand margin, the question and section of question being answered. Do not write in the right hand margin.

SCOTTISH
QUALIFICATIONS
AUTHORITY

©

SYLLABUS AREA 1—LIVING IN A DEMOCRACY

QUESTION 1

(a)

Describe **two** ways in which supporters of a candidate can help during an election campaign.

To answer this question, you may wish to use the drawing above.

(Knowledge & Understanding, **4** marks)

QUESTION 1 (CONTINUED)

(*b*)   Study the information below, then answer the question which follows.

Political Participation by British voters

Survey Result

Question: Which of the following political activities have you been involved in?

Activity	2001	2005
Signing a petition	43%	60%
Contacting your councillor	46%	43%
Attending a meeting or rally	38%	43%
Contacting a local council official	64%	41%
Taking part in a demonstration or protest	9%	22%
Contacting a government official	24%	20%
Contacting your Member of Parliament	33%	28%

Write down **two** conclusions about changes in political participation in Britain.

You must **only** use the information above.

You should write **one** conclusion about **each** of the following.

• The change in the most popular political activity from 2001 to 2005

• The activity which has shown the least change in participation from 2001 to 2005

(Enquiry Skills, **4** marks)

[Turn over

QUESTION 1 (CONTINUED)

(*c*)

> *Shop Stewards help union members in a number of different ways.*

Give **two** problems that a *Shop Steward might help their members* with.

For **one** of these problems, describe how the Shop Steward might help.

To answer this question, you may wish to use the drawing above.

(Knowledge and Understanding, **4** marks)

QUESTION 1 (CONTINUED)

(d)　Study Sources 1 and 2 below, then answer the question which follows.

SOURCE 1

UK Trade Union Membership 2001–2005

Year	Men	Women	Total
2001	3,636,000	3,210,000	6,846,000
2002	3,532,000	3,308,000	6,840,000
2003	3,500,000	3,320,000	6,820,000
2004	3,432,000	3,353,000	6,785,000
2005	3,311,000	3,356,000	6,667,000

SOURCE 2

The Daily Herald

Report About Pay

In 2005, the average hourly pay for all workers was £10·21 compared to only £8·75 in 2001. Workers who belong to a trade union enjoyed a pay rate of £11·38 in 2005, whereas workers who were not members got an average of £9·72. There are still big differences in the rates of pay received by different groups of workers.

Workers benefit from being members of a trade union. Membership of trade unions continued to increase for some groups of workers.

View of Salma Khan

Using **only** Sources 1 and 2, give **two** reasons to **support** the view of Salma Khan.

(Enquiry Skills, **4** marks)

[Turn over

SYLLABUS AREA 2—CHANGING SOCIETY

QUESTION 2

(a)   Study the information below, then answer the question which follows.

Information on Millie Smith

Millie Smith is 72 years old and lives in a 4 bedroomed house which is too big for her. Her husband died recently and she feels lonely. She has always enjoyed having a garden. She has recently had a hip operation and finds it more difficult to move about or do the housework. Millie is starting to feel the cold more and more.

Millie wants to buy another house. She has seen the two houses below but is not sure whether **House A or House B** would **better meet her needs.**

House A — Ground Floor Flat

A ground floor, 2 bedroomed flat in a two-storey building with a shared central entrance.

There is double-glazing. Some more insulation and draught proofing is needed but this would be easy to do.

Elderly people live in the other 3 flats. All residents share a conservatory which looks onto a colourful garden.

House B — Bungalow

A one-storey, 2 bedroomed house. It would be straightforward to build a ramp and rails at the front to give easy access.

It has an overgrown garden, with many shrubs, that needs some work. There is a very pleasant garden summer-house for sitting in.

The bungalow is fully double glazed throughout and has full gas central heating. It is cheap to heat in the winter.

Using the information above, decide which house, **House A or House B**, would be the **better** choice for Millie Smith to **meet her needs**.

Give **two** reasons to **support** your decision.

You **must** link the information about Millie Smith to the house you have chosen.

(Enquiry Skills, **4** marks)

QUESTION 2 (CONTINUED)

(b) | *Some elderly people are healthier than other elderly people.* |

Give **two** reasons to explain why *some elderly people are healthier than other elderly people.*

(Knowledge & Understanding, **4** marks)

(c)

| *The government tries to help meet the needs of elderly people.* |

Describe **two** ways in which *the government tries to help meet the needs of elderly people.*

To answer this question, you may wish to use the drawings above.

(Knowledge and Understanding, **4** marks)

[Turn over

QUESTION 2 (CONTINUED)

(*d*) Study Sources 1 and 2 below, then answer the question which follows.

SOURCE 1

Scots spend too much time at work and work too hard!

Trade unions estimate that 16% of Scottish workers work more than 48 hours per week. Investigations have shown that regularly working more than 48 hours a week increases the risk of illness.

A survey on holidays found some interesting results. About 73% of Scottish workers said they often failed to take all their annual holidays. 37% of workers said they had been too busy to take their annual holidays, while 20% simply said that they had forgotten to take them. 50% also said that their annual holiday allowance of 20 to 25 days was not enough and should be increased.

SOURCE 2

Average weekly working hours for men	
Belgium	39·1
France	40·3
Greece	41·7
Italy	39·7
Portugal	42·1
Scotland	45·4
Sweden	40·2
EU Average	**41·3**

- Scottish men are the only men who work more than the EU weekly average.
- Working long hours can damage a worker's health.
- Very few Scottish workers fail to take all their annual holidays.
- Belgian men work the lowest number of hours.

Statements made by Sandy Brown

Using **only** Sources 1 and 2 above, write down **two** statements made by Sandy Brown which are **exaggerated**.

Using the information in the Sources, give **one** reason why **each** of the statements you have chosen is **exaggerated**.

(Enquiry Skills, **4** marks)

[Turn over for Question 3 on *Page ten*

SYLLABUS AREA 3—IDEOLOGIES

QUESTION 3

Answer **ONE** section only: Section (A)—The USA on pages *ten* and *eleven*

OR Section (B)—Russia on pages *twelve* and *thirteen*

OR Section (C)—China on pages *fourteen* and *fifteen*

(A) THE USA

(a)

> *People in the USA have many rights. They also have responsibilities that go with them.*

Describe **one** *right* that American people have.

Describe **one** *responsibility* that American people have.

In your answer you **must** use American examples.

(Knowledge & Understanding, **4** marks)

(b)   Study the information below, then answer the question which follows.

The New York Herald

Bush wins again — 4 More Years

George Bush was returned to power for a second Presidential term in 2004.

Bush said to his opponents "To make this nation stronger and better, I will need your support and I will work to earn it." Bush told Kerry that he was "an admirable, worthy opponent."

Presidential Election Results (2004)

% vote for the candidates

1%

51%

48%

- Bush
- Kerry
- Others

Percentage of voters turning out to vote		
1996	–	49·0%
2000	–	49·3%
2004	–	59·8%

In the 2004 Presidential election, the winner had a large majority. It also showed greater participation in politics by voters in the USA.

View of Eva Kaye

Using **only** the information above, give **one** reason to **support** and **one** reason to **oppose** the view of Eva Kaye.

(Enquiry Skills, **4** marks)

QUESTION 3 (A) (CONTINUED)

(c)

My father was poor. However, thanks to all that America has to offer, I have become rich and successful.

Give **two** reasons to explain why many American people have become rich and successful.

In your answer you **must** use American examples.

(Knowledge & Understanding, **4** marks)

(d)   Study the information below, then answer the question which follows.

Opinion Poll — A Comparison

The percentage of American people who are supportive of President Bush's performance in selected policy areas

Policy Areas	2003	2004	2005
The economy	42%	46%	35%
Handling of the war in Iraq	52%	48%	32%
US campaign against terrorism	70%	57%	58%
Overall performance as President	**52%**	**47%**	**40%**

Statements made by Martin Baxter, an American journalist

- The lowest level of support for President Bush has always been in his campaign against terrorism.
- In 2005 less people approved of Bush's handling of the war in Iraq.
- Support for his handling of the economy has steadily fallen each year.
- The electorate's support for the President's overall performance has declined each year.

Using **only** the information above, write down **two** statements made by Martin Baxter which are **exaggerated.**

Using the information in the Opinion Poll, give **one** reason why **each** of the statements you have chosen is **exaggerated.**

(Enquiry Skills, **4** marks)

NOW GO TO QUESTION 4 ON PAGE SIXTEEN

QUESTION 3 (CONTINUED)

(B) **RUSSIA**

(*a*)

> *People in Russia have many rights. They also have responsibilities that go with them.*

Describe **one** *right* that Russian people have.

Describe **one** *responsibility* that Russian people have.

In your answer you **must** use Russian examples.

(Knowledge & Understanding, **4** marks)

(*b*)   Study the information below, then answer the question which follows.

MOSCOW JOURNAL

Putin Wins Again

President Putin has been returned to power by the Russian electorate. This represents a terrific result for him. Russia now has a strong President for the next four years.

The result means that he now has the backing of the Russian people to get all his policies into law.

Presidential Election Results (2004)

% vote for the candidates

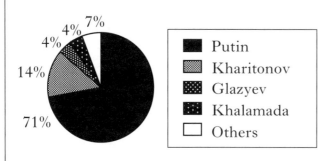

7%
4% 4%
4%
14%
71%

- Putin
- Kharitonov
- Glazyev
- Khalamada
- Others

Percentage of voters turning out to vote

1996	–	70%
2000	–	68%
2004	–	64%

> In the 2004 Presidential election, the winner had a large majority. It also showed greater participation in politics by voters in Russia.

View of Maria Chakvetadze

Using **only** the information above, give **one** reason to **support** and **one** reason to **oppose** the view of Maria Chakvetadze.

(Enquiry Skills, **4** marks)

QUESTION 3 (B) (CONTINUED)

(c)

My father was poor. However, thanks to all that Russia now offers, I have become rich and successful.

Give **two** reasons to explain why many Russian people have become rich and successful.

In your answer you **must** use Russian examples.

(Knowledge & Understanding, **4** marks)

(d) Study the information below, then answer the question which follows.

Opinion Poll — A Comparison

Question: How good a job is President Putin doing?

Comment	2000	2003	2005
Doing a good job	36%	42%	39%
Doing a fair job	20%	27%	32%
Doing a poor job	35%	27%	24%
Don't know	9%	4%	5%

Statements made by Alexia Gudrun, a Russian journalist

- More Russians thought Putin was "doing a good job" in 2005 than in previous years.
- In all three years, the majority of Russian people asked did not think he was "doing a fair job".
- In 2003, most Russians thought Putin was "doing a poor job".
- More Russians answered "Don't know" in 2000 than in other years.

Using **only** the information above, write down **two** statements made by Alexia Gudrun which are **exaggerated**.

Using the information in the Opinion Poll, give **one** reason why **each** of the statements you have chosen is **exaggerated**.

(Enquiry Skills, **4** marks)

NOW GO TO QUESTION 4 ON PAGE SIXTEEN

QUESTION 3 (CONTINUED)

(C) CHINA

(a) | *People in China have many rights. They also have responsibilities that go with them.*

Describe **one** *right* that Chinese people have.

Describe **one** *responsibility* that Chinese people have.

In your answer you **must** use Chinese examples.

(Knowledge & Understanding, **4** marks)

(b) Study the information below, then answer the question which follows.

Duyun Times

Amy Li's Surprise Win!

Communist Party candidate, Amy Li, won a place on the Duyun People's Congress yesterday.

She was not expected to win. Long serving representative, Zhao Lung, was a surprise loser. Amy has promised to work hard to improve the lives of all local people.

Duyun Peoples' Congress Elections (2005)

% vote for the candidates

14%

40%

46%

- ■ Amy Li
- □ Zhao Lung
- ▨ Xi Phuz

Percentage of voters turning out to vote

1995	–	85%
2000	–	88%
2005	–	91%

In the 2005 election, the winner had a large majority. It also showed greater participation in politics by voters in Duyun.

View of Zi Yan

Using **only** the information above, give **one** reason to **support** and **one** reason to **oppose** the view of Zi Yan.

(Enquiry Skills, **4** marks)

QUESTION 3 (C) (CONTINUED)

(c)

My father was poor. However, thanks to all that China now offers, I have become rich and successful.

Give **two** reasons to explain why many Chinese people have become rich and successful.

In your answer you **must** use Chinese examples.

(Knowledge & Understanding, **4** marks)

(d)   Study the information below, then answer the question which follows.

China's Urban/Rural split

Year	Total population	Urban population	Rural population
1995	1·21 billion	30%	70%
2000	1·29 billion	36%	64%
2005	1·30 billion	41%	59%
2010 (estimate)	1·31 billion	44%	56%

Statements made by Lye Zhang, a Chinese journalist

- The Chinese population has grown since 1995.
- The urban population of China will double between 1995 and 2010.
- The biggest rise in the total population came between 2000 and 2005.
- The urban population has always been smaller than the rural population.

Using **only** the information above, write down **two** statements made by Lye Zhang which are **exaggerated.**

Using **only** the information in the table, give **one** reason why **each** of the statements you have chosen is **exaggerated.**

(Enquiry Skills, **4** marks)

NOW GO TO QUESTION 4 ON PAGE SIXTEEN

SYLLABUS AREA 4—INTERNATIONAL RELATIONS

QUESTION 4

(*a*)

| Many different types of aid can help to meet the **needs** of some African countries. |

Describe **two** different types of aid which *help to meet the needs of some African countries.*

To answer this question, you may wish to use the drawing above.

(Knowledge & Understanding, **4** marks)

QUESTION 4 (CONTINUED)

(*b*)   Study Sources 1 and 2 below, then answer the question which follows.

SOURCE 1   SOURCE 2

NATO protects Afghans	Campaign proving difficult
Afghanistan is a poor country in Asia with Pakistan and Iran as neighbours. The mission by NATO forces in Afghanistan is the first they have undertaken outwith Europe.	NATO troops are involved in Afghanistan, a poor Asian country. Many local people have been forced to flee to refugee camps where the conditions are dangerous and filthy.
They are there to help train, build up and support the Afghan army in the war against the Taliban. They are being successful in making the lives of the people better and more secure by fighting the Taliban. Some Afghans have had to flee from the fighting but they have been moved to clean, safe refugee camps.	This is the first NATO campaign outside Europe and involves troops from many countries, including the United Kingdom. The campaign is very difficult with casualties mounting. The Taliban are proving hard to defeat as they are based in the mountains. Afghanistan is now suffering from lawlessness, misery and starvation.

Sources 1 and 2 give different views about **the involvement of NATO troops in Afghanistan**.

Write down **two** differences between these views.

You **must** only use information from the Sources above.

(Enquiry Skills, **4** marks)

[Turn over

QUESTION 4 (CONTINUED)

You are investigating the topic in the box below.

Scotland and the European Union (EU)

Answer questions (*c*), (*d*) and (*e*) which follow.

(*c*)   As part of the **Planning Stage**, give **two** relevant **aims** for your investigation.

(Enquiry Skills, **2** marks)

You decide to send an e-mail to your MEP to discover more about the topic.

(*d*)   Give **two** advantages of sending an e-mail as a way of finding out information for your investigation.

(Enquiry Skills, **2** marks)

QUESTION 4 (CONTINUED)

Whilst researching your investigation you discover the following website.

Use the information below to answer question (*e*).

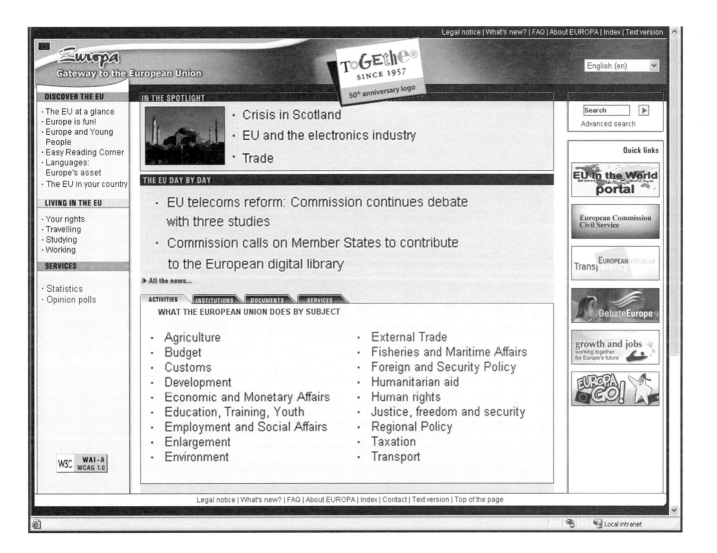

(*e*)   Give **two** ways you could use this website to find out more information for your investigation.

For **each** way, explain why it would be a **good** way to find out this information.

(Enquiry Skills, **4** marks)

[END OF QUESTION PAPER]

[BLANK PAGE]

STANDARD GRADE | CREDIT

2007

[BLANK PAGE]

C

2640/403

NATIONAL
QUALIFICATIONS
2007

TUESDAY, 22 MAY
1.00 PM – 3.00 PM

MODERN STUDIES
STANDARD GRADE
Credit Level

1 Read every question carefully.

2 Answer all questions as fully as you can.

3 If you cannot do a question, go on to the next one. Try again later.

4 In question 3, answer **one** section only: Section (A) The USA **or** Section (B) Russia **or** Section (C) China.

5 Write your answers in the answer book provided. Indicate clearly, in the left hand margin, the question and section of question being answered. Do not write in the right hand margin.

SCOTTISH
QUALIFICATIONS
AUTHORITY

©

[BLANK PAGE]

SYLLABUS AREA 1—LIVING IN A DEMOCRACY

QUESTION 1

(a)

The Daily Herald

OPPOSITION GROWS TO NEW GOVERNMENT LAWS

The Prime Minister has announced a package of new laws which he believes will improve the lives of the British people. They cover issues such as pensions, security and health. However, it is clear that many members of the public do not agree with these new laws and are ready to oppose the Government.

Describe, **in detail**, the rights that people have when opposing the introduction of new laws.

(Knowledge & Understanding, **4** marks)

(b)   Choose **one** of the following electoral systems.

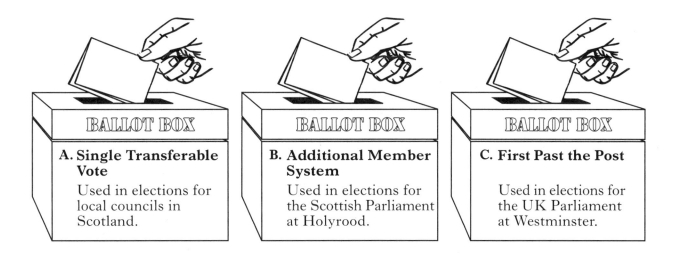

A. Single Transferable Vote

Used in elections for local councils in Scotland.

B. Additional Member System

Used in elections for the Scottish Parliament at Holyrood.

C. First Past the Post

Used in elections for the UK Parliament at Westminster.

Explain, **in detail,** the **advantages** of the electoral system you have chosen.

(Knowledge & Understanding, **6** marks)

[Turn over

QUESTION 1 (CONTINUED)

(c)   Study Sources 1, 2 and 3 below and opposite, then answer the question which follows.

SOURCE 1

UK General Election 2005: Selected Results

The UK RESULT			
Party	Vote (%)	MPs	Seats (%)
Cons	32	198	31
Labour	35	356	55
Lib Dem	22	62	10
SNP	2	6	1
Others	9	24	3

Scotland			
Party	Vote (%)	MPs	Seats (%)
Cons	16	1	2
Labour	39	41	69
Lib Dem	23	11	19
SNP	18	6	10
Others	4	0	0

Wales			
Party	Vote (%)	MPs	Seats (%)
Cons	21	3	8
Labour	43	29	72
Lib Dem	18	4	10
Plaid Cymru	13	3	8
Others	5	1	2

England			
Party	Vote (%)	MPs	Seats (%)
Cons	35·7	194	37
Labour	35·5	286	54
Lib Dem	22·9	47	8
Others	5·9	2	1

SOURCE 2

UK General Elections 1997 and 2005
Support for Selected Parties by Social class

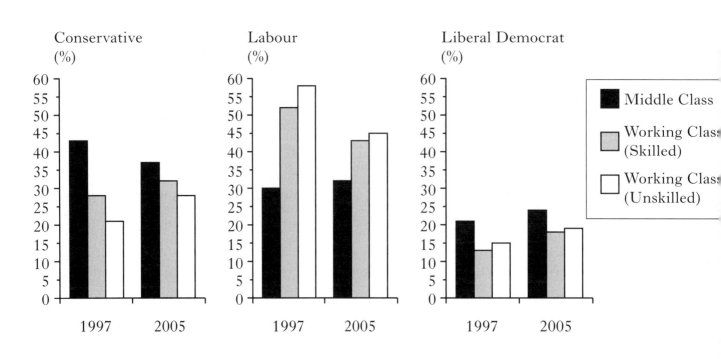

QUESTION 1 (c) (CONTINUED)

SOURCE 3

**UK General Elections 1997 and 2005
Support for Selected Parties by Age Range**

Age Range	Conservative		Labour		Lib Dem	
	1997 %	2005 %	1997 %	2005 %	1997 %	2005 %
18–24	25	24	50	42	17	26
25–34	27	24	50	42	17	26
35–64	31	33	43	38	18	22
65+	38	42	42	35	15	18

The Conservative Party did badly in all areas of the country. The Liberal Democrats, on the other hand, are the only party whose support increased amongst different age ranges and within different social classes compared with other parties, between 1997 and 2005.

View of Karen Mitchell

Using **only** Sources 1, 2 and 3, explain **the extent to which** Karen Mitchell could be accused of being **selective in the use of facts**.

(Enquiry Skills, **8** marks)

[Turn over

[BLANK PAGE]

SYLLABUS AREA 2—CHANGING SOCIETY

QUESTION 2

(a)

> *Some families are unable to meet the needs of their children.*

Explain, **in detail**, the reasons why *some families are unable to meet the needs of their children.*

(Knowledge and Understanding, **6** marks)

(b) Study the information below, then answer the question which follows.

Regional Unemployment in the UK (%)

Regions — North	1995	2005
Scotland	8·3	5·7
Northern Ireland	10·9	4·6
North East England	11·3	6·4
North West England	8·9	4·2
Yorkshire and Humber	8·6	5·0
West Midlands	8·9	4·3
Wales	8·8	4·4
Regions — South		
East Midlands	7·4	4·0
Eastern England	7·5	3·6
London	11·6	6·7
South East England	6·4	3·6
South West England	7·8	3·2
UK Average	**8·6**	**4·6**

In 1995, unemployment was a bigger problem in the North than it was in the South. Ten years on, the situation was the complete opposite.

View of Tom Hicks

Give **one** reason to **support** and **one** reason to **oppose** the view of Tom Hicks.

(Enquiry Skills, **4** marks)

QUESTION 2 (CONTINUED)

(c)   Study the information in the **"Focus on Families"** pamphlet below and opposite, then answer the question which follows.

Focus on Families

Introduction

Focus on Families looks at different types of families. Families in Britain have changed over the years.

Marriage and Divorce

More than 4 in 10 people over the age of 16 in the UK are married.

In 2005, the average age for first marriage was 31 for men and 29 for women. This had been 26 and 23 for men and women respectively 40 years earlier.

In 2005, the average age for divorce was 43 for men and 40 for women. This had been 39 and 37 for men and women respectively in 1995.

Marriages and Divorces in Britain

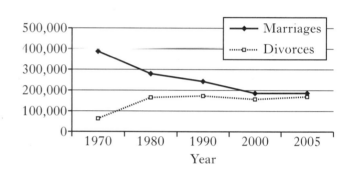

Family Structure

The total number of families reached 17 million in 2004. The "traditional" type of family has always been seen as a couple with dependent children. As the table shows, the percentage of families of each type in Britain has been changing. This may well have an impact on the welfare of dependent children.

People in each type of household (%)				
	1971	1981	1991	2004
One person	6	8	11	14
Families:				
Couple no children	19	20	23	25
Couple with dependent children	52	47	41	37
Couple with non-dependent children only	10	10	11	8
Lone parent family	4	6	10	12
Other households	9	9	4	4

QUESTION 2 (*c*) (CONTINUED)

Focus on Families (continued)

% of families that are lone parent families (Scotland)

Lone Parent Families

The main cities have a younger age structure than the overall population. As the map shows, there are wide variations in the distribution of lone parent families across Scotland.

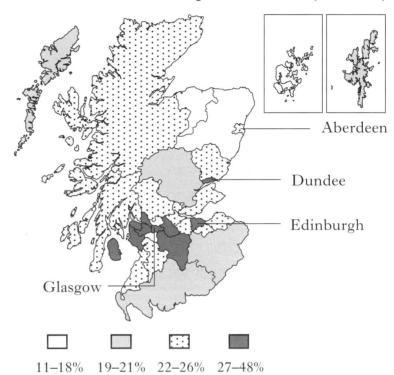

11–18% 19–21% 22–26% 27–48%

Families and Ethnicity

Some 9% of people in Britain are non-white. Ethnic groups differ in terms of family size and type.

62% of white families are married couples, 13% are cohabiting couples and 25% are lone parent families.

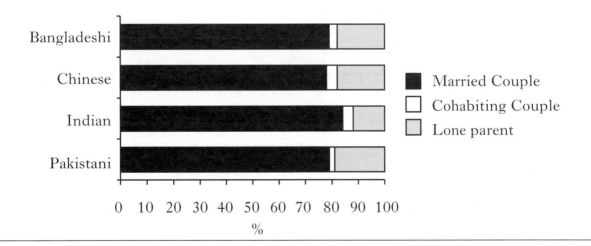

Using **only** the information from the "Focus on Families" pamphlet you must **make** and **justify** a conclusion about **all four** of the following headings.

* Changes in marriage and divorce in Britain.
* The link between changes in marriages and changes in the "traditional" family.
* The difference between the percentages of lone parent families in Britain and Scotland's four main cities.
* The main difference between ethnic minority families and white families.

(Enquiry Skills, **8** marks)

SYLLABUS AREA 3—IDEOLOGIES

QUESTION 3

Answer **one** section only: Section (A)—The USA on pages *ten* to *twelve*
                OR   Section (B)—Russia on pages *thirteen* to *fifteen*
                OR   Section (C)—China on pages *sixteen* to *eighteen*

(A) **THE USA**

(*a*)
> *Ethnic minority groups are now more likely to participate in politics in the USA.*

Explain, **in detail**, the reasons why *ethnic minority groups are now more likely to participate in politics in the USA*.

In your answer, you **must** use American examples.

(Knowledge and Understanding, **8** marks)

You have been asked to carry out **two** investigations.

The first investigation is on the topic in the box below.

> **Health care in the USA**

Now answer questions (*b*) and (*c*) which follow.

(*b*) State a relevant **hypothesis** for your investigation.

(Enquiry Skills, **2** marks)

(*c*) Give **two** relevant **aims** to help you prove or disprove your hypothesis.

(Enquiry Skills, **2** marks)

QUESTION 3 (A) (CONTINUED)

The second investigation is on the topic in the box below.

> **Education in the USA**

Now answer questions (*d*) and (*e*) which follow.

(*d*) While collecting information for your investigation you find out that your school has just started a twinning arrangement with a High School in the USA. You decide to **e-mail the Head Teacher** of the American school. You prepare the following e-mail. **Read it carefully**.

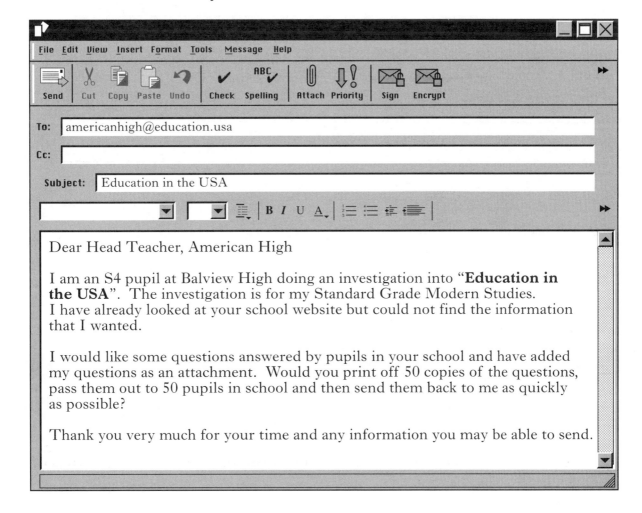

To: americanhigh@education.usa

Cc:

Subject: Education in the USA

Dear Head Teacher, American High

I am an S4 pupil at Balview High doing an investigation into "**Education in the USA**". The investigation is for my Standard Grade Modern Studies. I have already looked at your school website but could not find the information that I wanted.

I would like some questions answered by pupils in your school and have added my questions as an attachment. Would you print off 50 copies of the questions, pass them out to 50 pupils in school and then send them back to me as quickly as possible?

Thank you very much for your time and any information you may be able to send.

Give **one good point** and **one bad point** about **the content of the e-mail** above.

(Enquiry Skills, **2** marks)

QUESTION 3 (A) (CONTINUED)

(e)   Here is a copy of the questions you wish to send. **Read them carefully.**

EDUCATION IN THE USA
INVESTIGATION QUESTIONS FOR STUDENTS

Where there is a choice please circle your answer.

Question 1
Which racial group do you belong to?

White   Black   Hispanic   Asian   Native American   Other

Question 2
How many students in your school wear school uniform?

All   More than half   Less than half   None

Question 3
Are your school meals good and do students get them free?

Yes   No   Don't know

Question 4
Why do Blacks and Hispanics not do well at your school?

_____

_____

_____

Question 5
In what ways do you think your school could be improved?

_____

_____

After checking the questions with your teacher, you are told that **two** of the questions are **poorly worded**.

Identify the **two** questions that are **poorly worded** and then explain, **in detail**, why each needs to be changed.

(Enquiry Skills, **4** marks)

[NOW GO TO QUESTION 4 ON PAGE 19]

QUESTION 3 (CONTINUED)

(B) **RUSSIA**

(a)

> *Many people in Russia like the fact that they can participate in politics.*

Explain, **in detail**, the reasons why Russian people *participate in politics*.

In your answer, you **must** use Russian examples.

(Knowledge and Understanding, **8** marks)

You have been asked to carry out **two** investigations.

The first investigation is on the topic in the box below.

Health care in Russia

Now answer questions (*b*) and (*c*) which follow.

(b) State a relevant **hypothesis** for your investigation.

(Enquiry Skills, **2** marks)

(c) Give **two** relevant **aims** to help you prove or disprove your hypothesis.

(Enquiry Skills, **2** marks)

[Turn over

QUESTION 3 (B) (CONTINUED)

The second investigation is on the topic in the box below.

> **Education in Russia**

Now answer questions (*d*) and (*e*) which follow.

(*d*) While collecting information for your investigation you find out that your school has just started a twinning arrangement with a High School in Russia. You decide to **e-mail the Head Teacher** of the Russian school. You prepare the following e-mail. **Read it carefully**.

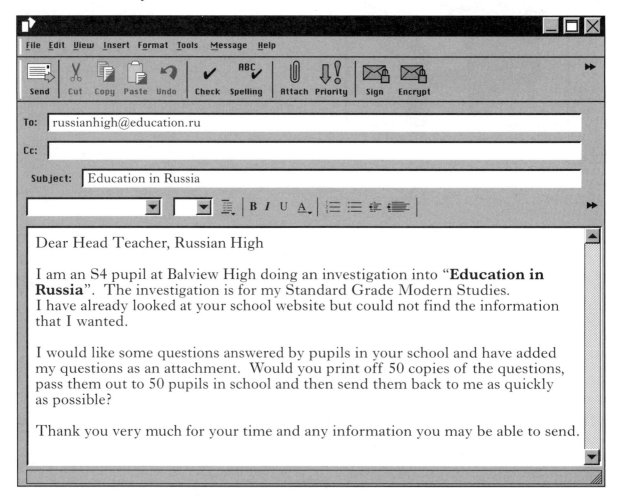

Give **one good point** and **one bad point** about the **content of the e-mail** above.

(Enquiry Skills, **2** marks)

QUESTION 3 (B) (CONTINUED)

(*e*) Here is a copy of the questions you wish to send. **Read them carefully.**

EDUCATION IN RUSSIA
INVESTIGATION QUESTIONS FOR STUDENTS

Where there is a choice please circle your answer.

Question 1
Which age group do you belong to?

11–12   13–14   15–16   17–18   Over 18

Question 2
How many students in your school wear school uniform?

All   More than half   Less than half   None

Question 3
Are your school meals good and do students get them free?

Yes   No   Don't know

Question 4
Why is it that girls always do better than boys at your school?

_____

_____

_____

Question 5
In what ways do you think your school could be improved?

_____

_____

After checking the questions with your teacher, you are told that **two** of the questions are **poorly worded**.

Identify the **two** questions that are **poorly worded** and then explain, **in detail**, why each needs to be changed.

(Enquiry Skills, **4** marks)

[NOW GO TO QUESTION 4 ON PAGE 19]

[Turn over

QUESTION 3 (CONTINUED)

(C)　**CHINA**

(a)　| *Many Chinese people have difficulties participating fully in politics.* |

Explain, **in detail**, the reasons why *many Chinese people have difficulties participating fully in politics.*

In your answer, you **must** use Chinese examples.

(Knowledge and Understanding, **8** marks)

You have been asked to carry out **two** investigations.

The first investigation is on the topic in the box below.

| **Health care in China** |

Now answer questions (b) and (c) which follow.

(b)　State a relevant **hypothesis** for your investigation.

(Enquiry Skills, **2** marks)

(c)　Give **two** relevant **aims** to help you prove or disprove your hypothesis.

(Enquiry Skills, **2** marks)

QUESTION 3 (C) (CONTINUED)

The second investigation is on the topic in the box below.

Education in China

Now answer questions (*d*) and (*e*) which follow.

(*d*) While collecting information for your investigation you find out that your school has just started a twinning arrangement with a High School in China. You decide to **e-mail the Head Teacher** of the Chinese school. You prepare the following e-mail. **Read it carefully**.

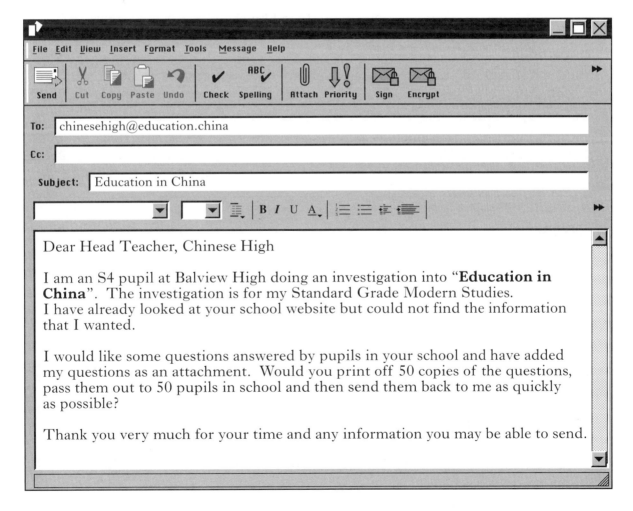

To: chinesehigh@education.china

Cc:

Subject: Education in China

Dear Head Teacher, Chinese High

I am an S4 pupil at Balview High doing an investigation into "**Education in China**". The investigation is for my Standard Grade Modern Studies.
I have already looked at your school website but could not find the information that I wanted.

I would like some questions answered by pupils in your school and have added my questions as an attachment. Would you print off 50 copies of the questions, pass them out to 50 pupils in school and then send them back to me as quickly as possible?

Thank you very much for your time and any information you may be able to send.

Give **one good point** and **one bad point** about the **content of the e-mail** above.

(Enquiry Skills, **2** marks)

QUESTION 3 (C) (CONTINUED)

(e)   Here is a copy of the questions you wish to send. **Read them carefully.**

EDUCATION IN CHINA
INVESTIGATION QUESTIONS FOR STUDENTS

Where there is a choice please circle your answer.

Question 1
Which ethnic group do you belong to?

Han   Zhuang   Uygur   Hui   Other

Question 2
How many students in your school wear school uniform?

All   More than half   Less than half   None

Question 3
Are your school meals good and do students get them free?

Yes   No   Don't know

Question 4
Why is it that children from rural areas always do worse at your school?

_____

_____

_____

Question 5
In what ways do you think your school could be improved?

_____

_____

After checking the questions with your teacher, you are told that **two** of the questions are **poorly worded**.

Identify the **two** questions that are **poorly worded** and then explain, **in detail**, why each needs to be changed.

(Enquiry Skills, **4** marks)

[NOW GO TO QUESTION 4 ON PAGE 19]

SYLLABUS AREA 4—INTERNATIONAL RELATIONS

QUESTION 4

(a)

> *The policies of the European Union (EU) try to meet the **needs** of member countries and their citizens.*

Choose **two** of the following policies.

- Single European Currency (Euro)
- Enlarged Membership
- Common Fisheries Policy
- Aid to the Regions
- European Defence Force
- Common Agricultural Policy

For **each** policy, describe, **in detail**, the ways in which it tries *to meet the **needs** of member countries and their citizens.*

In your answer, you **must** use recent examples you have studied.

(Knowledge & Understanding, **8** marks)

[Turn over

QUESTION 4 (CONTINUED)

(b)   Study the article below and the information in the radio debate opposite, then answer the question which follows.

FOCUS ON CHAD

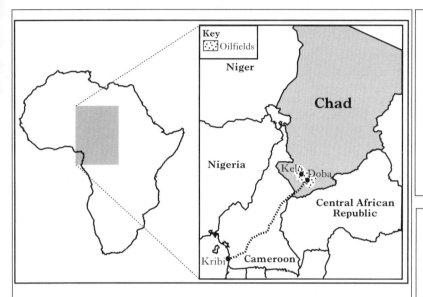

Health Services

There is a lack of access to medical services. Many remote villages never see trained medical professionals and people cannot afford to travel to modern hospitals in the cities. They rely on local people who lack proper training. Doctors expect to be paid in advance by patients before treatment and there is a shortage of drugs.

Economy

Over 80% of the population rely on basic farming and livestock for survival. 75% of the population live on less than a dollar a day.

Few people are sufficiently qualified to leave the land to seek well-paid employment. 80% of the population live below the poverty line. Over $1 billion is owed in debt. The World Bank helped Western businesses to develop an oil pipeline from Chad to Cameroon.

Introduction

Chad has many natural resources such as oil, uranium and gold which are under-developed. Only 200 sq km of farming land is currently irrigated and there are many natural hazards like drought. Lack of sanitation and clean water are major problems. The government is struggling to help its rapidly growing population.

People

Development Indicator	Chad	UK
Population	9·1 million	60·4 million
Population growth per year	3·0%	0·28%
Infant mortality per 1000 live births	94	5
Life expectancy	48 years	78 years
HIV/AIDS rate	5%	0·2%
Literacy rate	48%	99%

A conflict in Sudan has created a huge number of refugees which the government in Chad is trying to cope with.

Concerns of the people of Chad on selected issues

Question: What do you think is the most important issue facing Chad?

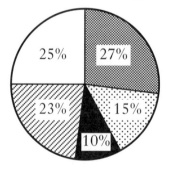

   �earth Health

   Education

   Employment

   Access to fresh water

   Farming improvement

QUESTION 4 (b) (CONTINUED)

RADIO DEBATE

World Radio brings you a studio discussion about the best way to tackle poverty in Africa. Today's debate focuses on Chad.

What makes your project best for Chad?
Hello. I'm **Simon Rose** and I represent Rose Energy. We believe in supporting governments such as Chad's as they understand local conditions. Large-scale projects such as oil production are the best way to develop a country.

Good morning. My name is **Chrissie Smith** and I work for a non-governmental organisation called Helping Hands. We help local communities develop at their own pace. Small-scale projects provide a long-term solution.

What would be the main focus of your project?
We are prepared to invest $1 billion to create a second oil field in Chad. We will build a new road network in the south of the country, benefiting other industries. We hope to build a city hospital close to our proposed oilfield. Villages along the pipeline will have water pumps installed. 2% of our profits will go to the government as tax which could be spent repaying debts.

Helping Hands believes that health care and contraception are the key issues facing Chad. We will train local women to provide free community health care, reducing the spread of HIV/AIDS. Ten clinics across Chad will be set up, each costing $20 000.

What other issues do you believe are important for the development of Chad?
Without oil I see no future for the country. The economy currently relies on cotton and cattle. Jobs and improved services will only come with the development of the oil field and new infrastructure. Big schemes are best as the money spreads down through society.

The other key areas are farming and education. We must improve the income of farmers. This is a major obstacle to development. Also, very few children go to school as they are needed on the farm. It is crucial to begin teaching these children so they can be offered a better future. Small locally managed community projects are best suited to countries such as Chad.

Project One
Rose Energy

Project Two
Helping Hands

Which one of these projects is more suitable for Chad?

Using only **Focus on Chad** and the **radio debate**, explain which project, Rose Energy or Helping Hands, would be **more suitable** to help Chad develop.

Give **detailed reasons** to explain your choice and also why you **rejected** the other option.

In your answer you must **relate** the information about Chad to the information about the **two** projects.

(Enquiry Skills, **10** marks)

[END OF QUESTION PAPER]

[BLANK PAGE]

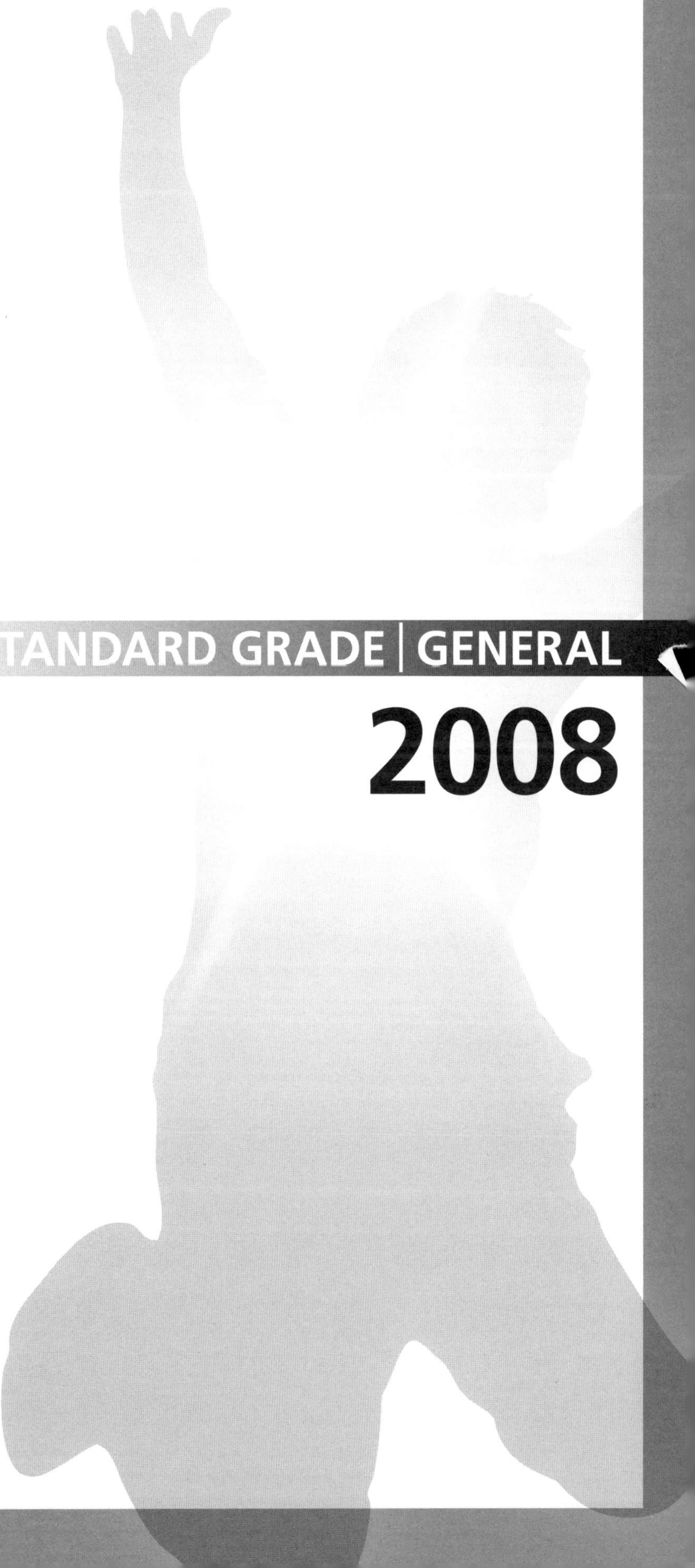

STANDARD GRADE | GENERAL

2008

[BLANK PAGE]

G

2640/402

NATIONAL
QUALIFICATIONS
2008

THURSDAY, 22 MAY
10.20 AM–11.50 AM

MODERN STUDIES
STANDARD GRADE
General Level

1   Read every question carefully.

2   Answer all questions as fully as you can.

3   If you cannot do a question, go on to the next one. Try again later.

4   In question 3, answer **one** section only; Section (A) The USA **or** Section (B) Russia **or** Section (C) China.

5   Write your answers in the answer book provided. Indicate clearly, in the left hand margin, the question and section of question being answered. Do not write in the right hand margin.

SYLLABUS AREA 1—LIVING IN A DEMOCRACY

QUESTION 1

(a)

> Members of pressure groups have rights and responsibilities.

Describe one **right** and one **responsibility** that members of a pressure group have.

To answer this question, you may wish to use the drawing above.

(Knowledge & Understanding, **4** marks)

(b)   Study Sources 1 and 2 below, then answer the question which follows.

SOURCE 1	**SOURCE 2**
VIEW OF MALCOLM BROWN	VIEW OF JANE RENNIE

SOURCE 1

VIEW OF MALCOLM BROWN

There are about 5 million members of ethnic minority groups in Britain. The number of MPs from such ethnic groups rose slightly in 2005.

We do not need special arrangements to attract more women into Parliament. After the 2005 General Election, the number of women in the House of Commons rose to a historic high. 128 female MPs were elected. This shows that women are now well represented in the UK.

This was election win number three for Prime Minister Blair and his party.

SOURCE 2

VIEW OF JANE RENNIE

The 2005 election was the third win in a row for Tony Blair and the Labour Party.

With 128 MPs, there are more women in the House of Commons than ever before. However, with less than 20% of the total, women in the UK are still poorly represented when compared to other European countries. We must find new ways to encourage more women to become MPs.

The number of representatives from Britain's 5 million or so ethnic minority population has increased a little from 13 to 15 MPs.

Sources 1 and 2 give different views about **representation in the House of Commons**.

Write down **two** differences between these views.

You **must** only use information from the Sources above.

(Enquiry Skills, **4** marks)

QUESTION 1 (CONTINUED)

You are investigating the topic in the box below.

> ### CAMPAIGNING IN ELECTIONS

Answer questions (*c*), (*d*) and (*e*) which follow.

(*c*) As part of the **Planning Stage**, give **two** relevant **aims** for your investigation.

(Enquiry Skills, 2 marks)

You decide to contact some political parties to help in your investigation.

(*d*) Give **two** ways in which you could contact the political parties.

For **each** way you have chosen, explain why it is a **good** way to get information to help in your investigation.

(Enquiry Skills, 4 marks)

You decide to use your local library to help with your investigation.

(*e*) Describe **one** way in which you could use your local library.

(Enquiry Skills, 2 marks)

[Turn over

SYLLABUS AREA 2—CHANGING SOCIETY

QUESTION 2

(a)

> The Government tries to help unemployed people find jobs.

Describe **two** ways in which *the Government tries to help unemployed people find jobs.*

To answer this question, you may wish to use the drawing above.

(Knowledge and Understanding, **4** marks)

QUESTION 2 (CONTINUED)

(*b*)

> *Technology has allowed many people to work from home.*

Give **two** ways in which *technology has allowed many people to work from home*.

For **each** way, explain why it has allowed many people to work from home.

To answer this question, you may wish to use the drawing above.

(Knowledge and Understanding, **4** marks)

[Turn over

QUESTION 2 (CONTINUED)

(c)   Study the information below, then answer the question which follows.

 **Inverdee Council**	**Inverdee Council to spend £150,000 on new scheme.** Inverdee wants to meet the needs of young unemployed people in one of its most deprived areas. These young people need help with completing job application forms. They also need to improve their interview skills and ICT skills.

Inverdee Council is not sure whether **Scheme A** or **Scheme B** would **best meet the needs of young unemployed people.**

Scheme A	**Scheme B**
A Digital Community Centre	**Personal Advisors**

This scheme digitally connects 12 local community centres in Inverdee. It aims to give local unemployed people basic to advanced ICT training. Locals will have access to multi-media technology, including computers, scanners, digital cameras and data projectors. The community centres will provide training, promote employment and assist in setting up new businesses. The scheme would target a range of groups including young people. Help will also be given in completing application forms for anyone who feels they need it.	Job hunters in Inverdee are to get help finding work. A local voluntary organisation wants to deliver a new service to help young people communicate better with possible employers. It will concentrate on improving interview skills but also offer work experience. The programme will be available to young people, aged 18 to 24, who are unemployed for six months or more. It will also give advice on filling in application forms for new jobs. The scheme is confident it will make a real difference in getting young people into quality employment in Inverdee.

Using the information above, decide whether **Scheme A** or **Scheme B**, would be the **better** choice for Inverdee Council to **meet the needs** of young unemployed people.

Give **two** reasons to **support** your decision.

You **must** link the information about the needs of the young unemployed people to the scheme you have chosen.

(Enquiry Skills, **4** marks)

QUESTION 2 (CONTINUED)

(d)   Study the table below, then answer the question which follows.

Self-employment by ethnic group			
	2001	**2003**	**2005**
White	11·0%	11·9%	12·0%
Pakistani	21·8%	22·5%	21·0%
Indian	12·5%	13·1%	12·5%
Chinese	19·1%	18·3%	16·0%
Black Caribbean	7·1%	9·7%	8·0%
Black African	6·6%	6·2%	6·0%
Bangladeshi	12·3%	9·9%	14·0%

Self-employment amongst Whites and Bangladeshis has grown every year.
Pakistanis had the largest decrease in self-employment between 2003 and 2005

View of Abigail Smith

Using **only** the table above, give **two** reasons to **disagree** with the view of Abigail Smith.

(Enquiry Skills, **4** marks)

[Turn over

SYLLABUS AREA 3 — IDEOLOGIES

QUESTION 3

Answer **ONE** section only: Section (A)—The USA on pages *eight* to *eleven*

OR Section (B)—Russia on pages *twelve* to *fifteen*

OR Section (C)—China on pages *sixteen* to *nineteen*

(A) THE USA

(a)

MAX'S TYRES Balance Sheet	
Sales:	$550,000
Profit:	$240,000
Tax:	$ 25,000

> *Starting up a business can improve the lives of some Americans.*

Describe **two** ways in which *starting up a business can improve the lives of some Americans.*

In your answer you **must** use American examples.

To answer this question, you may wish to use the drawings above.

(Knowledge & Understanding, **4** marks)

QUESTION 3 (A) (CONTINUED)

(b)   Study Sources 1 and 2 below, then answer the question which follows.

SOURCE 1

Information about selected countries		
Country	**Average Income ($)**	**Life Expectancy (Years)**
China	1,290	72
Japan	37,180	82
Russia	3,410	65
United Kingdom	33,940	79
United States	41,400	78

SOURCE 2

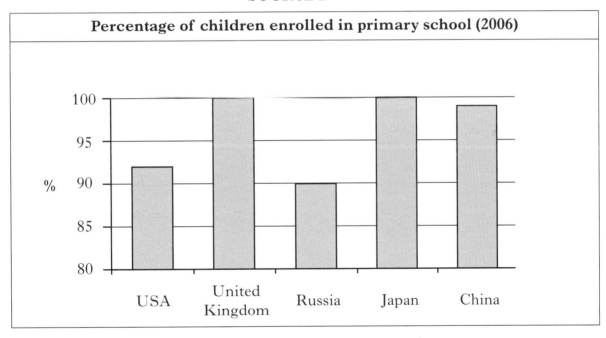

Percentage of children enrolled in primary school (2006)

The USA enrolls less of its children in primary school than most other major countries. However, people in the USA have both the highest average income and live the longest.

View of Kelly Halcomb

Using **only** Source 1 and Source 2 above, give **one** reason to **support** and **one** reason to **oppose** the view of Kelly Halcomb.

(Enquiry Skills, **4** marks)

[Turn over

QUESTION 3 (A) (CONTINUED)

(*c*)

ISSUES IN THE USA

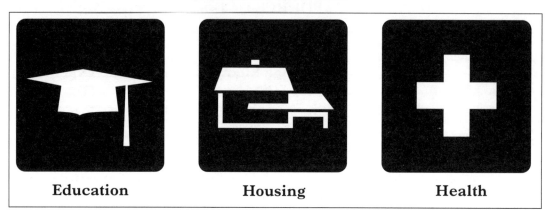

Education   Housing   Health

> *Some Americans are worse off than others.*

Choose **one** of the issues from the box above.

For the issue you have chosen, give **two** reasons why *some Americans are worse off than others*.

In your answer you **must** use American examples.

(Knowledge & Understanding, **4** marks)

QUESTION 3 (A) (CONTINUED)

(d)   Study Sources 1 and 2 below, then answer the question which follows.

SOURCE 1

Hurricane Katrina hit the Gulf Coast of the United States on 29 August 2005, destroying towns in the states of Mississippi and Louisiana. It made one million people homeless, and killed almost 1,800 others. Americans were upset at the size of the disaster and how poorly prepared all levels of government were to deal with the problem. The President agreed that the government had been slow to respond. He promised "one of the largest re-building efforts the world has ever seen" to repair the damage.

SOURCE 2

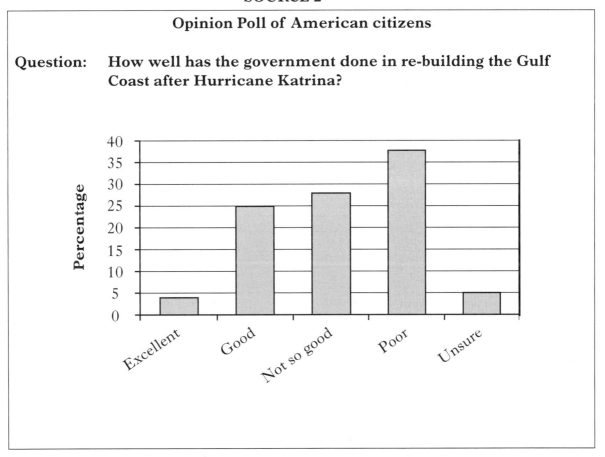

Opinion Poll of American citizens

Question: **How well has the government done in re-building the Gulf Coast after Hurricane Katrina?**

Hurricane Katrina caused a great deal of damage to the Gulf Coast area. However, the government was well equipped to respond to the disaster. President Bush has promised to re-build these states. The majority of people agree that the government is doing a good re-building job.

View of Reed Johnson

Using **only** Source 1 and Source 2 above, write down **two** statements made by Reed Johnson which are **exaggerated**.

Using the information in the Sources, give **one** reason why **each** of the statements you have chosen is **exaggerated**.

(Enquiry Skills, **4** marks)

NOW GO TO QUESTION 4 ON PAGE TWENTY

QUESTION 3 (CONTINUED)

(B) **RUSSIA**

(*a*)

Igor's Tyres
Balance Sheet
Sales: 550,000 roubles
Profit: 240,000 roubles
Tax: 25,000 roubles

> *Starting up a new business can improve the lives of some Russians.*

Describe **two** ways in which *starting up a business can improve the lives of some Russians.*

In your answer you **must** use Russian examples.

To answer this question, you may wish to use the drawings above.

(Knowledge & Understanding, **4** marks)

QUESTION 3 (B) (CONTINUED)

(b)   Study Sources 1 and 2 below, then answer the question which follows.

SOURCE 1

Information about selected countries		
Country	**Average Income ($)**	**Life Expectancy (Years)**
China	1,290	72
Japan	37,180	82
Russia	3,410	65
United Kingdom	33,940	79
United States	41,400	78

SOURCE 2

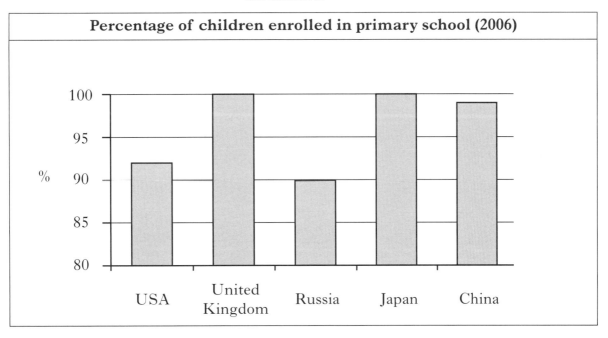

Percentage of children enrolled in primary school (2006)

Russia enrolls less of its children in primary school than most other major countries. People in Russia also have both the lowest average income and shortest life expectancy.

View of Georgi Safin

Using **only** Source 1 and Source 2 above, give **one** reason to **support** and **one** reason to **oppose** the view of Georgi Safin.

(Enquiry Skills, **4** marks)

[Turn over

QUESTION 3 (B) (CONTINUED)

(*c*)

ISSUES IN RUSSIA

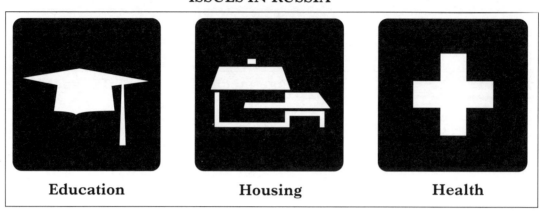

Education   Housing   Health

> *Some Russians are worse off than others.*

Choose **one** of the issues from the box above.

For the issue you have chosen, give **two** reasons why *some Russians are worse off than others*.

In your answer you **must** use Russian examples.

(Knowledge & Understanding, **4** marks)

QUESTION 3 (B) (CONTINUED)

(*d*)   Study Sources 1 and 2 below, then answer the question which follows.

SOURCE 1

The cost of living in Moscow has risen in the past ten years. Some tourists can spend as much as $390 a day whilst on holiday. Foreigners who live and work in Moscow admit a few items such as perfume can cost a little more than in their own country. However, shopping costs can be reduced by using shops on the outskirts of Moscow instead of the centre of the city. The majority of foreigners enjoy life in the Russian capital.

SOURCE 2

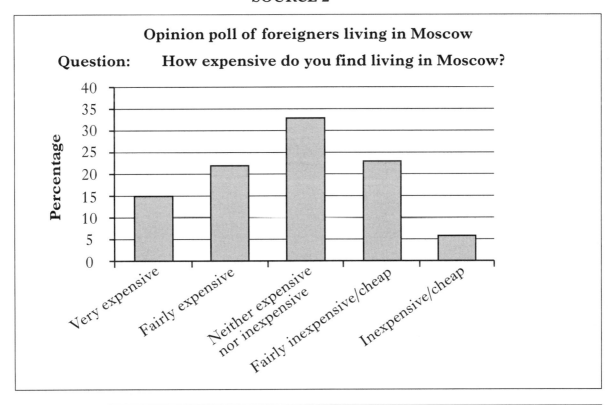

Opinion poll of foreigners living in Moscow

Question: How expensive do you find living in Moscow?

The cost of living continues to rise in Moscow. The majority of foreigners living in Moscow find the city expensive. Shopping costs are similar both in the centre and in the outskirts of Moscow. Foreign workers enjoy living and working in Moscow.

View of Maria Kirilenko

Using **only** Source 1 and Source 2 above, write down **two** statements made by Maria Kirilenko which are **exaggerated.**

Using the information in the Sources, give **one** reason why **each** of the statements you have chosen is **exaggerated.**

(Enquiry Skills, **4** marks)

NOW GO TO QUESTION 4 ON PAGE TWENTY

QUESTION 3 (CONTINUED)

(C) **CHINA**

(*a*)

> *Starting up a business can improve the lives of some Chinese people.*

Describe **two** ways in which *starting up a business can improve the lives of some Chinese people.*

In your answer you **must** use Chinese examples.

To answer this question, you may wish to use the drawings above.

(Knowledge & Understanding, **4** marks)

QUESTION 3 (C) (CONTINUED)

(b) Study Sources 1 and 2 below, then answer the question which follows.

SOURCE 1

Information about selected countries		
Country	**Average Income ($)**	**Life Expectancy (Years)**
China	1,290	72
India	620	64
Russia	3,410	65
United Kingdom	33,940	79
United States	41,400	78

SOURCE 2

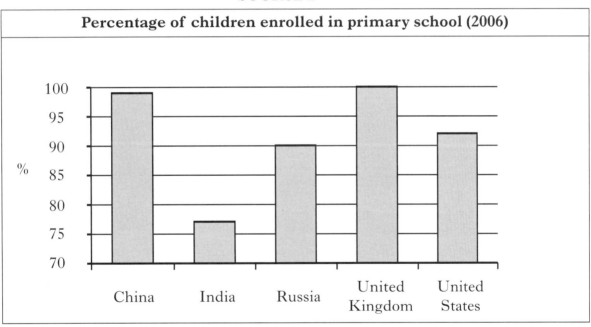

China enrolls more of its children in primary school than most other major countries. People in China also have both the second lowest average income and shortest life expectancy.

View of An Qi

Using **only** Source 1 and Source 2 above, give **one** reason to **support** and **one** reason to **oppose** the view of An Qi.

(Enquiry Skills, **4** marks)

[Turn over

QUESTION 3 (C) (CONTINUED)

(*c*)   **ISSUES IN CHINA**

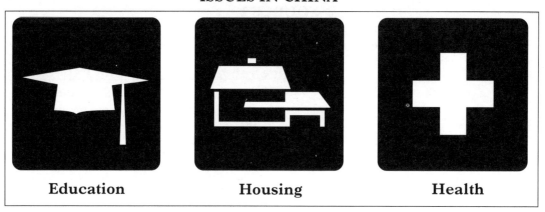

Education	**Housing**	**Health**

Some Chinese people are worse off than others.

Choose **one** of the issues from the box above.

For the issue you have chosen, give **two** reasons why *some Chinese people are worse off than others*.

In your answer you **must** use Chinese examples.

(Knowledge & Understanding, **4** marks)

QUESTION 3 (C) (CONTINUED)

(d) Study Sources 1 and 2 below, then answer the question which follows.

SOURCE 1

2008 Olympics – China spends big!

China has spent almost $39bn on preparations for the 2008 Olympic Games. Most of the cash was spent improving Beijing's transport links, with 132 kilometres of new rail and underground lines built. Beijing has also modernised roads, power stations and water supplies. Those in the countryside around Beijing have not been so fortunate as sixty-nine villages have been demolished to make way for the new Olympic facilities. China hopes to be the centre of attention in 2008 and attract more investment.

SOURCE 2

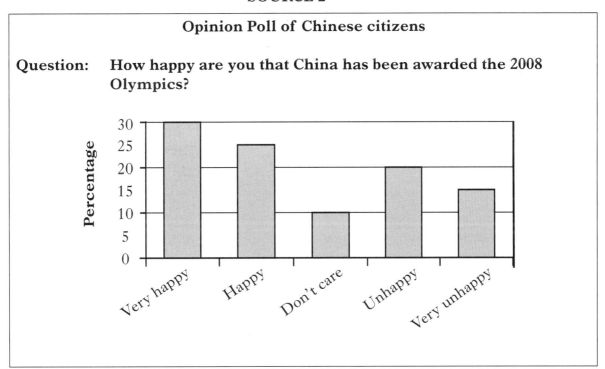

Opinion Poll of Chinese citizens

Question: How happy are you that China has been awarded the 2008 Olympics?

China has spent a lot of money preparing for the Olympics. The majority of Chinese people are not pleased about the Olympics coming to their country. However, everyone in the country should benefit from the Games. Beijing now has better transport links.

View of Zhan Zhenhua

Using **only** Source 1 and Source 2 above, write down **two** statements made by Zhan Zhenhua which are **exaggerated**.

Using the information in the Sources, give **one** reason why **each** of the statements you have chosen is **exaggerated**.

(Enquiry Skills, **4** marks)

NOW GO TO QUESTION 4 ON PAGE TWENTY

SYLLABUS AREA 4 - INTERNATIONAL RELATIONS

QUESTION 4

(a)

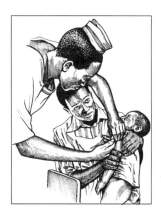

> *United Nations Agencies try to meet the needs of some people in less developed countries in Africa.*

Describe **two** ways in which *United Nations Agencies try to meet the needs of some people in less developed countries in Africa.*

To answer this question, you may wish to use the drawings above.

(Knowledge & Understanding, **4** marks)

QUESTION 4 (CONTINUED)

(b)   Study the information below, then answer the question which follows.

Data for selected NATO countries

Country	1990		2005	
	Numbers in Armed Forces ('000s)	Defence spending per person ($)	Numbers in Armed Forces ('000s)	Defence spending per person ($)
Greece	201	500	209	610
UK	308	770	216	530
USA	2,181	1,400	1,492	925
Turkey	769	110	816	115

Write down **two** conclusions about Armed Forces and Defence spending.

You should write **one** conclusion **with evidence** about **each** of the following.

*   The country with the biggest change in the numbers in its armed forces.

*   What happens to the numbers in the armed forces as defence spending rises.

You **must** only use the information above.

(Enquiry Skills, **4** marks)

[Turn over

QUESTION 4 (CONTINUED)

(c)

---

10 things you should know about the European Union (EU)

1. The European Union is a group of countries whose governments work together.

2. It's a bit like a club. To join you have to agree to follow the rules and in return you get certain benefits.

3. Each country has to pay money to be a member. They mostly do this through taxes.

4. The Single European Market has made trade between countries much easier.

5. There are 5 countries wishing to join at the moment.

6. 43% of all spending by the EU goes on Agriculture, Fisheries and helping the environment.

7. The EU has banned animal testing for cosmetics.

8. EU regional aid has raised living standards in poorer parts of Europe.

9. In 2006, 8 out of 10 EU citizens said they were fairly or very satisfied with living in the EU.

10. The EU has helped over 2 million young people study in another country.

Countries still wish to join the European Union.

Give **two** reasons why *countries still wish to join the European Union*.

To answer this question, you may wish to use the information above.

(Knowledge & Understanding, **4** marks)

QUESTION 4 (CONTINUED)

(*d*) Study the Timeline below, then answer the question which follows.

TIMELINE — NIGER FOOD CRISIS
KEY EVENTS 2004 – 2006

Date	Event
August 2004	Hardly any rain falls during what should be the rainy season. The crops which do grow are then eaten by several plagues of locusts.
November 2004	There are appeals for aid. Many people run out of food.
January 2005	Foodstocks are very low. There is very little food for people to buy. People march in the streets to draw attention to the problem.
July 2005	All Niger's debt is cancelled at the G8 summit. This should help greatly. Many children are dying of starvation.
August 2005	800,000 children under 5 are still going hungry. 40,000 tonnes of energy biscuits are sent to Niger by Italy.
September 2006	The rain fails to come again. A quarter of the population are reported to be hungry.

> Niger has suffered greatly due to a lack of rain. People in Niger protested about the situation. No food aid was received by Niger. Debt is still a major problem for the government.

View of Lyz Graham

Using **only** the information above, write down **two** statements made by Lyz Graham which are **exaggerated**.

Using the Timeline, give **one** reason why **each** of the statements you have chosen is **exaggerated**.

(Enquiry Skills, **4** marks)

[END OF QUESTION PAPER]

[BLANK PAGE]

2008

[BLANK PAGE]

C

2640/403

NATIONAL   THURSDAY, 22 MAY   MODERN STUDIES
QUALIFICATIONS   1.00 PM – 3.00 PM   STANDARD GRADE
2008   Credit Level

1   Read every question carefully.

2   Answer all questions as fully as you can.

3   If you cannot do a question, go on to the next one. Try again later.

4   In question 3, answer **one** section only: Section (A) The USA **or** Section (B) Russia **or** Section (C) China.

5   Write your answers in the answer book provided. Indicate clearly, in the left hand margin, the question and section of question being answered. Do not write in the right hand margin.

[BLANK PAGE]

SYLLABUS AREA 1—LIVING IN A DEMOCRACY

QUESTION 1

(a)

> *Trade union members have **rights during a dispute** with their employers.*

Describe, **in detail**, the **rights** trade union members have **during a dispute** with their employers.

(Knowledge & Understanding, **4** marks)

(b)

> *Women are better **represented** in the Scottish Parliament than they are at Westminster.*

Explain, **in detail**, the reasons why women are better **represented** in the Scottish Parliament than at Westminster.

(Knowledge & Understanding, **4** marks)

[Turn over

QUESTION 1 (CONTINUED)

(c)   Study the Background Information about Gleninch and Sources 1 and 2 on the next page, then answer the question which follows.

BACKGROUND INFORMATION ABOUT GLENINCH CONSTITUENCY

- Gleninch is a constituency in the north of Scotland with a population of 35 265 people. It is a largely rural area with only one town, Inverinch, and a large number of scattered villages. The traditional industries of farming and fishing have been in decline in recent years. The unemployment rate is well above the national average.
- Many young people leave the area, moving to the big cities throughout the UK to look for jobs or to attend college or university.
- Tourism is very important to the local economy, with a lot of people employed in hotels, bed and breakfast accommodation and restaurants. Tourists tend to visit the area for a few days on short breaks, attracted by rare wildlife and spectacular, unspoilt scenery. However, there are a number of transport problems in the constituency, including high petrol prices and poor public transport.
- There is a proposal to build a wind farm in the area. This would involve the construction of 6 large wind turbines along the coast, as well as a 15-mile long power line built on tall pylons to take electricity to the rest of the country. This would create a few temporary construction jobs but will disturb local wildlife and impact on the scenery of the area.
- An American mining company wants to build a huge "super-quarry" into a mountainside near Gleninch. This will produce crushed rock to build roads, railways and houses throughout the UK. The new quarry will create 150 new jobs in Gleninch.
- At the last General Election, the constituency was won by the Labour Party with a majority of just over 1000 votes. The Liberal Democrats came second. They are convinced that, with the right candidate, they can win the seat at the next election.

A Statistical Profile of Gleninch Constituency (2006)

	Gleninch	Comparison with Scottish Average
Average Income	£21 185	−14%
Income Support claimants	15·1%	+22%
Unemployment Rate	5·6%	+13%
School leavers with no qualifications	3·6%	−33%
School leavers with Highers	58·6%	+13%
Serious Assaults	8·8 (per 10 000 people)	−73%
Housebreaking	3·8 (per 10 000 people)	−93%
Road Accidents	57 casualties	−44%

Survey of Local Liberal Democrat Members

Question: *How important are these issues to people in the area?*

Issue	Unimportant	Not Very Important	Fairly Important	Very Important
Environment	5%	25%	40%	30%
Health	2%	10%	53%	35%
Jobs	0%	0%	48%	52%
Women in Parliament	15%	52%	22%	11%

QUESTION 1 (*c*) (CONTINUED)

There are two people hoping to be selected by the Liberal Democratic Party to be the Party's candidate at the next General Election. Here are extracts from speeches they have made.

SOURCE 1

EXTRACT FROM CAMPAIGN SPEECH BY KIRSTY REID

- I support the proposed wind farm as it will provide many local jobs and help the local environment.
- Our local schools provide an excellent education. If selected, I will work to ensure this continues.
- Women make up over half the country's population and yet there are still very few of us who are MPs. This is a major priority for local party members and is an important reason why I should be the candidate.
- The local economy has been in decline recently. We need more jobs to keep our young people in the area. The new quarry will help with this, and I will work hard to see that it is allowed to go ahead.
- To attract more people to the area we need to improve transport links. I will make this a priority.

SOURCE 2

EXTRACT FROM CAMPAIGN SPEECH BY ROBBIE McKAY

- Tourism is very important to the area and so I will oppose the new wind farm as it will be an ugly blot on the landscape and deter tourists.
- Crime in Gleninch is among the worst in Scotland. I will campaign to improve policing in the area.
- Although new jobs are important, local Liberal Democrats are much more concerned about the environment. The new quarry will put more heavy lorries on our roads which are already more dangerous than the rest of the country. I will oppose it going ahead.
- The issue of health will be one of my main concerns, just as it is for local party members.
- Compared to the rest of the country, the people of Gleninch are not well-off. I will do all I can to improve this.

Use **only** the information about Gleninch on *Page four* and Sources 1 and 2 above.

(i) State **which person** would be the **more suitable** to be selected by the Liberal Democratic Party as their candidate for this constituency at the next General Election.

(ii) Give **three detailed reasons to support your choice**.

(iii) Give **two detailed** reasons why you **rejected** the other candidate.

In your answer, you **must relate** information about the constituency to the information about the **two** candidates.

(Enquiry Skills, **10** marks)

SYLLABUS AREA 2—CHANGING SOCIETY

QUESTION 2

(a)   **TYPES OF CARE FOR THE ELDERLY**

Community Care within their own home	Sheltered Housing	Residential Care Homes

Choose **one** type of care from the options above.

Explain, **in detail**, the ways in which this type of care **meets the needs** of some elderly people.

(Knowledge and Understanding, **8** marks)

QUESTION 2 (CONTINUED)

You have been asked to carry out an investigation on the topic in the box below.

> **Help for families in the UK**

Now answer questions (*b*), (*c*), (*d*) and (*e*) which follow.

(*b*) State a relevant **hypothesis** for your investigation.

(Enquiry Skills, **2** marks)

(*c*) Give **two** relevant **aims** to help you prove or disprove your hypothesis.

(Enquiry Skills, **2** marks)

Your Modern Studies class decides to use **Video Conferencing** to do an interview to help the pupils with their investigations into "**Help for families in the UK**".

Your teacher contacted your MP at Westminster, who said she would be willing to be interviewed. The interview set up is shown below.

| Your MP in her office at Westminster | A secondary school classroom |

(*d*) Give **two relevant** questions which you could ask your MP to help with your investigation.

(Enquiry Skills, **4** marks)

[Turn over

QUESTION 2 (CONTINUED)

While collecting information for your investigation, you found the **Orinoco Web page** below which contained information about **Social Trends 2008**.

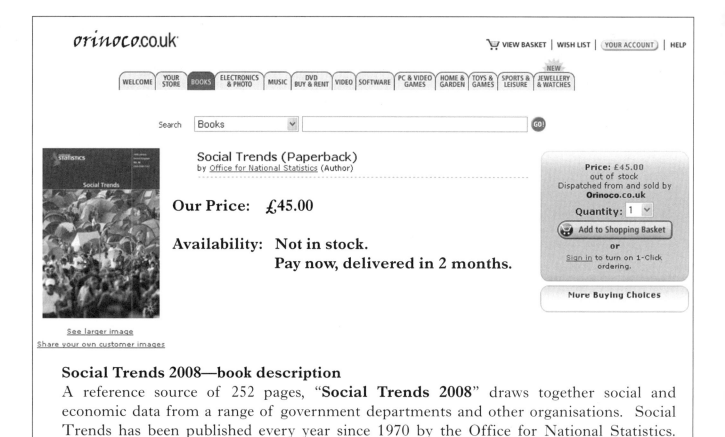

Social Trends 2008—book description

A reference source of 252 pages, "**Social Trends 2008**" draws together social and economic data from a range of government departments and other organisations. Social Trends has been published every year since 1970 by the Office for National Statistics. This annual publication provides a picture of life and lifestyle in the UK. Data is presented in a combination of tables, figures and text.

(*e*)　Using **only** the Orinoco Web page, give one **disadvantage** of **buying** from this website and one **advantage** of **using** Social Trends 2008 in your investigation.

(Enquiry Skills, **2** marks)

[Turn over for Question 3 on *Page ten*

SYLLABUS AREA 3—IDEOLOGIES

QUESTION 3

Answer **one** section only: Section (A)—The USA on pages *ten* to *thirteen*
           OR   Section (B)—Russia on pages *fourteen* to *seventeen*
           OR   Section (C)—China on pages *eighteen* to *twenty-one*

(A)   **THE USA**

(a) | *American citizens can **participate** in politics in many ways.* |

Describe, **in detail**, the ways in which *American citizens can **participate** in politics.*

In your answer, you **must** use American examples.

(Knowledge and Understanding, **8** marks)

QUESTION 3 (A) (CONTINUED)

(b)   Study Sources 1 and 2 below, then answer the question which follows.

SOURCE 1
Average Personal Income Level Per Person
in the 10 Wealthiest US States ($)

	2003	2004	2005
Colorado	34 500	36 000	37 500
Connecticut	42 000	45 400	47 500
Delaware	34 100	35 900	37 100
Maryland	37 500	39 200	42 000
Massachusetts	39 500	41 800	43 700
Minnesota	34 000	35 900	37 300
New Hampshire	35 100	37 000	37 800
New Jersey	39 600	41 300	43 800
New York	36 100	38 200	40 100
Virginia	33 700	35 500	37 600

SOURCE 2
Income Distribution in the USA

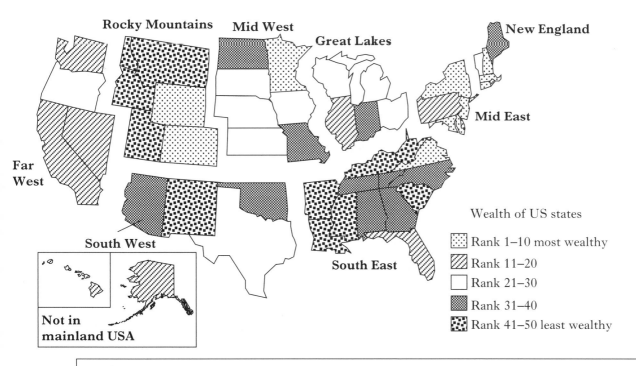

The biggest increase in personal income between 2003 and 2005 has been in Connecticut. The richest states in the US are all to be found in the Mid East of the country.

View of a Wall Street Economist

Using **only** the information above, give **one** reason to **support** and **one** reason to **oppose** the view of the Wall Street Economist.

(Enquiry Skills, **4** marks)

QUESTION 3 (A) (CONTINUED)

(c)   Study the information in Sources 1, 2 and 3 below and on the next page, then answer the question which follows.

SOURCE 1

The Rockford Record

Your local voice, free to all 10 000 homes in Rockford City (23 May 2008)

New Housing Project Causes Local Anger

A recent public meeting in Rockford City Hall was attended by 500 local people. They were told about plans for a new gated community of 700 houses called "Red Pines". It is to be built by the Allan Building Company.

The gated community of Red Pines would be a walled housing development to which public access would be restricted. It would be guarded using CCTV and security personnel. The complex would have its own supermarkets, restaurants and bars.

The people at the meeting showed mixed feelings, for and against the possible development.

In 2004, gated communities housed 16 million Americans, about 6% of all households. Homeowners in gated communities live in upmarket and mostly white developments. Affluent black American homeowners are less likely than white people to live in gated communities.

The Red Pines Area Now

At the moment Red Pines is a beautiful wooded area. It is used by Rockford residents for walking and exercise. There is a jogging track, 3 football pitches and a rowing club on the river. Unfortunately, it floods occasionally as it is near to the river.

Doctor Joan Quincy said, "It is well known that Rockford residents are not very good at taking exercise. Health statistics show that compared to the rest of the USA we need to take more exercise. We need the Red Pines area to keep our people healthy. We want to encourage more people to exercise in this area. Building houses would be a disaster for our community."

Health and Exercise Statistics	Rockford	USA
Overweight	48%	35%
Bicycle riding	6%	16%
Exercise walking	16%	32%
Running/Jogging	4%	10%

The building of Red Pines would also cause a great deal of disturbance in and around the town. There might be a few short-term benefits for the local community but long-term, there will be no real gain for the town as those living in Red Pines are unlikely to be spending much money in the shops in Rockford. They will get in their cars and drive to the city which is only 15 miles away.

Doctor Quincy is also Chairperson of the Rockford Residents' Association.

QUESTION 3 (A) (c) (CONTINUED)

SOURCE 2

What the people want

The Rockford Record decided to find out the views of local people about the "Red Pines" development. We conducted an opinion poll and received 8900 replies from 10 000 homes and feel that this survey shows the real views of the people.

The Questions: How Important	Unimportant	Not very important	Important	Very important
is it that Rockford stays a racially mixed town?	20%	15%	25%	40%
a problem is jobs to the people of Rockford?	15%	25%	20%	40%
is the Red Pines area for exercise?	20%	10%	45%	25%

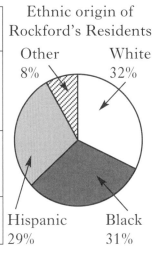

Ethnic origin of Rockford's Residents

Other 8%
White 32%
Hispanic 29%
Black 31%

SOURCE 3

Leaflet from Allan Building Company

I am Chairman of the Allan Building Company and I was born in Rockford. I have stayed here all my life and want to do the best for Rockford. There is great demand for this type of housing from middle and upper income groups who would not live in Rockford because of their fear of rising crime there. We already have 500 new families from outwith Rockford, wanting to move into Red Pines whenever it is built. They are a mixture of young and old with an ethnic mix of 50% White, 25% Hispanic, 24% Black and 1% other groups.

Impact on Rockford

SHORT-TERM IMPACT	LONG-TERM IMPACT
• Skilled workers employed in the building of Red Pines. • Unskilled workers also needed. • Workers on-site spend money in local shops. • Building supply companies will increase trade.	• Unskilled jobs will be available, eg cleaners. • Jobs will be available in the new shops and restaurants. • Shops in Rockford will gain extra business from the new residents close-by. • Local shops have the opportunity to become suppliers to the new restaurants and bars which will open. • Flood prevention measures will stop flooding.

The Red Pines gated development will cause many problems for our health and change the ethnic mix of Rockford. It will bring few benefits to the people of Rockford.

View of Findlay Smith, Editor, The Rockford Record

Using **only** the information in Sources 1, 2 and 3, explain, **in detail**, **the extent to which** Findlay Smith could be accused of being **selective in the use of facts**.

(Enquiry Skills, **8** marks)

[NOW GO TO QUESTION 4 ON PAGE 22]

QUESTION 3 (CONTINUED)

(B)   RUSSIA

(a) | *Russian citizens can **participate** in politics in many ways.*

Describe, **in detail**, the ways in which *Russian citizens can **participate** in politics.*
In your answer, you **must** use Russian examples.

(Knowledge and Understanding, **8** marks)

QUESTION 3 (B) (CONTINUED)

(b)   Study Sources 1 and 2 below, then answer the question which follows.

SOURCE 1
Index of growth of Industry and Agriculture in Russia

Sector	2001	2002	2003	2004	2005
Industry	1108	1443	1601	1681	2995
Agriculture	204	287	309	302	625

SOURCE 2
The ways in which the Russian people spend their money
(% of total)

	2002	2003	2004	2005
Foodstuffs	50·2	45·8	53·4	53·7
Alcohol	2·5	2·8	2·6	2·5
Non-foods	31·3	36·5	30·1	30·8
Services	16·0	14·9	13·9	13·0

Both Industry and Agriculture have grown each year between 2002 and 2005. The amount spent on foodstuffs is the only one which has seen a rise between 2002 and 2005.

View of a Russian Economist

Using **only** the information above, give **one** reason to **support** and **one** reason to **oppose** the view of the Russian Economist.

(Enquiry Skills, **4** marks)

[Turn over

QUESTION 3 (B) (CONTINUED)

(c) Study the information from Sources 1, 2 and 3 below and on the next page, then answer the question which follows.

SOURCE 1

The Vorkuta Reporter

Your local voice, free to all 10 000 homes in Vorkuta (23 May 2008)

New Housing Project Causes Local Anger

A recent public meeting in Vorkuta Town Hall was attended by 500 local people. They were told about plans for a new gated community of 700 houses called "Sosny Woods". It is to be built by the Andropov Building Company.

The gated community of Sosny Woods would be a walled housing development to which public access would be restricted. It would be guarded using CCTV and security personnel. The complex would have its own supermarkets, restaurants and bars.

The people at the meeting showed mixed feelings, for and against the possible development.

Gated communities have been around for a long time in Russia. It used to be the case that they were only built for high-ranking political officials. This is changing and more and more are being built for Russians who are rich enough to be able to buy them.

The Sosny Woods Area Now

At the moment, the Sosny Woods area is a beautiful wooded area. It is used by Vorkuta residents for walking and exercise. There is a jogging track, 3 football pitches and a rowing club on the river. Unfortunately, it floods occasionally as it is near to the river.

Doctor Yuri Press said, "It is well known that Vorkuta residents are not very good at taking exercise. Health statistics show that compared to the rest of Russia we need to take more exercise. We need

Health and Exercise Statistics	Vorkuta	Russia
Overweight	48%	35%
Bicycle riding	6%	16%
Exercise walking	16%	32%
Running/Jogging	4%	10%

the Sosny Woods area to keep our people healthy. We want to encourage more people to exercise in this area. Building houses would be a disaster for our community."

The building of Sosny Woods would also cause a great deal of disturbance in and around the town. There might be a few short-term benefits for the local community but long-term, there will be no real gain for the town as those living in Sosny Woods are unlikely to be spending much money in the shops in Vorkuta. They will get in their cars and drive to the city which is only 15 miles away.

Doctor Press is also chairperson of the Vorkuta Residents' Association.

QUESTION 3 (B) (c) (CONTINUED)

SOURCE 2

What the people want

The Vorkuta Record decided to find out the views of local people about the "Sosny Woods" development. We conducted an opinion poll and received 8900 replies from 10 000 homes and feel that this survey shows the real views of the people.

The Questions: How Important	Unimportant	Not very important	Important	Very important
is it that Vorkuta keeps in-comers to a minimum?	20%	15%	25%	40%
a problem is jobs to the people of Vorkuta?	20%	40%	25%	15%
is the Sosny Woods area for exercise?	20%	10%	45%	25%

SOURCE 3

Leaflet from Andropov Building Company

I am Chairman of the Andropov Building Company and I was born in Vorkuta. I have stayed here all my life and want to do the best for the town. There is a great demand for this type of housing from middle and upper income groups. They are keen to move to Vorkuta because of their fear of rising crime in nearby cities. We already have 500 new families wanting to move into Sosny Woods whenever it is built. They are a mixture of age ranges and backgrounds. 73% are people with no connection to the town, 17% are people who live in nearby towns and 10% are Vorkuta residents.

Benefits to Vorkuta

SHORT-TERM IMPACT	LONG-TERM IMPACT
• Skilled workers employed in the building of Sosny Woods. • Unskilled workers also needed. • Workers on-site spend money in local shops. • Building supply companies will increase trade.	• Unskilled jobs will be available, eg cleaners. • Jobs will be available in the new shops and restaurants. • Shops in Vorkuta will gain extra business from the new residents close-by. • Local shops have the opportunity to become suppliers to the new restaurants and bars which will open. • Flood prevention measures will stop flooding.

The Sosny Woods Gated Development will cause many problems for our health and allow outsiders to dominate Vorkuta. It will bring few benefits to the people of Vorkuta.

View of Dmitri Arshavin, Editor, The Vorkuta Reporter

Using **only** the information in Sources 1, 2 and 3, explain, **in detail**, **the extent to which** Dmitri Arshavin could be accused of being **selective in the use of facts**.

(Enquiry Skills, **8** marks)

[NOW GO TO QUESTION 4 ON PAGE 22]

QUESTION 3 (CONTINUED)

(C) **CHINA**

(a) | *Chinese citizens can **participate** in politics in many ways.*

Describe, **in detail**, the ways in which *Chinese citizens can **participate** in politics*.
In your answer, you **must** use Chinese examples.

(Knowledge and Understanding, **8** marks)

QUESTION 3 (C) (CONTINUED)

(b)   Study Sources 1 and 2 below, then answer the question which follows.

SOURCE 1
Average Personal Income
Top Ten Chinese Regions (Yuan)

Region	2003	2004	2005
Beijing	35 000	37 000	39 500
Tianjin	29 500	31 500	34 000
Hebei	13 000	13 500	13 500
Liaoning	15 000	16 500	17 000
Heilongjiang	13 000	14 000	15 500
Shanghai	51 000	55 500	61 000
Zhejiang	21 000	24 000	25 000
Fujian	15 500	17 000	18 000
Shangdong	16 000	17 000	17 500
Guangdong	18 500	20 000	21 000

SOURCE 2
China's Ten Richest Regions

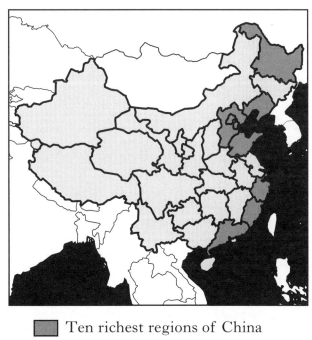

▇ Ten richest regions of China
▢ Rest of China

The greatest increase in personal income has been experienced by those living in Shanghai. However, the wealthiest regions are evenly distributed throughout China.

View of Chinese Economist

Using **only** the information above, give **one** reason to **support** and **one** reason to **oppose** the view of the Chinese Economist.

(Enquiry Skills, **4** marks)

QUESTION 3 (C) (CONTINUED)

(c) Study the information from Sources 1, 2 and 3 below and on the next page, then answer the question which follows.

SOURCE 1

The Hankou Herald

Free to all 50 000 residents. Published by the Peoples' Congress of Hankou.

Joy as riverside housing is opened

The city authorities announced yesterday that the brand new "Riverside Garden" development of top quality houses is to open next month. The development (next to the Anze river) attracted 300 building jobs to the area, which have benefited Hankou's economy.

The new housing is known as a "Gated Community". This means that a wall will surround the 500 houses and local people will be employed as security guards and CCTV operators.   Around 300 local people will have well-paid jobs in the community's facilities, eg medical centre, golf course, tennis courts, shops and gym.

The housing is very high quality and will attract many of the region's most successful business people who are looking for an escape from the city, and the chance to relax, play sport and socialise.

It will raise the profile of the area and possibly tempt more people to open new businesses in Hankou which is depressed economically and in need of a boost.

The Riverside area before

The area was only used by a few fishermen. Wages were poor and it was the only work available.

The town's people rarely went there. Sports facilities in all parts of the town, including the Riverside area, were very poor.

Local doctor speaks out

Dr Pu Zihao says, "It is well known that Hankou residents are not very good at taking exercise.   Health statistics show that compared to the rest of China we need to be more active. We need new sporting facilities in the Riverside area to keep our people healthy. Building these houses is good for our community".

"Anyone will be able to use the sports facilities if they are willing to pay the yearly Sports Club membership fee of only 50 yuan."

(Dr Pu is a member of the "Healthy Hankou Campaign".)

Health and Exercise Statistics	Hankou	China
Overweight	27%	21%
Regular cyclists	64%	73%
Regular walkers	51%	78%
Regular golf/tennis players	1%	8%

An economic boost!

The people of Hankou have tried for many years to lift themselves out of poverty but they have not succeeded. Average wages are lower than the Chinese average and have shown little improvement in the last few years.

Average Wages (yuan)

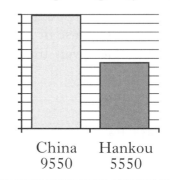

China 9550   Hankou 5550

QUESTION 3 (C) (*c*) (CONTINUED)

SOURCE 2

What the people want

We decided to find out the views of the local people about the Riverside development. We sent questionnaires to 10 000 local homes and received 8900 replies. The views of local people really have been heard.

Question: How important are the following things for Hankou?

	Unimportant	Not very important	Important	Very important
Higher pay	13%	13%	20%	54%
Attracting new businesses	5%	14%	30%	51%
Protecting existing farmers and fishermen	40%	25%	26%	9%

View of Li Jie – a local fisherman

I have lost my job and so have six of my friends. Hankou fishermen are all against this new housing development. Riverside Garden might bring a few short-term benefits for the local community but, in the long term, there will be no real gain for the town. Those living in Riverside Garden are unlikely to be spending much money in the shops in Hankou. They will only use the shops in Riverside Garden as there will be little to interest them in Hankou or they will get in their cars and drive to the city which is only one hour's drive away.

SOURCE 3

Leaflet from Hankou Authorities

IMPACT ON HANKOU

- Unskilled jobs will be available, eg cleaners.
- Jobs will be available in the new shops and restaurants.
- Shops in Hankou will gain extra business from the new residents close-by.
- Local shops have the opportunity to become suppliers to the new restaurants and bars which will open.
- Affordable sports facilities

The Riverside Gated Development will improve the health of people living in Hankou. It will bring much needed benefits to the people of Hankou. Everyone living in Hankou is excited by the opening of Riverside Garden.

View of Pu Wei, Editor, The Hankou Herald

Using **only** the information in Sources 1, 2 and 3, explain, **in detail**, **the extent to which** Pu Wei could be accused of being **selective in the use of facts**.

(Enquiry Skills, **8** marks)

[NOW GO TO QUESTION 4 ON PAGE 22]

SYLLABUS AREA 4—INTERNATIONAL RELATIONS

QUESTION 4

(a)   **SELECTED ISSUES IN AFRICA**

HIV/AIDS on the increase in large parts of Africa	Civil wars rage on in parts of Africa	Prices fall on a number of raw materials produced in some African countries

Choose **one** issue from the boxes above.

Explain, **in detail**, why your chosen issue may prevent some African governments **meeting the needs** of their people.

(Knowledge & Understanding, **4** marks)

QUESTION 4 (CONTINUED)

(b)

> *European governments have taken actions to protect their populations from possible threats to their security.*

Describe, **in detail**, some of the actions taken by *European governments to protect their populations from possible threats to their security*.

(Knowledge & Understanding, **4** marks)

[Turn over

QUESTION 4 (CONTINUED)

(c)   Study the information in Sources 1, 2 and 3 below and on the next page, then answer the question which follows.

SOURCE 1
Millennium Development Goals

The Millennium Development Goals were agreed by 189 countries in New York in 2000.

Selected Millennium Development Goals

1:    **Reduce child mortality**

2:    **Achieve primary education for all**

3:    **Remove extreme poverty and hunger**

4:    **Combat diseases**

These goals represented a commitment by rich and poor nations to expand social and economic progress in all regions of the world, as well as creating a global partnership for reducing levels of poverty and suffering in less developed countries by 2015.

Many are now questioning the commitment of the More Developed Countries to making these goals a reality as few MDCs give the UN recommended 0·7% of Gross National Income (GNI).

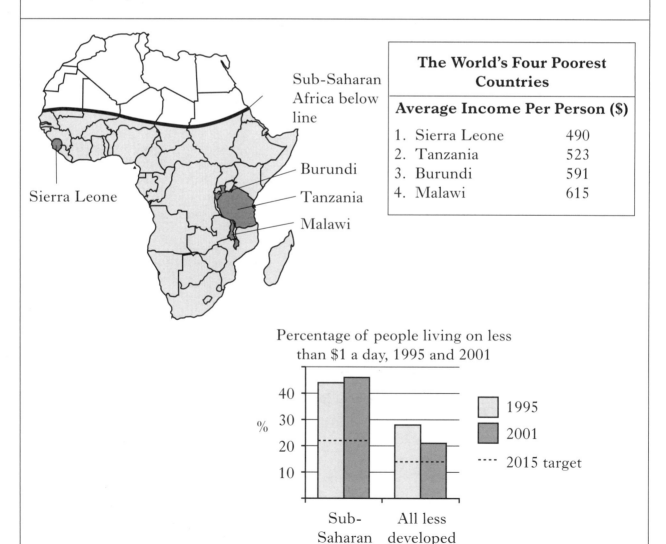

Sub-Saharan Africa below line

Burundi

Tanzania

Malawi

Sierra Leone

The World's Four Poorest Countries	
Average Income Per Person ($)	
1. Sierra Leone	490
2. Tanzania	523
3. Burundi	591
4. Malawi	615

Percentage of people living on less than $1 a day, 1995 and 2001

1995
2001
---- 2015 target

Sub-Saharan Africa   All less developed countries

QUESTION 4 (c) (CONTINUED)

SOURCE 2: Aid given by selected Donor Countries

Selected Donor Countries	Aid Given		% increase	Largest recipients ($ millions)
	2004 $ billions (% of GNI)	2010 (prediction) $ billions (% of GNI)		
UK	7·88 (0·36)	14·60 (0·59)	85	1. India ($419) 2. Bangladesh ($267) 3. Tanzania ($265)
USA	19·7 (0·17)	24·00 (0·18)	22	1. Iraq ($2286) 2. Congo ($804) 3. Egypt ($767)
Portugal	1·03 (0·63)	0·93 (0·51)	−10	1. Angola ($367) 2. Cape Verde ($39) 3. Timor ($34)
Italy	2·46 (0·15)	9·26 (0·51)	276	1. Dem. Rep. Congo ($235) 2. China ($52) 3. Tunisia ($41)

SOURCE 3

Four Poorest African Countries – Progress on selected Millennium Development Goals								
	Sierra Leone		Tanzania		Burundi		Malawi	
Selected Indicators \ Year	1996	2006	1996	2006	1996	2006	1996	2006
% of population undernourished	44	50	50	44	63	67	50	34
Child Mortality (per 1000 births)	293	283	159	126	190	190	216	175
% 1 year olds vaccinated against measles	37	64	49	91	80	75	90	80
% Primary school enrolment	43	73	94	95	43	57	48	98

Using **only** the information above and opposite, you must **make** and **justify** conclusions about progress towards the Millennium Development Goals using the **four** headings below.

* Progress towards Millennium Development Goal 1
* Progress towards **all** of Millennium Development Goal 3
* The commitment of More Developed Countries to meeting the UN aid recommendation
* The commitment of Donor Countries to the world's **four poorest** nations

(Enquiry Skills, **8** marks)

[END OF QUESTION PAPER]

[BLANK PAGE]

[BLANK PAGE]

G

2640/402

NATIONAL
QUALIFICATIONS
2009

MONDAY, 25 MAY
10.20 AM–11.50 AM

MODERN STUDIES
STANDARD GRADE
General Level

1   Read every question carefully.

2   Answer all questions as fully as you can.

3   If you cannot do a question, go on to the next one. Try again later.

4   In question 3, answer **one** section only: Section (A) The USA **or** Section (B) China.

5   Write your answers in the answer book provided. Indicate clearly, in the left hand margin, the question and section of question being answered. Do not write in the right hand margin.

SYLLABUS AREA 1—LIVING IN A DEMOCRACY

QUESTION 1

(a) | *Members of the Scottish Parliament (MSPs) can represent their constituents in many ways.*

Extract from an MSP's diary

MAY 2009

Monday 18

> 2·00pm : Meet constituents at Holyrood

Tuesday 19

> 10·30 pm : Interview with journalist

Wednesday 20

> 11·00 am : Health Committee Meeting in Room 2

Thursday 21

> 12 noon : First Minister's Questions

Friday 22

> 10·00am – 4·00pm : Constituency Office

Describe **two** ways in which MSPs **represent** their constituents.

To answer this question, you may wish to use the information above.

(Knowledge & Understanding, **4** marks)

QUESTION 1 (CONTINUED)

(b)   Study Sources 1 and 2 below, then answer the question which follows.

Election Information, 2007 Scottish Parliament

SOURCE 1
Percentage of Spoilt Ballot Papers in the Scottish Parliament Election in 2007

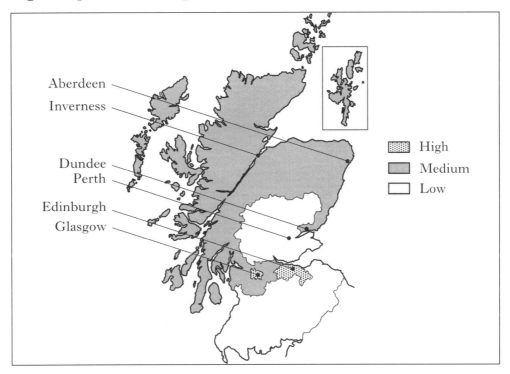

SOURCE 2
The Number of Spoilt Ballot Papers and Majorities in Selected Constituencies (2007)

Constituency	Spoilt Ballot Papers (Number of votes not counted in result)	Majority (Number of votes candidate won by)
Aberdeen North	1173	3749
Airdrie and Shotts	1536	1446
Cunninghame South	1055	2168
Dumfries	1006	2839
Midlothian	1649	1702

> Edinburgh and Glasgow have the highest percentage of spoilt ballot papers. The number of spoilt ballot papers did not affect the result in any of the selected constituencies.

View of Holly Kerr

Using **only** Sources 1 and 2 above, give **one** reason to **support** and **one** reason to **oppose** the view of Holly Kerr.

(Enquiry Skills, **4** marks)

QUESTION 1 (CONTINUED)

(c)

Many workers choose to join a trade union. As members of a trade union, workers have rights that are important to them.

Give **two rights** that members of a trade union have.

Choose **one** of these **rights** and explain why it is important to workers.

To answer this question, you may wish to use the drawing above.

(Knowledge and Understanding, **4** marks)

QUESTION 1 (CONTINUED)

(d)   Study Sources 1 and 2 below, then answer the question which follows.

Information about Industrial Disputes in the UK
SOURCE 1

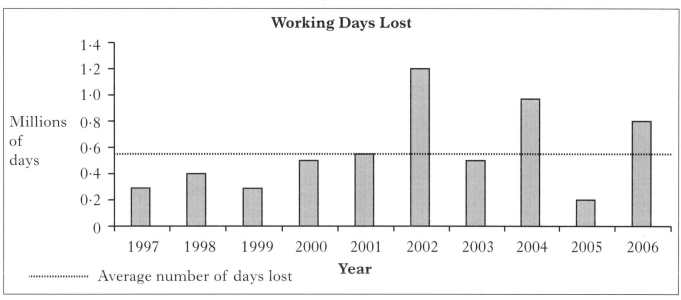

SOURCE 2

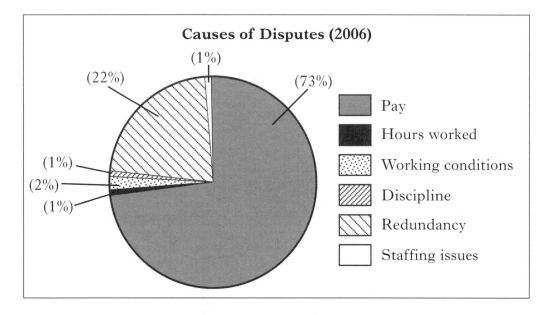

Write down **two** conclusions about industrial disputes in the UK.

You should write **one** conclusion **with evidence** about **each** of the following.

- The main cause of industrial disputes in 2006.

- The year which was the furthest from the average for working days lost.

Your answer **must** be based entirely on the Sources above.

(Enquiry Skills, **4** marks)

[2640/402]   *Page five*   **[Turn over**

SYLLABUS AREA 2—CHANGING SOCIETY

QUESTION 2

(a) | *Sheltered housing can help meet the **needs** of elderly people.* |

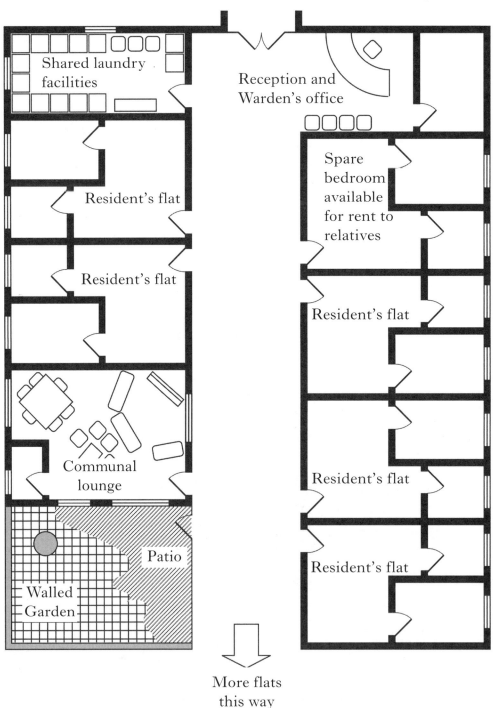

Describe **two** ways in which *sheltered housing can help meet the **needs** of elderly people.*

To answer this question you may wish to use the drawing above.

(Knowledge and Understanding, **4** marks)

QUESTION 2 (CONTINUED)

(b)   Study Sources 1 and 2 below, then answer the question which follows.

SOURCE 1

> **The Scottish Workforce**
>
> In 2006, Scotland's population was 5,116,900. It was 5,094,800 the previous year, and 5,064,200 in 2001.
>
> The number of people in employment is called the workforce. In 2006, there were 2,500,000 people in work in Scotland. The number of male workers had increased by 5·6% since 1996, and the number of females had gone up by 11·2%.

SOURCE 2

Unemployment in Scotland, 2000–2006 (%)			
Year	Male	Female	Total
2000	6·4	2·2	4·5
2001	5·9	1·9	4·0
2002	5·8	1·8	3·9
2003	5·5	1·8	3·7
2004	5·1	1·7	3·5
2005	4·7	1·6	3·2
2006	4·8	1·7	3·3

> **Statements made by Betty Hill**
>
> * The population has increased in recent years.
> * The percentage of male workers has increased much more than the percentage of female workers.
> * Female unemployment has always been lower than male unemployment.
> * Total unemployment has fallen every year since 2000.

Using **only** Sources 1 and 2 above, write down **two** statements made by Betty Hill which are **exaggerated.**

Using the information in the Sources, give **one** reason why **each** of the statements you have chosen is **exaggerated**.

(Enquiry Skills, **4** marks)

[Turn over

QUESTION 2 (CONTINUED)

(c) | *Some elderly people are wealthier than other elderly people.*

Give **two** reasons to explain why *some elderly people are wealthier than other elderly people*.

(Knowledge and Understanding, **4** marks)

(d) Study Sources 1 and 2 below, then answer the question which follows.

SOURCE 1   **SOURCE 2**

VIEW OF ALEX BROWN
The number of unemployed people in the United Kingdom has fallen in recent years.
Jobseeker's Allowance (JSA) was introduced by the Government to replace Unemployment Benefit. It is a weekly payment which is just enough to meet an unemployed person's basic needs.
To receive this benefit, an unemployed person must be aged 18 years or over, and actively seeking work.
JSA aims to get unemployed people into a job that best suits their qualifications.

VIEW OF NICOLA McLEAN
Jobseeker's Allowance (JSA) tries to push people off benefits and into any low paid job that's available.
Any unemployed person who is looking for a job, and is 18 or over, can apply.
The money is paid every week, but it is not enough for unemployed people to live on.
The Government brought in JSA as a replacement for Unemployment Benefit.
In the last few years there has been a decrease in the level of unemployment in the United Kingdom.

Sources 1 and 2 give different views about the **Jobseeker's Allowance**.

Write down **two** differences between these views.

You **must** only use information from the Sources above.

(Enquiry Skills, **4** marks)

SYLLABUS AREA 3 — IDEOLOGIES

QUESTION 3

Answer **ONE** section only: Section (A)—The USA on pages *nine* to *twelve*

OR Section (B)—China on pages *thirteen* to *sixteen*

(A) **THE USA**

(a) | *American people can **participate** in politics in many ways.* |

Describe **two** ways in which *American people can **participate** in politics* in the USA.

In your answer, you **must** use American examples.

To answer this question, you may wish to use the drawings above.

(Knowledge & Understanding, **4** marks)

[Turn over

QUESTION 3 (A) (CONTINUED)

(b)   Study Sources 1 and 2 below, then answer the question which follows.

SOURCE 1
USA Ethnic Minority Unemployment Rate

Year	Ethnic Minority Groups		
	Black	Hispanic	Asian
1998	8·9%	7·2%	3·8%
2000	7·6%	5·7%	3·6%
2002	10·2%	7·5%	5·9%
2004	10·4%	7·0%	4·4%
2006	8·9%	5·2%	3·0%

SOURCE 2

The Rockford Record
Home Ownership Today

Home ownership is seen as an important part of the American Dream in the USA.

In 2006, home ownership was 75% for White families but only 47% for Black, 50% for Hispanic and 60% for Asian families. Compared to 1998, this is an increase of 3% for White families, 2% for Black families, 5% for Hispanic families and for Asian families the increase is 8%.

Today, there are still big differences in the rates of home ownership between whites and other ethnic minority groups.

In 2006, unemployment was at its lowest for all ethnic minority groups. The group with the lowest unemployment in 2006 has seen the greatest increase in home ownership.

View of Ann Struther

Using **only** Source 1 and Source 2 above, give **one** reason to **support** and **one** reason to **oppose** the view of Ann Struther.

(Enquiry Skills, **4** marks)

QUESTION 3 (A) (CONTINUED)

You are investigating the topic in the box below.

CRIME IN THE USA

Answer questions (*c*), (*d*) and (*e*) which follow.

(*c*)   As part of the **Planning Stage**, give **two** relevant **aims** for your investigation.

(Enquiry Skills, **2** marks)

Relatives from the USA are visiting Scotland on holiday and you decide to talk to them about your investigation.

(*d*)   Give **two** advantages of talking to your relatives from the USA as a way of finding out information for your investigation.

(Enquiry Skills, **2** marks)

[Turn over

QUESTION 3 (A) (CONTINUED)

You find out that your relatives have brought a copy of the "**Rockford Record**" with them. You find the page below in the newspaper.

Use the newspaper page below to answer question (*e*).

The Rockford Record   page 2

	California	Texas	Mississippi	New York
High School Graduates	77%	76%	73%	79%
People living in poverty	13%	16%	19%	14%
Violent crimes per 100,000	526	529	278	445
Unemployment rate	5%	5%	7%	4%

Special Reports

America at War
Full coverage of the conflicts in Iraq and Afghanistan and of the "War on Terror" on pages 12 and 13.

Crime in the USA
See "Crime in the USA – Special Report" on pages 10 and 11.

The Top Schools
Find your school in our 2009 Index – is your school the best or the worst?

E-MAIL NEWSLETTERS
Sign up for your weekly newsletter. These specialised e-mails give extra information on each topic.

News –	Breaking news
Politics –	The 2008 Elections
Issues –	Youth Crime
Life –	Personal Health
Sports –	Baseball

Crime in Rockford

There will be a public meeting about local crime in the town hall on Friday. Come along and make your views known to the Chief of Police who will be there.

(*e*) Give **two** ways in which you could use the newspaper page above to help with your investigation into "Crime in the USA".

For **each** way, explain why it would be a **good** way to help you with your investigation.

(Enquiry Skills, **4** marks)

NOW GO TO QUESTION 4 ON PAGE SEVENTEEN

QUESTION 3 (CONTINUED)

(B) **CHINA**

(a) | *Chinese people can **participate** in politics in many ways.* |

Describe **two** ways in which *Chinese people can **participate** in politics* in China.

In your answer, you **must** use Chinese examples.

To answer this question, you may wish to use the drawings above.

(Knowledge & Understanding, **4** marks)

[Turn over

QUESTION 3 (B) (CONTINUED)

(b)   Study Sources 1 and 2 below, then answer the question which follows.

SOURCE 1

Unemployment Rate in Selected Chinese Regions

Year	Beijing	Guangdong	Henan
1998	0·8%	3·0%	3·0%
2000	0·9%	3·2%	3·1%
2002	1·4%	3·4%	3·5%
2004	2·3%	3·6%	4·7%
2006	2·5%	3·7%	4·8%

SOURCE 2

The Nanchong News

Report about the Wealth Gap

Unemployment in China is increasing the gap between rich and poor.

Unemployed people in Henan province struggle to live on $12 per month in benefits whereas the average monthly wage is $64. The average monthly wage in Beijing is $138 and in Guangdong it is $149.

Different education levels affect the differences in income.

The highest ownership of cars was in Beijing where 20% of households owned a car whereas in Guangdong it was 8% and in Henan 3%.

Since 1998, unemployment has increased in all the selected regions. The region with the lowest rate of unemployment in 2006 had the highest average monthly income.

View of Kathy Lou

Using **only** Source 1 and Source 2 above, give **one** reason to **support** and **one** reason to **oppose** the view of Kathy Lou.

(Enquiry Skills, **4** marks)

QUESTION 3 (B) (CONTINUED)

You are investigating the topic in the box below.

CRIME IN CHINA

Answer questions (*c*), (*d*) and (*e*) which follow.

(*c*)   As part of the **Planning Stage**, give **two** relevant **aims** for your investigation.

(Enquiry Skills, **2** marks)

Relatives from China are visiting Scotland on holiday and you decide to talk to them about your investigation.

(*d*)   Give **two** advantages of talking to your relatives from China as a way of finding out information for your investigation.

(Enquiry Skills, **2** marks)

[Turn over

QUESTION 3 (B) (CONTINUED)

You find out that your relatives have brought a copy of the "**Kowloon Herald**" with them. You find the page below in the newspaper.

Use the newspaper page below to answer question (*e*).

The Kowloon Herald — page 2
Hong Kong's Biggest English Speaking Newspaper

	Hong Kong	Guangzhou	Sichuan	Henan
High School Graduates	96%	91%	72%	75%
People living in poverty	18%	16%	27%	27%
Violent crimes per 100,000	138	147	68	62
Unemployment rate	4%	3%	4·5%	5%

Special Reports

The Chinese Economy
Analysis of the rapid growth in the Chinese economy. Could the economy "overheat"? Turn to pages 7 and 8 to find out.

Crime in China
See "Crime in China – Special Report" on pages 10 and 11.

Olympic Impact
Turn to pages 12 and 13 to find out how the Beijing Olympics boosted Chinese tourism.

E-MAIL NEWSLETTERS
Sign up for your weekly newsletter. These specialised e-mails give extra information on each topic.

News –	Breaking news
Politics –	Voting in the Party Congress
Issues –	Youth Crime
Life –	Has the One Child Policy worked?
Sports –	World Cup 2010

Crime in Hong Kong

The head of the Ministry for Public Security will be in Hong Kong on Friday to hear your views on the issue of crime. Come along and make your views known.

(*e*)   Give **two** ways in which you could use the newspaper page above to help with your investigation into "Crime in China".

For **each** way, explain why it would be a **good** way to help you with your investigation.

(Enquiry Skills, **4** marks)

NOW GO TO QUESTION 4 ON PAGE SEVENTEEN

SYLLABUS AREA 4 - INTERNATIONAL RELATIONS

QUESTION 4

(*a*)   **Problems faced by some African countries**

War/Conflict	**Debt**	**HIV/AIDS**	**Unsafe water**

Choose **two** of the problems shown above.

Describe how **each of the problems you have chosen** affects some African countries.

*(Knowledge & Understanding, **4** marks)*

[Turn over

QUESTION 4 (CONTINUED)

(b)   Study Sources 1 and 2 below, then answer the question which follows.

SOURCE 1

EU Reform Treaty – The governments say "YES"

In 2007, all 27 European Union (EU) governments agreed a new treaty. It is called the EU Reform Treaty. European governments believe that it will give better security for all and help improve living standards for EU citizens. However, there are many people in Europe who do not support the Reform Treaty, particularly in France and Denmark.

The UK Government believes that British people support the treaty. They do not think a referendum on the EU Reform Treaty is necessary.

SOURCE 2

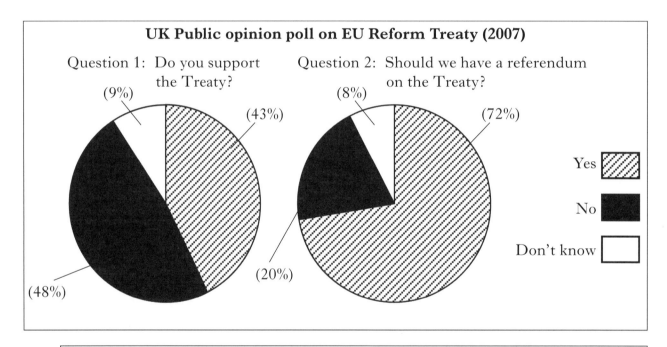

Statements made by John O'Donovan, Journalist

- All of the EU member governments have said "yes" to the Treaty.
- Almost half of the UK population are against the Reform Treaty.
- A large percentage of the UK's population are undecided about the Treaty.
- Most people agree with the UK government about a referendum on the Treaty.

Using **only** Source 1 and Source 2 above, write down **two** statements made by John O'Donovan which are **exaggerated**.

Using **only** the information in the Sources, give **one** reason why **each** of the statements you have chosen is **exaggerated**.

(Enquiry Skills, **4** marks)

QUESTION 4 (CONTINUED)

(c)
> *Countries like the UK can benefit from being members of the European Union.*

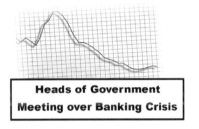

Give **two** ways in which a country *like the UK can benefit from being a member of the European Union.*

For **one** of these ways, describe how a country like the UK could benefit.

To answer this question, you may wish to use the drawings above.

(Knowledge & Understanding, **4** marks)

[Turn over for Question 4 (d) on *Page twenty*

QUESTION 4 (CONTINUED)

(*d*)   Study the information below, then answer the question which follows.

	**Information about Tonu** Tonu is a town in the African country of Ghana. Tonu's population is around 23,000. Many of the people are very poor and half of them live on less than one dollar per day. The average income in the town is only $500 per year. Ghana is a democratic country, with elections being held every four years. It is difficult to improve standards of living as only 58% of Tonu's population can read and write.

Ghana's government wants to solve some of Tonu's problems. They are not sure if **Project A** or **Project B** would **best solve these problems**.

<table>
<tr><th>PROJECT A</th><th>PROJECT B</th></tr>
<tr><td>

BS Industries – New factories

A new factory will be built in Tonu on land which will have to be cleared of rubbish. Electrical goods will be produced and sold throughout the world. Wages are likely to be around $1000 each per year for the 110 permanent workers.

The jobs will be low skilled and require little education. Some temporary jobs will be created to clear the land. The building work itself will take around four months to complete.

</td><td>

Ghana Learning Foundation – Schools

This charity works in many different parts of Ghana. Five new primary schools will be built in Tonu, giving around two thousand children access to education for the first time.

Each school will serve a main housing area. Schools will be built on land that is not being currently used. The building work will take around 6 months to complete. 100 local people will be trained as teachers. They will then earn around $1200 per year.

</td></tr>
</table>

Using **only** the information above, decide which project, **Project A** or **Project B**, would be the **better** choice for Ghana's government to **solve Tonu's problems**.

Give **two** reasons to **support** your decision.

You **must** link the information about Tonu to the project you have chosen.

(Enquiry Skills, **4** marks)

[END OF QUESTION PAPER]

[BLANK PAGE]

C

2640/403

NATIONAL
QUALIFICATIONS
2009

MONDAY, 25 MAY
1.00 PM – 3.00 PM

MODERN STUDIES
STANDARD GRADE
Credit Level

1 Read every question carefully.

2 Answer all questions as fully as you can.

3 If you cannot do a question, go on to the next one. Try again later.

4 In question 3, answer **one** section only: Section (A) The USA **or** Section (B) China.

5 Write your answers in the answer book provided. Indicate clearly, in the left hand margin, the question and section of question being answered. Do not write in the right hand margin.

[BLANK PAGE]

SYLLABUS AREA 1—LIVING IN A DEMOCRACY

QUESTION 1

(a)

> *There are many ways for people in the UK to **participate** in **election campaigns**.*

Describe, **in detail**, the ways in which people in the UK can **participate** in **election campaigns**.

(Knowledge & Understanding, **6** marks)

(b)

> *Pressure Groups have many **responsibilities**.*

Choose **two** of the following **responsibilities**.

The pressure group should:

- inform the police before a demonstration
- keep protests within the law
- represent members' views
- only use accurate information during campaigns.

For **each responsibility** you have chosen, explain, **in detail**, why it is important.

(Knowledge & Understanding, **4** marks)

[Turn over

QUESTION 1 (CONTINUED)

(c)   Study Sources 1, 2 and 3 below and on the next page, then answer the question which follows.

SOURCE 1

**What should happen to Scotland after the 2007 Scottish Parliament Election
Views of Main Parties**

LIBERAL DEMOCRATS	LABOUR	CONSERVATIVE	SNP	GREENS
Increased powers for the Scottish Parliament but "no" to independence	Scotland to remain in the United Kingdom	Scotland remains in the UK but willing to debate issues about devolved powers	Scotland to become independent after a referendum	Scotland to become an independent country

Seats in Scottish Parliament 2003 and 2007

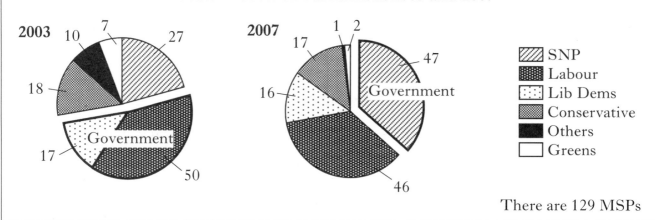

There are 129 MSPs

SOURCE 2

**Scottish Parliament Elections (2003 & 2007)
Regional Turnout**

Region	Turnout 2003	Turnout 2007
1. Central Scotland	48·5%	50·5%
2. Glasgow	41·5%	41·6%
3. Highlands and Islands	52·3%	54·7%
4. Lothians	50·5%	54·0%
5. Mid-Scotland and Fife	49·7%	52·8%
6. North East Scotland	48·3%	50·7%
7. South of Scotland	52·3%	53·6%
8. West of Scotland	53·3%	56·5%
Scotland (Total)	**49·4%**	**51·7%**

QUESTION 1 (c) (CONTINUED)

SOURCE 3

National Identity and the Scottish Parliament

People have different views on what makes a Scot. Is it supporting our football and rugby teams; is it a willingness to wear a kilt; is it a liking for traditional Scottish music or shortbread or the consumption of our national drink?

What makes a Scot?

A person's accent appears to be a very important factor when people are deciding if

somebody is Scottish or not. A recent survey showed that 70% of Scottish people felt that a non-white person with a Scottish accent was Scottish whilst 54% believed that a person with an English accent living in Scotland, was not Scottish.

In 1999, prior to the opening of the Scottish Parliament, research carried out for the Government

showed 25% of people in Scotland felt "Scottish not British" and 11% said they would describe themselves as "British not Scottish". SNP voters and young people were much more likely to say they were Scottish whilst the elderly and Conservative voters were more likely to say they were "British". When the research was repeated in 2006, 32% of Scottish people said they would describe themselves as "Scottish not British" and only 9% of those asked said that they were "British not Scottish".

The West of Scotland Region had the largest increase in voter turnout. In 2007, there were more MSPs in favour of independence than ever before and, since the opening of the Scottish Parliament, people feel more Scottish.

View of Callum Wishart

Using **only** Sources 1, 2 and 3, explain **the extent to which** Callum Wishart could be accused of being **selective in the use of facts.**

(Enquiry Skills, **8** marks)

[Turn over

SYLLABUS AREA 2—CHANGING SOCIETY

QUESTION 2

(a)   **Government Policies to help Families with Dependent Children (2007)**

Education Maintenance Allowance	SureStart	Child Benefit
Child Tax Credits	Child Trust Fund	New Deal

Different governments at different times have introduced policies which they believed would help families with dependent children in a number of different ways.

Choose **two** policies from the six above.

For **each** policy, describe, **in detail**, the ways in which they helped families with dependent children.

(Knowledge and Understanding, **6** marks)

QUESTION 2 (CONTINUED)

(b)   Study Sources 1 and 2 below, then answer the question which follows.

SOURCE 1

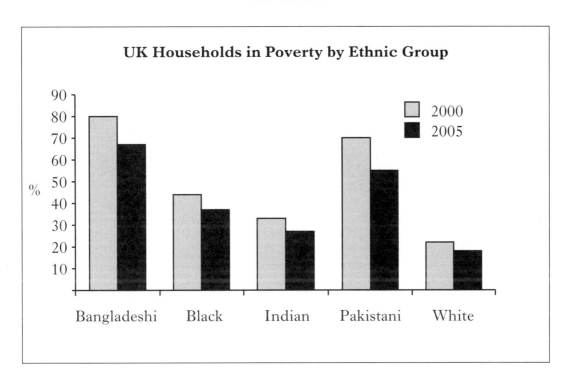

SOURCE 2

Average hourly Pay for Workers aged 18 and over (£ per hour)		
	2000	**2005**
Bangladeshi	6·00	7·60
Black	7·04	7·33
Indian	6·57	8·41
Pakistani	4·94	6·25
White	6·76	8·00

Pakistani households have had a bigger fall in poverty than all other ethnic groups. The group with the smallest increase in hourly pay had the smallest drop in poverty.

View of Asif Iqbal

Give **one** reason to **support** and **one** reason to **oppose** the view of Asif Iqbal.

(Enquiry Skills, **4** marks)

QUESTION 2 (CONTINUED)

(c) Study the information about London and Sources 1, 2, 3 and 4 below and on the next page, then answer the question which follows.

Focus on London

- In 2005, there were 7,428,600 people in London.
- The city is divided into 32 boroughs.
- It is by far the largest city in the United Kingdom accounting for 12·5% of the country's population.
- Many immigrants have moved to London making it very ethnically mixed.

The Population of London: Ethnic Composition (2005)

	Number	%
White	5,182,200	70·0
Black	809,000	10·2
Indian	473,800	6·5
Bangladeshi	165,900	2·3
Pakistani	161,800	2·2
Chinese	103,000	1·5
Others	532,900	7·3

1 Barking and Dagenham
2 Brent
3 Kensington and Chelsea
4 Newham
5 Sutton

SOURCE 1

Resident Population by Ethnic Group in Selected London Boroughs (%)

Ethnic Group	Barking and Dagenham	Brent	Kensington and Chelsea	Newham	Sutton
White	85·2	45·3	78·6	39·4	89·2
Black	7·0	19·9	7·0	21·6	2·6
Indian	2·3	18·5	2·0	12·1	2·3
Bangladeshi	0·4	0·5	0·7	8·8	0·3
Pakistani	1·8	4·0	0·8	8·5	0·7
Chinese	0·5	1·0	1·6	1·0	0·7
Others	2·8	10·8	9·3	8·6	4·2

SOURCE 2

Crime in Selected London Boroughs (Rates per 10,000 people)

Type of Crime	Barking and Dagenham	Brent	Kensington and Chelsea	Newham	Sutton
Violence	321	308	181	340	178
Robbery	47	88	49	101	23
Burglary	68	96	85	108	38
Car Crime	200	180	169	282	132
Total Crime	**652**	**684**	**495**	**847**	**381**

QUESTION 2 (c) (CONTINUED)

SOURCE 3

Employment Statistics for Selected London Boroughs (%)

	Employment Rate	Self-employed	Unemployment Rate
Barking and Dagenham	62·0	12·8	9·6
Brent	68·3	17·1	7·7
Kensington and Chelsea	67·2	25·7	6·3
Newham	59·4	12·8	8·7
Sutton	88·3	11·6	4·9

SOURCE 4

Education and Earnings in Selected London Boroughs

	Percentage of pupils achieving 5 or more exam passes by age 16	Average Weekly Income
Barking and Dagenham	55·8	£478·30
Brent	61·4	£467·50
Kensington and Chelsea	63·0	£818·40
Newham	52·8	£460·40
Sutton	70·8	£506·00

Using **only** the information about London and Sources 1, 2, 3 and 4, what **conclusions** can be drawn about London and some of its boroughs?

You must **make** and **justify** a conclusion about **each** of the following headings.

- The relationship between education and unemployment
- The relationship between total crime and income
- The borough whose ethnic mix is **most** like that of London as a whole
- The borough that would be the most desirable to live in

(Enquiry Skills, **8** marks)

[Turn over

[BLANK PAGE]

SYLLABUS AREA 3—IDEOLOGIES

QUESTION 3

Answer **one** section only: Section (A)—The USA on pages *eleven* to *thirteen*

            OR   Section (B)—China on pages *fifteen* to *seventeen*

(A) **THE USA**

(*a*) | *In the USA, social and economic inequalities continue to exist.* |

Explain, **in detail**, why *in the USA, social and economic inequalities continue to exist.*

In answering this question, you must:

• describe the inequalities which exist

• explain the reasons why they exist.

In your answer, you **must** use American examples.

(Knowledge and Understanding, **8** marks)

[Turn over

QUESTION 3 (A) (CONTINUED)

(b)   Study the information on **The Illegal Immigration Debate** and **Sources 1** and **2** on the next page, then answer the question which follows.

The Illegal Immigration Debate

For centuries, the USA has attracted immigrants in search of "The American Dream". Today, Americans are deeply divided about how to deal with the illegal immigrants who enter the USA through the border with Mexico. The best place to see, at first hand, the issue of immigration is in California. Here, for instance, you can find Mexican nannies collecting the children of rich Californians from suburban schools or Mexicans cleaning toilets. Many are part of the 7% of California's population that are illegal immigrants. California has one third of all illegal immigrants in the USA.

USA Illegal Immigrants (millions)

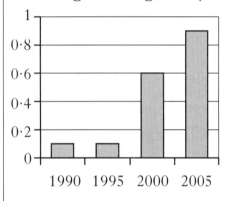

Illegal Immigrants – % of Californian workforce

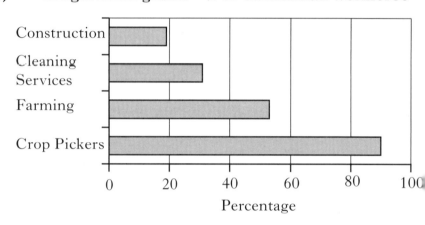

Unemployment is not a problem in California. It is less than 5%. 70% of Californians think that illegal immigrants are doing jobs that others do not want. Many Californians are concerned that illegal immigrants often live and work as "modern-day slaves" because they work for low wages and have no paid holidays or sick pay. However, some argue that illegal immigrants are a financial burden on California as they cost $650 million in health care, $2·2 billion in education with an overall cost of $5 billion a year.

One new suggestion to stop these illegal immigrants is to improve existing border security by building a high-tech fence at a cost of $5 billion to the Federal Government.

Proposed high-tech fence on the 140 mile Californian/Mexican Border

Californian voter opinion on how to deal with illegal immigrants	Yes	No	No opinion
Increase the number of border guards	71%	25%	4%
Introduce a Temporary Worker Programme	68%	28%	4%
Build a high-tech fence along sections of the border	36%	59%	5%

QUESTION 3 (A) (b) (CONTINUED)

The two people below are hoping to become Governor of California. Here are extracts from speeches they have made.

SOURCE 1

Corrine Padilla I am an American citizen but my Grandfather was an illegal immigrant from Mexico chasing the American Dream. I am not concerned about illegal immigration as the numbers entering the US are not rising steeply.

I, like many Californians, feel that illegal immigrants in California are exploited. My first priority will be to improve their pay and working conditions.

Although illegal immigration continues to occur, many Californians are not in favour of a high-tech fence. I agree with them as it will not prevent illegal immigration.

Border guards do a very difficult job but we do not need to increase their numbers and most Californians agree with me on this issue.

California needs workers to come and help our farmers pick their crops. If David Beckham can come and play football for LA Galaxy for a short time then a Mexican labourer should be able to come and work for a short time then go back to Mexico.

SOURCE 2

Peter Head My ancestors came from Scotland and I am proud of this. Although California only has a very small percentage of all US illegal immigrants, I am still concerned about this.

Illegal immigrants already in California cost a lot of money. Because of this they should become legal citizens so that they pay their taxes. This is my main aim.

I, like most Californians, believe that illegal immigrants take the jobs that Californians want, so we need to do something to stop it.

The high-tech fence should not be built as it will not protect all of the Californian/Mexican border. This means that illegal immigration would just continue.

The money saved by not having the high-tech fence would be better spent on more guards patrolling the border, which is what Californians want.

Use **only** the information about **The Illegal Immigration Debate** and **Sources 1** and **2** above.

(i) State **which person** would be the **more suitable** to become Governor of California.

(ii) Give **three detailed reasons to support your choice**.

(iii) Give **two detailed reasons** why you **rejected** the other person.

In your answer, you **must relate** information about the Illegal Immigration Debate to the information about the **two** people.

(Enquiry Skills, **10** marks)

NOW GO TO QUESTION 4 ON PAGE EIGHTEEN

[BLANK PAGE]

QUESTION 3 (CONTINUED)

(B) **CHINA**

(a) | *In China, social and economic inequalities continue to exist.*

Explain, **in detail**, why *in China, social and economic inequalities continue to exist.*

In answering this question, you must:

- describe the inequalities which exist

- explain the reasons why they exist.

In your answer, you **must** use Chinese examples.

(Knowledge and Understanding, **8** marks)

[Turn over

QUESTION 3 (B) (CONTINUED)

(b)   Study the information on **The Migration Debate** and **Sources 1** and **2** on the next page, then answer the question which follows.

The Migration Debate

The difference in the standard of living between the cities and countryside in China is among the larg[e] in the world. As a result, many poor farmers are moving to the eastern cities where a lot of new buildi[ng] is taking place. This migration is necessary to provide labour for the factories that are turning Chi[na] into the "workshop of the world". Without these workers, China's economy would suffer. The m[ost] common destinations for migrants are the cities of Beijing, Shanghai and Guangzhou. It is estimat[ed] that 60% of China's population will live in towns and cities by 2020.

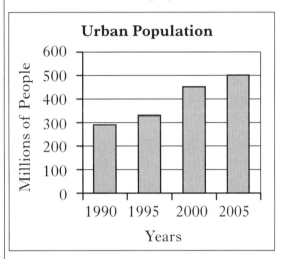

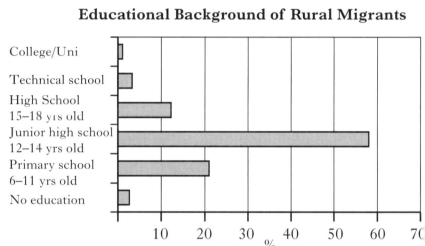

Educational Background of Rural Migrants

Unemployment is low in China. The rate in Beijing is 2·5% whilst it is 3·4% in Guangzhou. The migrants who move to these cities often work in clothing factories, shops, restaurants or in construction crews. Most plan to work for a year or two and then return home to have a family. Often they do not receive their whole wage on time as some is withheld to make sure that they stay for a full year. Since urban workers earn three times that of farmers, they send home part of their pay to help ageing parents or to educate younger brothers or sisters. Many Chinese are concerned about this wealth gap and President Hu Jintao has promised greater spending on health and education in rural areas in order to reduce the differences.

Many feel that the cities cannot cope with the growing numbers of migrants. Problems include a gr[eat] shortage of housing, hospitals, power and transport. It is also claimed that in big cities more th[an] 70% of crime is caused by temporary rural migrants.

Beijing residents' opinions on how to deal with migration	Yes	No	No opinion
Allow temporary migrant workers to become permanent	74%	14%	12%
Impose an additional tax on migrant workers in the city	24%	62%	14%
Make foreign firms invest in rural development when they locate in China	52%	27%	21%

QUESTION 3 (B) (CONTINUED)

The two people below are hoping to become the "Beijing Migration Officer". Here are extracts from speeches they have made.

SOURCE 1

Liu Wang I moved from the countryside to the city 15 years ago in order to improve my standard of living. Many migrants are college educated or better which is good for our cities and I will work to see this continue.

I, like many other Beijing residents, feel that temporary migrant workers are exploited. My first priority will be to make them permanent residents.

These migrant workers are required to fill jobs in construction, manufacturing and services. However, it is no good if only the cities are rich. I believe it is important that something is also done to raise the standard of living in the countryside.

In my opinion, it is no good punishing workers who continue to move to the city with additional taxes and most people agree with me on this issue.

As Chinese citizens, we believe that it is important to look after ourselves and most of Beijing realises that we should not rely on investment from foreign firms for development in rural areas.

SOURCE 2

Cho Yuen My ancestors moved from the countryside many years ago and I am proud of this. I am not concerned about rural migration as the numbers moving to the cities are small and not rising steeply.

I, like many others in Beijing, believe that temporary rural migrants fit in well and make Beijing a better place to live. My first priority will be to encourage further migration.

The income which these migrant workers send home is vital to the rural economy. I aim to allow this to continue so that city growth benefits those still living in the countryside.

Until President Hu Jintao has reduced the differences in education, I will work to allow migrants to come to Beijing in order to gain more than basic schooling so that better paid and better quality jobs are available to them.

Finally, China has become the "workshop of the world" and many international companies benefit from our labour. I am not alone in believing that we should make foreign firms invest in the development of rural China since they are using our labour to make profits.

Use **only** the information about **The Urban Migration Debate** and **Sources 1** and **2** above.

(i) State **which person** would be the **more suitable** to become Beijing Migration Officer.

(ii) Give **three detailed reasons to support your choice**.

(iii) Give **two detailed reasons** why you **rejected** the other person.

In your answer, you **must relate** information about The Migration Debate to the information about the **two** people.

(Enquiry Skills, **10** marks)

NOW GO TO QUESTION 4 ON PAGE EIGHTEEN

SYLLABUS AREA 4—INTERNATIONAL RELATIONS

QUESTION 4

(a)

> A number of European countries have faced threats to their security. They have responded in different ways.

Describe, **in detail**:

- the threats these countries have faced
- the ways in which they have responded to these threats.

(Knowledge & Understanding, **8** marks)

QUESTION 4 (CONTINUED)

You have been asked to carry out **two** investigations.

The first investigation is on the topic in the box below.

> **HIV/Aids in Africa**

Now answer questions (*b*) and (*c*) which follow.

(*b*)   State a relevant **hypothesis** for your investigation.

(Enquiry Skills, **2** marks)

(*c*)   Give **two** relevant **aims** to help you prove or disprove your hypothesis.

(Enquiry Skills, **2** marks)

The second investigation is on the topic in the box below.

> **The benefits of EU expansion**

Now answer questions (*d*) and (*e*) which follow.

(*d*)   Describe, **in detail, two** factors that must be taken into account when designing and carrying out a survey.

(Enquiry Skills, **4** marks)

[Turn over for Question 4 (*e*) on *Page twenty*

QUESTION 4 (CONTINUED)

(e)   You also decide to carry out a search on the Internet.

You enter the phrase, "Benefits of EU expansion" into an Internet search engine.

Six results are shown below.

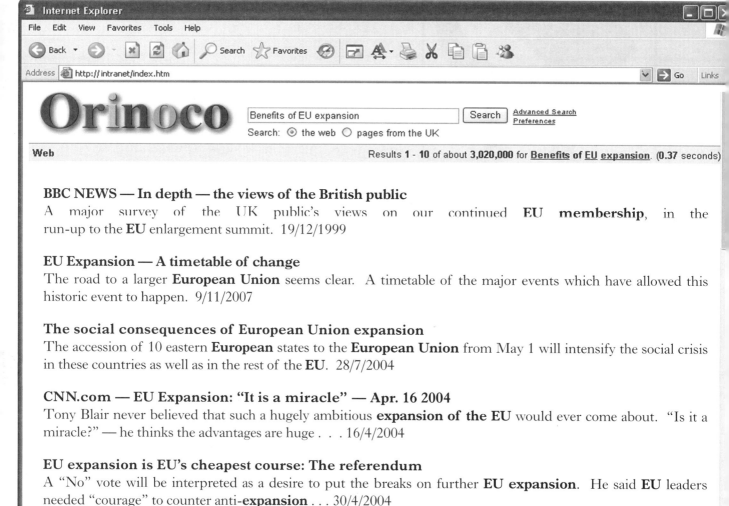

BBC NEWS — In depth — the views of the British public
A major survey of the UK public's views on our continued **EU membership**, in the run-up to the **EU** enlargement summit. 19/12/1999

EU Expansion — A timetable of change
The road to a larger **European Union** seems clear. A timetable of the major events which have allowed this historic event to happen. 9/11/2007

The social consequences of European Union expansion
The accession of 10 eastern **European** states to the **European Union** from May 1 will intensify the social crisis in these countries as well as in the rest of the **EU**. 28/7/2004

CNN.com — EU Expansion: "It is a miracle" — Apr. 16 2004
Tony Blair never believed that such a hugely ambitious **expansion of the EU** would ever come about. "Is it a miracle?" — he thinks the advantages are huge . . . 16/4/2004

EU expansion is EU's cheapest course: The referendum
A "No" vote will be interpreted as a desire to put the breaks on further **EU expansion**. He said **EU** leaders needed "courage" to counter anti-**expansion** . . . 30/4/2004

EU expansion and EU growth — The benefits explained
Countries have benefited from the formation and the later **expansion of the EU**. An outline of the benefits of European **expansion** and integration, which appear to be numerous . . .9/5/2009

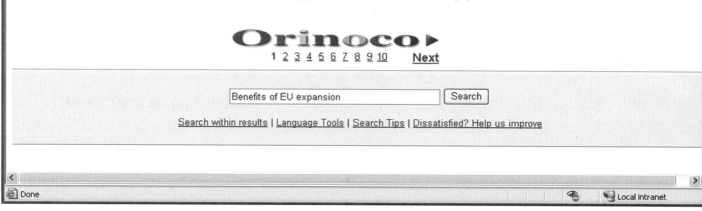

Which result do you think would be **most useful**? **Explain** your answer.

(Enquiry Skills, **2** marks)

[END OF QUESTION PAPER]

[BLANK PAGE]

2640/402

NATIONAL
QUALIFICATIONS
2010

TUESDAY, 25 MAY
10.20 AM–11.50 AM

MODERN STUDIES
STANDARD GRADE
General Level

1   Read every question carefully.

2   Answer all questions as fully as you can.

3   If you cannot do a question, go on to the next one. Try again later.

4   In question 3, answer **one** section only: Section (A) The USA **or** Section (B) China.

5   Write your answers in the answer book provided. Indicate clearly, in the left hand margin, the question and section of question being answered. Do not write in the right hand margin.

SYLLABUS AREA 1—LIVING IN A DEMOCRACY

QUESTION 1

(a)

(i) Give **two** ways in which a Councillor **can find out** about a local problem.

(ii) Describe **one** action a local Councillor could take to help **solve** a local problem.

To answer this question, you may wish to use the drawings above.

(Knowledge & Understanding, **4** marks)

QUESTION 1 (CONTINUED)

(*b*)   Study Sources 1 and 2 below, then answer the question which follows.

SOURCE 1

UK Election Results in Glasgow East Constituency

	Number of Votes 2005	Number of Votes 2008
Conservative Party	2135	1639
Labour Party	18 775	10 912
Liberal Democrat Party	3665	915
Scottish National Party	5268	11 277
Scottish Socialist Party	1096	555

SOURCE 2

Changes in the Scottish Parliament

The Scottish Parliament was set up in 1999 and since then has made many changes to life in Scotland.

There are 129 seats in the Scottish Parliament. In 1999, the Labour Party was the largest group in the Scottish Parliament with 56 seats. Labour formed a coalition government with the Liberal Democrats. The closest party to Labour was the SNP with 35 seats. In the 2007 election, the SNP won 47 seats compared to Labour who won 46. The next election to the Scottish Parliament will be held in 2011.

In Glasgow East, the support for all political parties decreased between 2005 and 2008.

Labour continues to be the largest party in the Scottish Parliament.

View of Iain McEwan

Using **only** Sources 1 and 2 above, give **two** reasons to **oppose** the view of Iain McEwan.

(Enquiry Skills, **4** marks)

[Turn over

QUESTION 1 (CONTINUED)

(c) | *People have **rights** and **responsibilities** when they belong to a Pressure Group.*

Describe one **right** and one **responsibility** that people have when they belong to a Pressure Group.

To answer this question, you may wish to use the drawing above.

(Knowledge and Understanding, **4** marks)

QUESTION 1 (CONTINUED)

(d)   Study Sources 1 and 2 below, then answer the question which follows.

SOURCE 1

The SNP's First Year in Government (2007–2008)

In May 2007, less than a month after they came to power, the SNP abolished road tolls on all Scottish bridges. In December 2007, the SNP announced that they would abolish NHS prescription charges by 2011. In February 2008, SNP MSPs voted to scrap the one-off student fee which students must pay when they graduate. Labour and Conservative MSPs voted against this policy. In the Spring of 2008, the Scottish Government urged people not to "panic buy" petrol when oil refineries closed due to industrial action. Fuel was shipped from England to ensure Scotland did not run out.

SOURCE 2
Opinion Poll (May 2008)
Question: Which party would you vote for?

Party	In a Scottish Parliament Election	In a UK Parliament Election
Conservative	13%	17%
Labour	31%	34%
Liberal Democrat	15%	14%
SNP	36%	30%

STATEMENTS MADE BY SADIA NAVEED

- The Conservative Party would get least votes in an election for the Scottish Parliament.
- The SNP and the Conservative Party agreed on all policies during the year.
- The SNP promised to abolish prescription charges.
- The SNP is likely to get most votes in a UK Parliament Election.

Using **only** Sources 1 and 2 above, write down **two** statements made by Sadia Naveed which are **exaggerated**.

Using the information in the Sources, give **one** reason why **each** of the statements you have chosen is **exaggerated**.

(Enquiry Skills, **4** marks)

SYLLABUS AREA 2—CHANGING SOCIETY

QUESTION 2

(a) | Elderly people make more use of the National Health Service (NHS) than other groups.

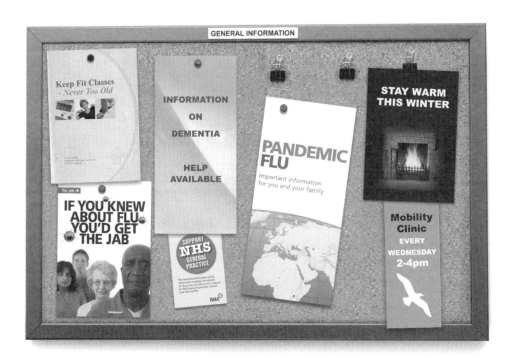

Give **two** reasons why *elderly people make more use of the NHS than other groups.*

To answer this question, you may wish to use the drawing above.

(Knowledge and Understanding, **4** marks)

QUESTION 2 (CONTINUED)

(b)   Study Sources 1 and 2 below, then answer the question which follows.

<table>
<tr><td align="center">**SOURCE 1**</td><td align="center">**SOURCE 2**</td></tr>
<tr><td>

VIEW OF KIRSTY LAWRENCE

The number of UK households in fuel poverty has risen to over 3·5 million.   This is a rise of over 900 000 in a single year.

Huge rises in gas and electricity bills are the main causes of this increase in fuel poverty.

The Government has spent over £20 billion in recent years on a variety of schemes to help those in fuel poverty.

The best way to solve fuel poverty is to increase State benefits to vulnerable groups such as the elderly and families with children.

</td><td>

VIEW OF GORDON MUIR

The main cause of fuel poverty is poor insulation in many houses allowing heat to escape through walls, windows and roof.

Over the past few years, the UK Government has introduced a variety of measures to try to end fuel poverty.   This has cost more than £20 billion.

However, there has been a recent increase from 2·6 million, to just over 3·5 million households who suffer from fuel poverty.

The Government should provide better insulation for homes to help reduce fuel poverty.

</td></tr>
</table>

Sources 1 and 2 give different views about **fuel poverty**.

Write down **two** differences between these views.

You **must** only use the information from the Sources above.

(Enquiry Skills, **4** marks)

[Turn over

QUESTION 2 (CONTINUED)

You are investigating the topic in the box below.

> **FAMILIES WITH YOUNG CHILDREN**

Answer questions (*c*), (*d*) and (*e*) which follow.

(*c*) As part of the **Planning Stage**, give **two** relevant **aims** for your investigation.

(Enquiry Skills, **2** marks)

You decide to **visit** a local **Nursery** to speak to parents about your investigation.

(*d*) Describe **two** things that you would need to do to **prepare** for your **visit** to a local Nursery.

(Enquiry Skills, **4** marks)

QUESTION 2 (CONTINUED)

You decide to carry out a survey of parents at the Nursery.

You write some questions and show them to your teacher.

Your teacher says that one of your questions is really good.

Use the survey below to answer question (*e*).

Auldtown Academy
Modern Studies Department
Survey

(Please circle answers as required)

1. How long have you been unemployed?   (*a*)   1–2 months
                                             (*b*)   3–6 months
                                             (*c*)   6 months–1 year
                                             (*d*)   over 1 year

2. What do you think about the level of Child Benefit?

    Too high   About right   Too low

3. Do you receive . . .   (*a*)   a state pension?
                                             (*b*)   a work pension?
                                             (*c*)   a private pension?

(*e*)   Choose the **one** question which would **best** help with your investigation into "Families with young children".

Explain why this question would help with your investigation.

*(Enquiry Skills, **2** marks)*

[Turn over

SYLLABUS AREA 3 — IDEOLOGIES

QUESTION 3

Answer **ONE** section only: Section (A)—The USA on pages *ten* to *thirteen*

                                    OR Section (B)—China on pages *fourteen* to *seventeen*

(A) **THE USA**

(a)

> *American citizens may disagree with decisions taken by their Government.*

Describe **two** actions American citizens can take when they *disagree with decisions taken by their Government*.

In your answer, you **must** use American examples.

(Knowledge & Understanding, **4** marks)

QUESTION 3 (A) (CONTINUED)

(b)   Study the timeline below, then answer the question which follows.

TIMELINE

THE USA PRESIDENTIAL ELECTION
KEY EVENTS 2007–2009

Date	Event
Early 2007	Politicians who want to be President of the USA start to raise money and gather support. The major candidates are from the two main parties, the Democrats and Republicans.
January to June 2008	The Primary elections are held. The Democrat and Republican party members start to vote for their choice of candidate.
August to September 2008	At the Democratic Convention, Barack Obama is chosen as their candidate. The Republican Convention chooses John McCain as their candidate.
October 2008	Barack Obama and John McCain take part in TV debates. These debates are watched by many Americans. Issues like the economy, healthcare, immigration and Iraq are discussed.
November 4th 2008	On Election Day, US citizens across all 50 states cast their votes for the President. The winner is Barack Obama with 365 Electoral College votes and 52·5% of the popular vote.
January 20th 2009	The Inauguration of Barack Obama as the 44th President takes place on the steps of Capitol Hill in Washington D.C.

> The USA's main political parties are the Democrat and Republican parties. Both the Democrats and Republicans held a Convention to choose their candidate in August and September. Few Americans watched the TV debates between Obama and McCain. Unfortunately, the President was elected with less than half the popular vote.

View of Lucy Smith, US Politics Expert

Using **only** the timeline above, write down **two** statements made by Lucy Smith which are **exaggerated**.

Using the information in the timeline, give **one** reason why **each** of the statements you have chosen is **exaggerated**.

(Enquiry Skills, **4** marks)

[Turn over

QUESTION 3 (A) (CONTINUED)

(c) | *Many American people have become rich and successful.*

Describe **two** ways in which *many American people have become rich and successful.*

In your answer, you **must** use American examples.

To answer this question, you may wish to use the drawings above.

(Knowledge & Understanding, **4** marks)

QUESTION 3 (A) (CONTINUED)

(*d*)   Study the information below, then answer the question which follows.

USA Enquirer

January 2009

New policies from Barack Obama

President Barack Obama's plan is to tackle the problems within the USA. He campaigned on the idea that the USA can change.

President Obama wants to make the economy stronger and make life better for hard working Americans.

Average income per person ($)   **Percentage living below the poverty line (2008)**

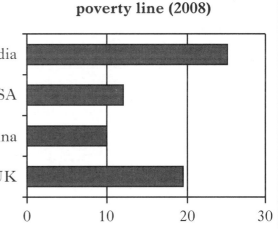

In recent years, there has been a continuous increase in the average income of people in the USA. The USA has the lowest percentage of its population living below the poverty line.

View of Emma Steele

Using **only** the information above, give **one** reason to **support** and **one** reason to **oppose** the view of Emma Steele.

(Enquiry Skills, **4** marks)

NOW GO TO QUESTION 4 ON PAGE EIGHTEEN

QUESTION 3 (CONTINUED)

(B) **CHINA**

(*a*)

Crime	Housing	Health

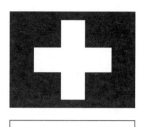

Choose **one** of the topics above.

For the topic you have chosen, give **two** reasons why some Chinese are **worse off** than others.

In your answer, you **must** use Chinese examples.

(Knowledge & Understanding, **4** marks)

QUESTION 3 (B) (CONTINUED)

(b)   Study the timeline below, then answer the question which follows.

TIMELINE

**BEIJING OLYMPICS 2008
SELECTED EVENTS 2001–2008**

Date	Event
July 2001	Beijing is announced as the host city for the 2008 Olympic Games. The unsuccessful cities are Toronto, Paris, Istanbul and Osaka.
May 2004	Construction begins on the Beijing National Stadium. It later becomes known as the "Bird's Nest" due to the way it looks.
August 2007	A human rights group based in Switzerland states that 1·5 million people have lost their homes to provide land for Olympic venues.
March 2008	The torch-lighting ceremony takes place in Olympia, Greece, home of the ancient Olympics. It is then carried round the world to Beijing.
April 2008	Thousands of protesters wave Tibetan flags and shout "Shame on China" as the Olympic torch relay passes through London. Protests continue in San Francisco, New Delhi and Canberra.
August 2008	The Chinese Government promises to give greater freedom to the press during the Olympics. It fails to do so as many Internet sites are blocked to reporters.

> The new National Stadium was designed to look like a bird's nest. Many Chinese people had lost their homes due to new Olympic buildings being built. Protests about human rights only took place in London. Reporters were given greater freedom during the Olympics.

Statements made in a speech by Sue Chan

Using **only** the timeline above, write down **two** statements made by Sue Chan which are **exaggerated**.

Using the information in the timeline, give **one** reason why **each** of the statements you have chosen is **exaggerated**.

(Enquiry Skills, **4** marks)

QUESTION 3 (B) (CONTINUED)

(c) | *Many Chinese people have become rich and successful.*

Describe **two** ways in which *many Chinese people have become rich and successful.*

In your answer, you **must** use Chinese examples.

To answer this question, you may wish to use the drawings above.

(Knowledge & Understanding, **4** marks)

QUESTION 3 (B) (CONTINUED)

(*d*)   Study the information below, then answer the question which follows.

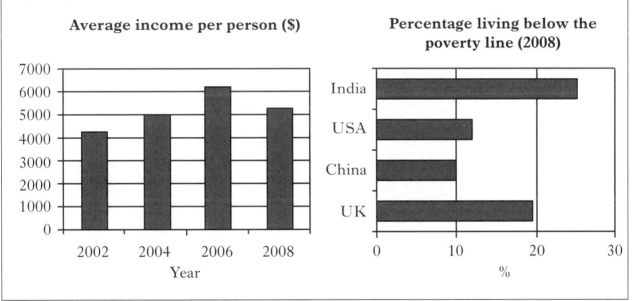

China Today

January 2009

New policies from Hu Jintao

President Hu Jintao's plan is to tackle the problems within China. He promotes the idea of a society where all Chinese people are happy and doing well.

China still has a number of poor people and it is Jintao's vision to make rural areas wealthier and reduce the number of people living in poverty.

Average income per person ($)

Percentage living below the poverty line (2008)

In recent years, there has been a continuous increase in the average income of people in China. China has the lowest percentage of its population living below the poverty line.

View of Li Yifan

Using **only** the information above, give **one** reason to **support** and **one** reason to **oppose** the view of Li Yifan.

(Enquiry Skills, **4** marks)

NOW GO TO QUESTION 4 ON PAGE EIGHTEEN

SYLLABUS AREA 4 - INTERNATIONAL RELATIONS

QUESTION 4

(a) | *The North Atlantic Treaty Organisation (NATO) is a military alliance that countries wish to join.*

Give **two** reasons why some countries want to join the NATO military alliance.

To answer this question, you may wish to use the drawing above.

(Knowledge & Understanding, **4** marks)

QUESTION 4 (CONTINUED)

(b)   Study the information below, then answer the question which follows.

SCOT AID	SCOTAID to spend £50000 in Cameroon
	Scottish charity, SCOTAID, wants to meet the needs of young people in Cameroon, which is one of Africa's poorest countries. SCOTAID has 3 main aims. • To improve education for young people • To improve basic health care • To improve child care in Cameroon

SCOTAID is not sure if **Project A** or **Project B** would **best meet its aims**.

<table>
<tr><th>PROJECT A</th><th>PROJECT B</th></tr>
<tr><td>

School Bus Project in Chomba

Chomba is an isolated village where many people are farmers. Due to the steep hillsides, farming can be very difficult.

A school bus would be purchased. This would allow an extra fifty children to attend school every day. Two local people would be employed as part-time drivers.

Every weekend the bus would be used to bring supplies such as medicines, bandages and ointments from the city of Bamenda.

The cost of this project is £50000.

</td><td>

Community Centre Project in Soppo

A new community centre would be built.

One full-time caretaker would be employed.

This project would cost £50000.

Many of Soppo's women would like to work. The new community centre will have a children's nursery.

The centre would be fully equipped with ten wind-up laptop computers that the young people could use to gain qualifications.

</td></tr>
</table>

Using **only** the information above, decide which project, **Project A** or **Project B**, would be the **better** choice to meet **SCOTAID's aims**.

You **must** link SCOTAID's aims to the project you have chosen.

Give **two** reasons to **support** your decision.

(Enquiry Skills, **4** marks)

QUESTION 4 (CONTINUED)

(c) | *Rich countries have power over poor countries in Africa.*

Describe **two** ways in which *rich countries have power over poor countries in Africa.*

To answer this question, you may wish to use the photographs above.

(Knowledge & Understanding, **4** marks)

QUESTION 4 (CONTINUED)

(d)   Study the information below, then answer the question which follows.

Daily Oil Production and Imports ('000s of barrels)
Selected EU countries

Country	2005		2008	
	Production	Imports	Production	Imports
France	70	1900	70	1900
Germany	140	2900	150	2100
Poland	30	480	33	410
UK	1800	1600	2070	1080

Write down **two** conclusions about oil production and oil imports in the European Union.

You should write **one** conclusion **with evidence** about **each** of the following.

• The country with the biggest change in oil production.

• What happens to oil imports as a country's oil production rises.

You **must** only use the information above.

(Enquiry Skills, **4** marks)

[END OF QUESTION PAPER]

[BLANK PAGE]

[BLANK PAGE]

C

2640/403

NATIONAL
QUALIFICATIONS
2010

TUESDAY, 25 MAY
1.00 PM – 3.00 PM

MODERN STUDIES
STANDARD GRADE
Credit Level

1 Read every question carefully.

2 Answer all questions as fully as you can.

3 If you cannot do a question, go on to the next one. Try again later.

4 In question 3, answer **one** section only: Section (A) The USA **or** Section (B) China.

5 Write your answers in the answer book provided. Indicate clearly, in the left hand margin, the question and section of question being answered. Do not write in the right hand margin.

[BLANK PAGE]

SYLLABUS AREA 1—LIVING IN A DEMOCRACY

QUESTION 1

(a)

> *Members of the Scottish Parliament (MSPs) **represent** their constituents **within** the Scottish Parliament at Holyrood.*

Describe, **in detail**, the ways in which MSPs **represent** their constituents **within** the Scottish Parliament at Holyrood.

(Knowledge & Understanding, **4** marks)

(b)

> *In 2008, almost 8 million workers in the UK were members of a trade union.*

Explain, **in detail**, why a worker may choose to join a trade union.

(Knowledge & Understanding, **4** marks)

[Turn over

QUESTION 1 (CONTINUED)

You have been asked to carry out **two** investigations.

The first investigation is on the topic in the box below.

> **Representation in the House of Commons**

Now answer questions (*c*) and (*d*) which follow.

(*c*) State a relevant **hypothesis** for your investigation.

(Enquiry Skills, **2** marks)

(*d*) Give **two** relevant **aims** to help you prove or disprove your hypothesis.

(Enquiry Skills, **2** marks)

QUESTION 1 (CONTINUED)

The second investigation is on the topic in the box below.

> **Participation of young people in elections**

Now answer questions (*e*) and (*f*) which follow.

Your Modern Studies class decides to use **video conferencing** to do an interview to help the pupils with their investigations into **"Participation of young people in elections"**.

Your teacher sets up a link with a school in Austria where people can vote from 16 years of age. The video conference is shown below.

| A Scottish secondary classroom | An Austrian classroom |

(*e*) Describe, **in detail**, **two** problems that need to be taken into account when setting up the video conference.

(Enquiry Skills, **4** marks)

(*f*) Describe, **in detail**, **one** advantage of using video conferencing as a method of research for an investigation.

(Enquiry Skills, **2** marks)

[Turn over

SYLLABUS AREA 2—CHANGING SOCIETY

QUESTION 2

(*a*)

Groups of people who might have difficulty in finding a suitable job

Parents with young children	People with disabilities	Older people	Minority Ethnic Groups

Choose **two** of the groups of people shown above.

For **each**, explain, **in detail**, the reasons why members of that group might have difficulty in finding a suitable job.

(Knowledge and Understanding, **8** marks)

QUESTION 2 (CONTINUED)

(b)   Study Sources 1 and 2 below, then answer the question which follows.

SOURCE 1

Child poverty rates in selected European countries (%)			
	1999	**2003**	**2006**
Austria	14	16	15
Denmark	7	9	10
Finland	7	10	9
France	17	15	13
Greece	17	21	22
Netherlands	14	18	14
UK	29	22	24

SOURCE 2

	UK child poverty (2007–2011)				
	Position in 2007	**2011 projection based on current government spending plans**		**2011 projection based on an additional £4 billion government spending**	
Group	Children within group living in poverty	Children within group living in poverty	Change in size of group	Children within group living in poverty	Change in size of group
Lone Parent	48%	49%	+30 000	38%	−320 000
Lone Parent not working	72%	74%	+30 000	58%	−240 000
Family with 3 children	30%	29%	−30 000	19%	−240 000

> Two European countries have shown a continuous decline in child poverty rates. Spending an additional £4 billion would help more children than current government spending plans.

View of Fiona Clark

Using **only** the information above, give **one** reason to **support** and **one** reason to **oppose** the view of Fiona Clark.

(Enquiry Skills, **4** marks)

QUESTION 2 (CONTINUED)

(c)   Study Sources 1, 2 and 3 below and on the next page, then answer the question which follows.

SOURCE 1

Free personal and nursing care in Scotland

At home, people aged 65 and over can no longer be charged for personal care services they receive. In 2004, 33,030 received free personal care at home. By 2008 this figure was 42,400. However, they can be charged for domestic services such as help with shopping or housework. This charge varies with their income.

People aged 65 and over who live in care homes are entitled to receive free personal care. There were 8340 people in care homes receiving free personal care in 2004. By 2008 this figure was 9600.

Nursing care can also be provided for people resident in care homes. 5270 people got nursing care in 2004 and by 2008 the figure was 6160. The remainder of the care home fees, known as the "hotel" costs, must still be paid for by themselves. "Hotel" charges can be thought of as the normal costs of living, such as accommodation, food and water, electricity and gas.

SOURCE 2

Care homes for the elderly in selected Scottish Local Authority areas (2003–2007)

Local Authority	Places Available			Spending (£ million)		
	2003	2005	2007	2003	2005	2007
East Lothian	690	701	698	7·1	8·5	9·7
Falkirk	927	935	930	8·5	9·0	9·7
Fife	2458	2670	2572	21·7	31·0	33·4
Inverclyde	580	608	678	7·5	5·8	8·5
Midlothian	586	591	588	7·2	7·6	8·2
Moray	555	582	580	7·2	6·7	7·4
North Lanarkshire	1830	1960	1982	24·7	28·9	28·2
Orkney	100	100	130	2·3	2·2	3·0
Renfrewshire	1208	1270	1276	14·5	15·6	16·5
South Lanarkshire	2926	2869	2796	24·4	18·3	28·7
West Dunbartonshire	557	623	608	7·1	8·4	10·3

QUESTION 2 (c) (CONTINUED)

SOURCE 3

Number of adults attending day care services (2007)

Reason	Under 65		Over 65	
	Male	Female	Male	Female
Dementia	89	98	997	2634
Mental Health	176	217	135	321
Physical Disability	994	944	2097	5769
Drug/Alcohol problems	152	39	28	19
Learning Disabilities	3270	3842	236	349
Other	183	62	122	238

The numbers of people receiving free personal care at home and in care homes have both risen. All local authorities that spent more in 2007 than 2003 on care homes have seen an increase in the places available between these years. Older females, for every reason, make more use of day care services than every other group.

View of Cameron Petrie

Explain, **in detail, the extent to which** Cameron Petrie could be accused of being **selective in the use of facts**.

Use **only** Sources 1, 2 and 3 above and opposite.

In your answer, you should:

- explain, **in detail**, why each of the statements made by Cameron Petrie are either correct **or** incorrect;
- reach an **overall** conclusion **on the extent to which** Cameron Petrie has been **selective in the use of facts**.

(Enquiry Skills, **8** marks)

[Turn over

[BLANK PAGE]

SYLLABUS AREA 3—IDEOLOGIES

QUESTION 3

Answer **one** section only: Section (A)—The USA on pages *eleven* to *thirteen*
                OR   Section (B)—China on pages *fifteen* to *seventeen*

(A)   **THE USA**

(*a*)   **Rights and Responsibilities in the USA**

American citizens have political rights and responsibilities.

Describe, **in detail**, the ***political rights*** and ***responsibilities*** of American citizens.

In your answer, you **must** use American examples.

                              (Knowledge and Understanding, **8** marks)

                                       [Turn over

QUESTION 3 (A) (CONTINUED)

(b) Study the information about the USA and Sources 1, 2, 3 and 4 below and on the next page, then answer the question which follows.

Information about the USA

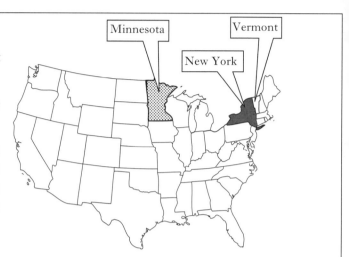

The USA is made up of 50 very different states.

The average annual income across the whole of the USA is $40,800.

According to recent figures, 22% of children under 18 live in poverty in the USA. Also the teen birth rate is 39·9 per 1000 of the population. The murder rate is running at 5·7 per 100,000 people.

SOURCE 1

Population statistics for selected states in the USA

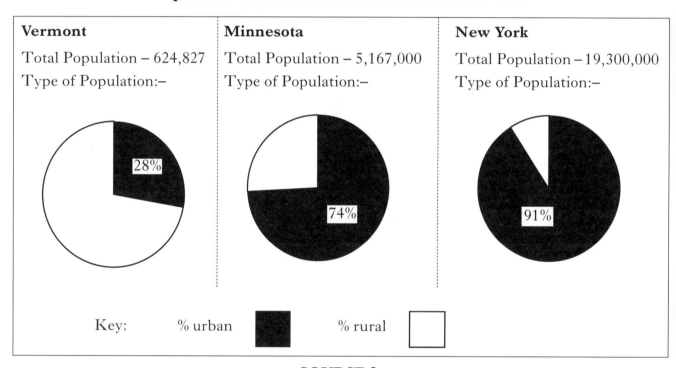

Vermont

Total Population – 624,827

Type of Population:–

28%

Minnesota

Total Population – 5,167,000

Type of Population:–

74%

New York

Total Population – 19,300,000

Type of Population:–

91%

Key: % urban [■] % rural [□]

SOURCE 2

Crime in selected states

	Vermont	Minnesota	New York
Violent crimes per 100,000 population	137	312	435
Property crimes per 100,000 population	2304	3079	2052
Murders per 100,000 population	1·9	2·4	4·8

QUESTION 3 (A) (*b*) (CONTINUED)

SOURCE 3

Social and economic statistics for selected states

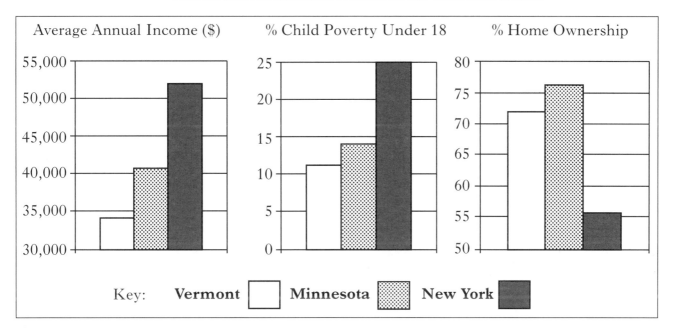

Key: **Vermont** □   **Minnesota** ▨   **New York** ■

SOURCE 4

Health issues in selected states

	Vermont	Minnesota	New York
% of population with no health insurance	10·9	8·6	13·5
Doctors per 100,000 population	362	281	389
Teen birth rate per 1000 population	18·6	26·1	26·5
Infant deaths per 1000 births	5·5	4·8	6·0
Nurses per 100,000 population	911	1014	867

Using **only** the information about the USA and Sources 1, 2, 3 and 4 above and opposite, you must **make** and **justify** conclusions about similarities and differences between the states using the **four** headings below.

- The relationship between the **total population** of these states and **violent crime**.

- The relationship between the **type of population** of these states and **income**.

- The relationship between **the percentage of the population with no health insurance** in each of these states and **infant deaths**.

- The state which is **most like the USA** as a whole.

(Enquiry Skills, **8** marks)

NOW GO TO QUESTION 4 ON PAGE EIGHTEEN

[BLANK PAGE]

QUESTION 3 (CONTINUED)

(B) **CHINA**

(*a*)

Rights and Responsibilities in China

Chinese citizens have political rights and responsibilities.

Describe, **in detail**, the ***political rights*** *and* ***responsibilities*** *of Chinese citizens.*

In your answer, you **must** use Chinese examples.

(Knowledge and Understanding, **8** marks)

[Turn over

QUESTION 3 (B) (CONTINUED)

(b)   Study the information about China and Sources 1, 2, 3 and 4 below and on the next page, then answer the question which follows.

Information about China

China is made up of 23 provinces.

The average annual income across the whole of China is $5400.

42% of the Chinese population live in urban areas and 58% in rural areas.

Average life expectancy in China is 73 years.

Adult literacy in China is 92%.

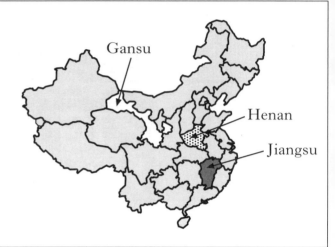

SOURCE 1

Population statistics for selected provinces in China

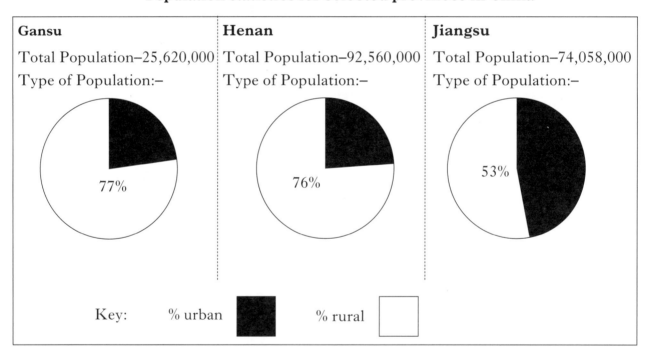

Gansu	Henan	Jiangsu
Total Population–25,620,000	Total Population–92,560,000	Total Population–74,058,000
Type of Population:–	Type of Population:–	Type of Population:–
77%	76%	53%

Key: % urban ■   % rural □

SOURCE 2

Education in selected provinces

	Gansu	Henan	Jiangsu
Literacy rate	88%	86%	93%
Average number of years per person spent in education	7	8	10
Pupils per teacher	28	21	21

QUESTION 3 (B) (CONTINUED)

SOURCE 3

Social and economic issues in selected provinces

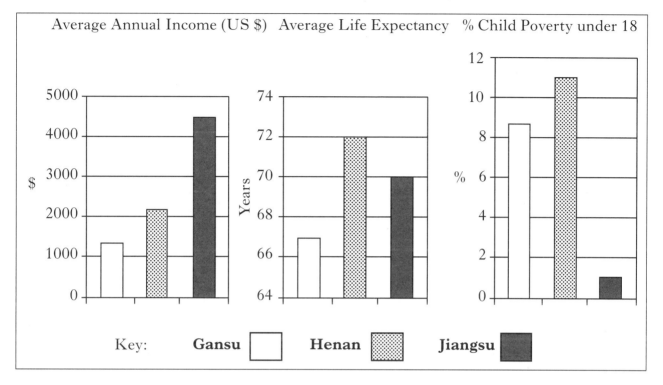

Average Annual Income (US $)   Average Life Expectancy   % Child Poverty under 18

Key: **Gansu** □   **Henan** ▨   **Jiangsu** ■

SOURCE 4

Health issues in selected provinces

	Gansu	Henan	Jiangsu
Birth rate per 1000 population	14	13	12
Infant mortality per 1000 births	21	13	8
% of under 5's who are under-weight	13·5	16	7
Doctors per 100,000 of population	1·2	1·5	3·4
% of population aged over 65	5	7	9

Using **only** the information about China and Sources 1, 2, 3 and 4 above and opposite, you must **make** and **justify** conclusions about similarities and differences between the provinces using the **four** headings below.

- The relationship between the **literacy rate** of the provinces and **percentage of children under 18 living in poverty**.

- The relationship between the **type of population** of the provinces and **income**.

- The relationship between **doctors per 100,000** and **infant mortality**.

- The province which is **most like China** as a whole.

(Enquiry Skills, **8** marks)

NOW GO TO QUESTION 4 ON PAGE EIGHTEEN

SYLLABUS AREA 4—INTERNATIONAL RELATIONS

QUESTION 4

(*a*)   **United Nations Agencies**

| UNICEF | WHO | UNESCO | FAO | WFP |

Choose **two** of the UN agencies shown above.

For **each** agency, describe, **in detail**, the ways in which it tries to meet the **needs** of some African countries.

(Knowledge & Understanding, **8** marks)

[Turn over for Question 4(*b*) on *Pages twenty* and *twenty-one*

QUESTION 4 (CONTINUED)

(b) Study the **European Union Factfile** below and **Sources 1 and 2** on the next page, then answer the question which follows.

EUROPEAN UNION (EU) FACTFILE

- The EU has grown over the years. In 2009, it had 27 member states and a population close to 500 million. Average life expectancy in the EU is 78 years and child mortality is 5 per 1000 live births. More countries still wish to join.

- 48% of the EU's budget is spent supporting agriculture and fishing although these industries employ only 4% of the workforce. This support is planned to fall over the next few years and many member governments see this as a necessity.

- The EU's growing economy needs more university graduates. EU countries are among the most technologically advanced in the world. At the moment, 51% of school leavers go to university.

- Across all member states, schools in the EU have achieved a 96% literacy level. Any country wishing to join must be able to come close to this figure.

- Trade between EU member states contributes to the high standard of living within the EU. On average, a worker in the EU earns €23,100. Several member states are concerned about the number of poor countries applying to join.

- The EU has to import 11 million barrels of oil every day from countries like Russia. Many people in the EU worry that it is too dependent on Russia for oil and would like to admit new members with large oil reserves.

- EU health and welfare systems are among the best in the world. Groups such as the elderly and children are well looked after. Any new members must try to match these standards.

Survey of EU Public Opinion

Question: How important is it that new EU members have:

	Unimportant	Not very important	Fairly important	Very important
Strict policies on crime?	4%	8%	38%	50%
Low unemployment?	0%	0%	48%	52%
A good record on human rights?	2%	10%	53%	35%

QUESTION 4 (*b*) (CONTINUED)

Country A and Country B are **Candidate Countries** hoping to be allowed to join the European Union. Source 1 and 2 contain information about both countries taken from their applications.

SOURCE 1

CANDIDATE COUNTRY "A"

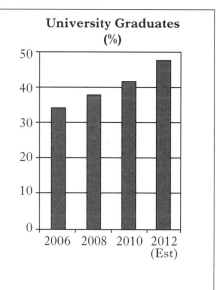

University Graduates (%)

- This country has a small population of 4·5 million people and an average income of only €11,200.

- The police have worked hard to catch drug traffickers Many have been given long jail sentences.

- Country A allows its citizens many rights and freedoms. It would meet the criteria of the European Convention on Human Rights.

- UNICEF and several large childrens' charities have criticised Country A for its social care system. Investigations have shown that many elderly people and children are cared for in terrible conditions.

SOURCE 2

CANDIDATE COUNTRY "B"

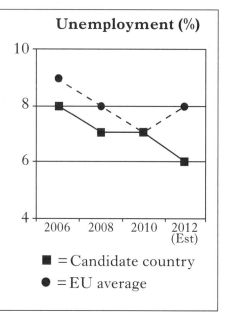

Unemployment (%)

■ = Candidate country
● = EU average

- Country B produces 32 million barrels of oil per day and only uses 13 million barrels. It wants to export more.

- Healthcare is poor in Country B. Life expectancy is low at 58 and child mortality is high at 11 per 1000 live births.

- In Country B, 36% of the population still work on farms. The EU would be asked to spend money to improve agriculture.

- UNESCO has praised the primary education system in Country B as levels of illiteracy have fallen to below 10%.

Use **only** the European Union Factfile on *Page twenty* and Sources 1 and 2 on *Page twenty-one*.

   (i)   State **which candidate country** would be the **more suitable** to become a member of the European Union (EU).

   (ii)   Give **three detailed reasons to support your choice**.

   (iii)   Give **two detailed reasons** why you **rejected** the other country.

In your answer, you **must relate** information from the EU Factfile to the information about Candidate Countries A and B.

(Enquiry Skills, **10** marks)

[END OF QUESTION PAPER]

[BLANK PAGE]

[BLANK PAGE]

G

2640/402

NATIONAL
QUALIFICATIONS
2011

TUESDAY, 10 MAY
10.20 AM – 11.50 AM

MODERN STUDIES
STANDARD GRADE
General Level

1 Read every question carefully.

2 Answer all questions as fully as you can.

3 If you cannot do a question, go on to the next one. Try again later.

4 In question 3, answer **one** section only: Section (A) The USA **or** Section (B) China.

5 Write your answers in the answer book provided. Indicate clearly, in the left hand margin, the question and section of question being answered. Do not write in the right hand margin.

SYLLABUS AREA 1—LIVING IN A DEMOCRACY

QUESTION 1

(a)

Candidates and their supporters campaign in many ways before an election.

Describe **two** ways in which candidates and their supporters campaign **before** an election.

To answer this question, you may wish to use the drawing above.

(Knowledge and Understanding, **4** marks)

QUESTION 1 (CONTINUED)

(b) Study Sources 1 and 2 below, then answer the question which follows.

SOURCE 1

Opinion Poll — At what age should Scots be allowed to vote?

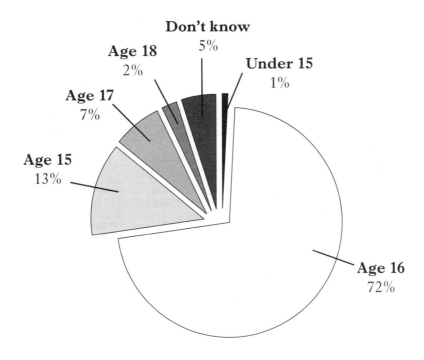

SOURCE 2

Voting Age and Voter Turnout

Country	Minimum Voting Age	Voter Turnout
Austria	16	79%
Brazil	16	83%
Canada	18	60%
UK	18	61%
USA	18	57%

Write down **two** conclusions about voting age.

You should write **one** conclusion **with evidence** about **each** of the following.

• The age that most people think Scots should be allowed to vote.

• The link between Minimum Voting Age and Voter Turnout.

Your answer **must** be based entirely on the Sources above.

(Enquiry Skills, **4** marks)

QUESTION 1 (CONTINUED)

(*c*)

> *Trade Union members have both **rights** and **responsibilities**.*

Describe **one** right and **one** responsibility that trade union members have.

To answer this question, you may wish to use the drawing above.

(Knowledge and Understanding, **4** marks)

QUESTION 1 (CONTINUED)

(*d*)   Study Sources 1 and 2 below, then answer the question which follows.

SOURCE 1

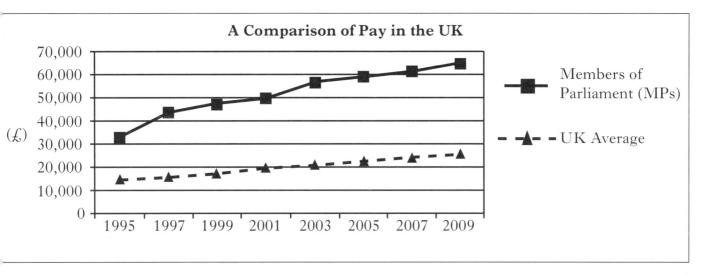

SOURCE 2

MPs' Expenses Row

MPs are paid a salary but are also allowed to claim money to cover expenses. For example, in 2009, they could claim £24,000 so that they could afford to live in London and over £100,000 to pay for office staff.

In 2009, The Daily Telegraph published a story about MPs' expenses. Amongst other things, the newspaper revealed that two MPs had broken the rules by claiming money for houses they no longer owned.

However, most MPs showed that they could only do their job properly because they received these expenses.

Statements made by Chloe Carstairs

- MPs' pay has increased every year.
- MPs are allowed to claim expenses to employ staff.
- MPs' pay is similar to the average pay in the UK.
- All MPs' claims for expenses were shown to be within the rules.

Using **only** Sources 1 and 2 above, write down **two** statements made by Chloe Carstairs which are **exaggerated**.

Using the information in the Sources, give **one** reason why **each** of the statements you have chosen is **exaggerated**.

(Enquiry Skills, **4** marks)

SYLLABUS AREA 2—CHANGING SOCIETY

QUESTION 2

(a) | *Unemployed people in the UK have many **needs**.* |

Describe **two needs** that unemployed people in the UK have.

(Knowledge and Understanding, **4** marks)

(b)   Study the information about Bill Laird below and the plan of Craigloch on *Page seven*, then answer the question which follows.

Information about Bill Laird and his needs

Bill is 80 years old, and lives alone in a big house in the town of Craigloch. He is keen to move to a smaller house.

Bill has a number of **needs** which are important to him.

- He needs to visit the Post Office to collect his pension and pay bills.

- Bill needs to visit the Community Nurse after suffering a mild heart attack recently.

- He needs to feel safe as his house was broken into recently and he is frightened it will happen again.

- Bill has friends from his working days and he needs to continue seeing them. He would like to be able to go out for lunch nearby with them occasionally.

QUESTION 2 (b) (CONTINUED)

Bill has been to see the two houses shown in the plan below, but is not sure whether the **location** of **House A** or **House B** would better meet his needs.

PLAN OF CRAIGLOCH

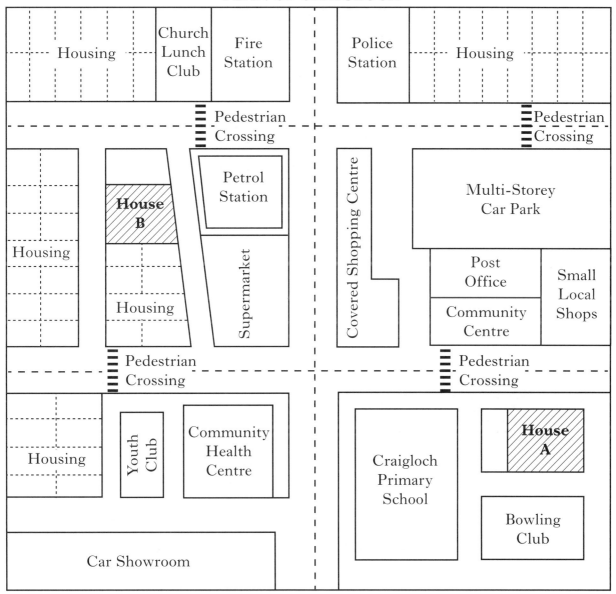

Using **only** the information in the plan above, decide which house, **House A** or **House B**, would be the **better** choice for Bill Laird to **meet his needs**.

You **must** link the information about Bill Laird to the house you have chosen.

Give **two** reasons to **support** your decision.

(Enquiry Skills, **4** marks)

[Turn over

QUESTION 2 (CONTINUED)

(c)   *The Government provides help for families.*

Government Help for Families (2010)

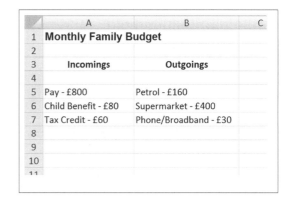

Give **two ways** in which the Government provides help for families.

Choose **one** of these **ways** and explain why the Government gives this help.

To answer this question, you may wish to use the drawings above.

(Knowledge and Understanding, **4** marks)

QUESTION 2 (CONTINUED)

(d)   Study Sources 1 and 2 below, then answer the question which follows.

SOURCE 1

Low Pay and Ethnic Groups

Whites are the largest ethnic group in the UK. There are big variations in pay between the various ethnic groups. For example, more than half of people from the Bangladeshi and Pakistani communities are in low paid employment. The percentage of people on low pay from an Indian background is 28% whilst for Whites it is 20%. The figure for Black Africans is 46% whilst for Black Caribbeans it is 30%.

SOURCE 2

Unemployment Rate by Ethnic Group (%)		
	2007	**2009**
Bangladeshi	12·5	13·2
Black African	10·2	11·9
Black Caribbean	10·0	13·0
Indian	5·2	7·8
Pakistani	14·0	14·3
White	4·5	5·8

Whites have fewer people on low pay than any other ethnic group. The biggest rise in unemployment between 2007 and 2009 was amongst people from the Pakistani community.

View of Asif Khan

Using **only** the information above, give **one** reason to **support** and **one** reason to **oppose** the view of Asif Khan.

(Enquiry Skills, **4** marks)

[Turn over

SYLLABUS AREA 3—IDEOLOGIES

QUESTION 3

Answer **ONE** section only: Section (A)—The USA on pages *ten* to *thirteen*

OR   Section (B)—China on pages *fourteen* to *seventeen*

(A)   **THE USA**

(*a*) | *Not all American citizens are equal.*

Give **two** ways in which American citizens are not equal.

For **one** of these ways, explain why *not all American citizens are equal*.

In your answer, you **must** use American examples.

To answer this question, you may wish to use the drawings above.

(Knowledge and Understanding, **4** marks)

QUESTION 3 (A) (CONTINUED)

(b)   Study Sources 1 and 2 below, then answer the question which follows.

SOURCE 1

Between 2000 and 2010, the American people saw the biggest change in unemployment for many years. In 2000, the figure was 4·0% while in 2010, it was 10·0%. One of the effects of unemployment was that many Americans lost their houses as they could not afford to pay for them.

In 2009, President Obama signed the "American Recovery and Reinvestment Act", which was a plan to spend $539 billion to help the country recover. The government believes that these measures have already helped the economy to improve as the number of companies closing down has fallen.

SOURCE 2

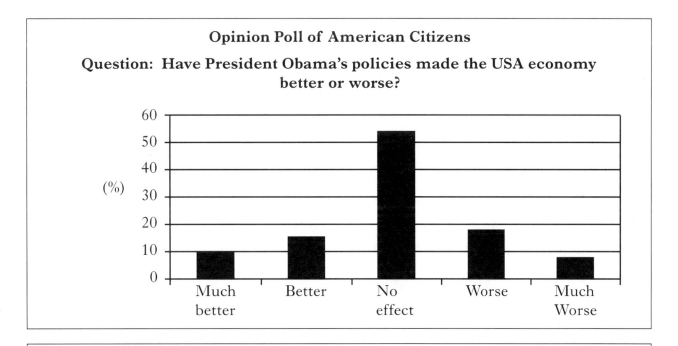

Opinion Poll of American Citizens

Question: Have President Obama's policies made the USA economy better or worse?

Statements made by Paul Douglas

- The link between unemployment and losing your house is very strong.
- The majority of people agree that President Obama is doing a good job with the economy.
- A minority of people think that President Obama has made the economy much worse.
- The "American Recovery and Reinvestment Act" has not helped the economy.

Using **only** Sources 1 and 2 above, write down **two** statements made by Paul Douglas which are **exaggerated**.

Using the information in the Sources, give **one** reason why **each** of the statements you have chosen is **exaggerated**.

(Enquiry Skills, **4** marks)

QUESTION 3 (A) (CONTINUED)

(*c*) | *American citizens can use the media to influence the decisions of the American Government.*

Describe **two** ways in which *American citizens can use the media to influence the decisions of the American Government.*

In your answer, you **must** use American examples.

To answer this question, you may wish to use the drawing above.

(Knowledge and Understanding, **4** marks)

QUESTION 3 (A) (CONTINUED)

(d)   Study Sources 1 and 2 below, then answer the question which follows.

SOURCE 1

State	Ethnic Minority Owned Businesses (%)		
	Asian	Black	Hispanic
Arizona	2·7	1·7	9·2
California	12·8	3·9	14·7
Florida	2·7	6·6	17·3
Georgia	4·0	13·2	2·7
New York	8·5	7·6	9·6
Oklahoma	1·6	2·6	1·9

SOURCE 2

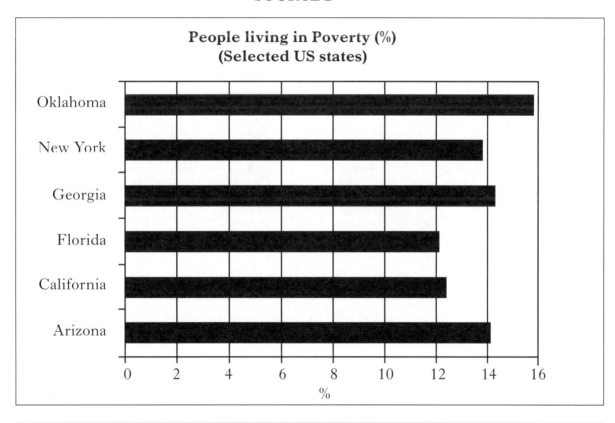

People living in Poverty (%)
(Selected US states)

California has the highest percentage of Hispanic owned businesses. California and Florida are the two states with the lowest percentages of people in poverty.

View of Drew Laburn

Using **only** Source 1 and Source 2 above, give **one** reason to **support** and **one** reason to **oppose** the view of Drew Laburn.

(Enquiry Skills, **4** marks)

NOW GO TO QUESTION 4 ON PAGE EIGHTEEN

QUESTION 3 (CONTINUED)

(B) **CHINA**

(*a*)

> *Not all Chinese citizens are equal.*

Give **two** ways in which Chinese citizens are not equal.

For **one** of these ways, explain why *not all Chinese citizens are equal*.

In your answer, you **must** use Chinese examples.

To answer this question, you may wish to use the drawings above.

(Knowledge and Understanding, **4** marks)

QUESTION 3 (B) (CONTINUED)

(b) Study Sources 1 and 2 below, then answer the question which follows.

SOURCE 1

Since the world recession, around 20 million rural migrants have returned home to the countryside. There are no longer jobs for them in China's coastal cities. However, it is not only migrant workers who are struggling to find jobs. In China, 32% of the 6·11 million graduates have not yet found work. The Chinese Government has promised to do what it can to tackle the problem of unemployment. It is planning to spend $585 billion to try to help the country's economy recover.

SOURCE 2

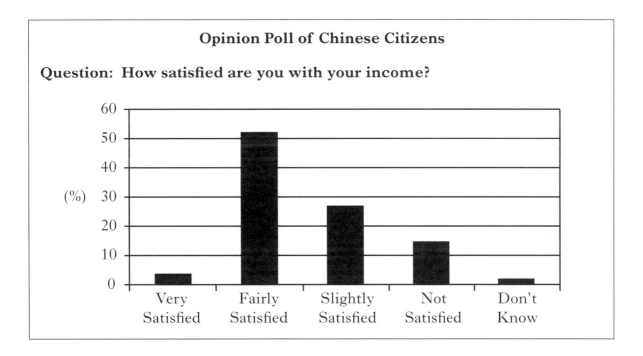

Opinion Poll of Chinese Citizens

Question: How satisfied are you with your income?

Statements made by Amy Yip

- The Chinese Government has promised to spend large amounts of money to help the economy.

- Few rural migrants are returning home to the countryside to work.

- A small percentage of Chinese people are very satisfied with their income.

- The majority of people surveyed are not satisfied with their income.

Using **only** Sources 1 and 2 above, write down **two** statements made by Amy Yip which are **exaggerated**.

Using the information in the Sources, give **one** reason why **each** of the statements you have chosen is **exaggerated**.

(Enquiry Skills, **4** marks)

QUESTION 3 (B) (CONTINUED)

(c) | *Chinese people who criticise their government can find themselves in major trouble.*

Describe **two** actions which the Chinese Government might take to deal with those who criticise the Government.

In your answer, you **must** use Chinese examples.

To answer this question, you may wish to use the drawings above.

(Knowledge and Understanding, **4** marks)

QUESTION 3 (B) (CONTINUED)

(*d*)   Study Sources 1 and 2 below, then answer the question which follows.

SOURCE 1

Selected data on Chinese provinces

Province	Value of foreign trade ($ billion)	Average income per person (Yuan)	Pupils completing junior secondary school (%)
Gansu	1·33	12,000	25
Qinghai	0·26	17,000	23
Heilong	1·52	22,000	35
Zhejiang	6·68	42,000	93
Sichuan	1·0	15,000	32
Fujian	2·6	30,000	85

SOURCE 2

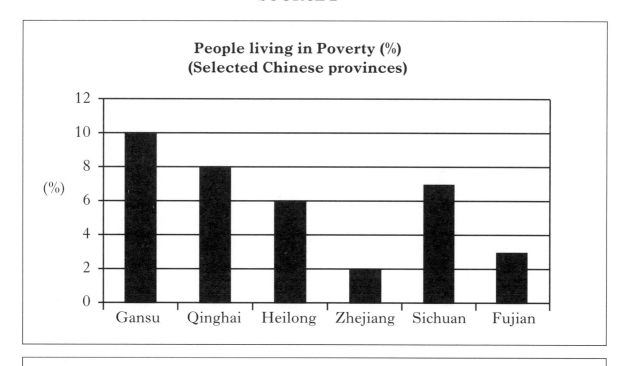

People living in Poverty (%)
(Selected Chinese provinces)

Gansu and Sichuan have the biggest percentage of people living in poverty. The province with the greatest level of foreign trade also has the highest average income and the highest percentage of pupils completing junior secondary school.

View of Jinqu Zou

Using **only** Source 1 and Source 2 above, give **one** reason to **support** and **one** reason to **oppose** the view of Jinqu Zou.

(Enquiry Skills, **4** marks)

NOW GO TO QUESTION 4 ON PAGE EIGHTEEN

SYLLABUS AREA 4—INTERNATIONAL RELATIONS

QUESTION 4

(a)   **United Nations projects helping some African countries.**

Choose **two** of the United Nations projects shown above.

Describe how **each of the projects you have chosen** *can help to meet the needs of some people in Africa.*

(Knowledge and Understanding, **4** marks)

QUESTION 4 (CONTINUED)

(b)   Study Sources 1 and 2 below, then answer the question which follows.

The War in Afghanistan (2009)

SOURCE 1

VIEW OF LYNSEY LEWIS

When the International Security Assistance Force (ISAF), backed by NATO, was sent to Afghanistan, it was NATO's first operation outside Europe.

As of October 2009, ISAF had 67,700 troops from 42 different countries in Afghanistan. The largest contributing nations are the USA with 32,000 troops and the UK with 9000 troops.

NATO has brought peace and stability to the government of Afghanistan. It is also involved in training the Afghan National Army.

It is hoped that in the near future much of the Taleban's funding which comes from the trade in heroin will stop as ISAF takes back the areas where the illegal production of heroin is based.

SOURCE 2

VIEW OF KIRSTY GRAHAM

The number of ISAF troops has grown from 5000 to almost 68,000. This International Security Assistance Force is the first time NATO has sent combat troops outside Europe.

Although many NATO members have sent equipment to help, only a few countries have sent troops.

The UK and the USA remain the largest contributors of troops. Some of these troops are training the Afghan army to fight the Taleban. So far, NATO hasn't managed to stop the Taleban's civil war against the Afghan Government.

One of the main sources of income for the Taleban is the trade in heroin. The Taleban control much of the territory where the heroin is produced.

Sources 1 and 2 give different views about **NATO's forces in Afghanistan**.

Write down **two** differences between these views.

You **must** only use information from the Sources above.

(Enquiry Skills, **4** marks)

[Turn over

QUESTION 4 (CONTINUED)

You are investigating the topic in the box below.

WAR IN AFRICA

Answer questions (*c*), (*d*) and (*e*) which follow.

(*c*)   As part of the **Planning Stage**, give **two** relevant **aims** for your investigation.

(Enquiry Skills, **2** marks)

Mrs Watt, a teacher in your school, has just come back from a visit to the African country of Sudan. You decide to interview her for your investigation into "War in Africa".

(*d*)   Give **two** advantages of an interview as a way of finding out information for your investigation.

(Enquiry Skills, **2** marks)

After the interview with Mrs Watt, she gives you a website address.

When you go to the website you find the webpage opposite.

QUESTION 4 (CONTINUED)

(*e*)   Use the website page below to answer the question which follows.

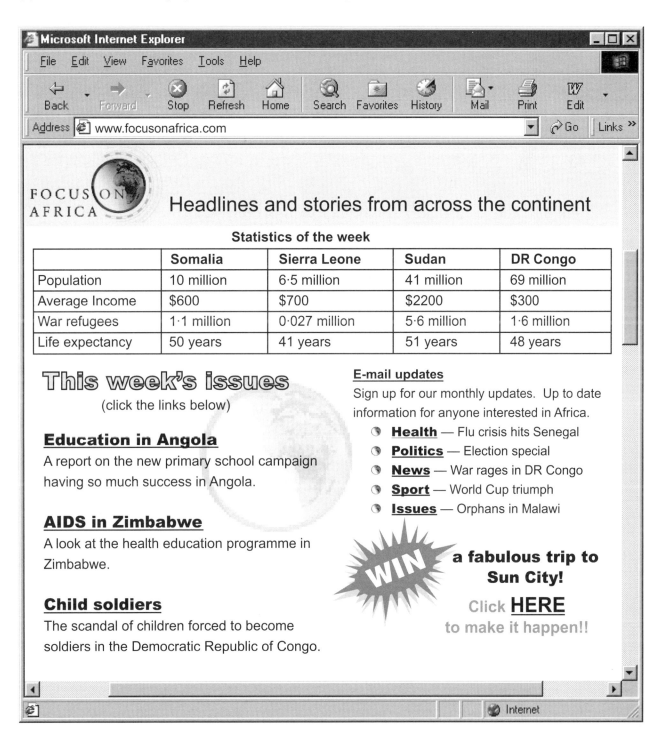

Give **two** ways in which you could use the website page to help with your investigation into "War in Africa".

For **each** way, explain why it would be a **good** way to help you with your investigation.

(Enquiry Skills, **4** marks)

[*END OF QUESTION PAPER*]

[BLANK PAGE]

STANDARD GRADE | CREDIT

2011

[BLANK PAGE]

C

2640/403

NATIONAL
QUALIFICATIONS
2011

TUESDAY, 10 MAY
1.00 PM – 3.00 PM

MODERN STUDIES
STANDARD GRADE
Credit Level

1 Read every question carefully.

2 Answer all questions as fully as you can.

3 If you cannot do a question, go on to the next one. Try again later.

4 In question 3, answer **one** section only: Section (A) The USA **or** Section (B) China.

5 Write your answers in the answer book provided. Indicate clearly, in the left hand margin, the question and section of question being answered. Do not write in the right hand margin.

[BLANK PAGE]

SYLLABUS AREA 1—LIVING IN A DEMOCRACY

QUESTION 1

(*a*) Choose **one** of the following electoral systems.

Single Transferable Vote Used in Scottish Local Council elections 	**Additional Member System** Used in Scottish Parliament elections 
First Past the Post Used in UK Parliament elections 	**Regional List** Used in European Parliament elections 

Explain, **in detail**, the **advantages** and **disadvantages** of the electoral system you have chosen.

(Knowledge & Understanding, **8** marks)

[Turn over

QUESTION 1 (CONTINUED)

(b) Study the information in the "**Spotlight on Trade Unions**" pamphlet below and opposite, then answer the question which follows.

Spotlight on Trade Unions

Introduction

"Spotlight on Trade Unions" gives an understanding of Trade Unions in Great Britain today. Trade Unions are involved in trying to get better pay, better conditions and in trying to reduce unemployment.

Union membership in Great Britain

There are over 6·7 million union members in GB today. This is a 42% decrease from 1979 which was the peak year for union membership when there were 13·2 million union members. Membership is projected to decrease further in the future. In the past, union membership was strong in the traditional industries of mining, quarrying and the utilities such as gas, electricity and water.

Trade union membership by employment sector		
	%	% change from 1998
Public administration	56	-4·5
Education	54	+1·0
Utilities	42	-14·6
Health and social work	41	-5·9
Transport and communication	39	-3·6
Manufacturing	21	-9·5
Mining and quarrying	18	-10·4
Construction	14	-5·8
Retail and motor trade	12	+0·9
Agriculture, forestry and fishing	7	-6·0
Hotels and restaurants	5	-1·3

Trade union membership – ethnicity and gender

The rate of union membership for employees in the whole of the UK was 27% in 2009. Trade union membership varies between both ethnic group and gender.

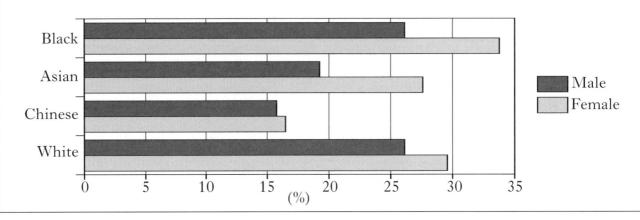

QUESTION 1 (*b*) (CONTINUED)

Regional union membership in Great Britain (2010)

The North East was the region with the highest union membership at 35·7% followed by Wales at 35·4%. Membership in the North West was 32·1% followed by Scotland at 31·8%. In other regions within Britain, union membership varied greatly with the South East having the lowest percentage of workers belonging to a trade union.

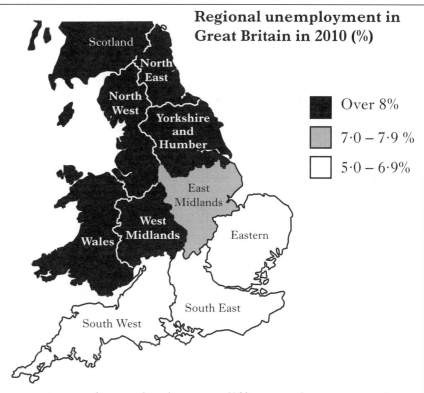

Regional unemployment in Great Britain in 2010 (%)

- Over 8%
- 7·0 – 7·9 %
- 5·0 – 6·9%

Wages and earnings

Two aims of Trade Unions are to improve pay and to maintain wage differences between trade union members and non-trade union members.

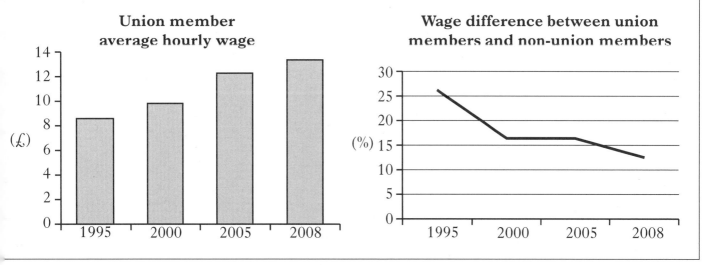

Union member average hourly wage

Wage difference between union members and non-union members

Using **only** the information from the "**Spotlight on Trade Unions**" pamphlet above and opposite, what **conclusions** can be drawn about trade unions in GB?

You must **make** and **justify** a conclusion about **each** of the following headings.

- The change in union membership within "Traditional Industries".
- The link between gender and trade union membership across all ethnic groups.
- The link between regional unemployment and regional trade union membership.
- The success of trade unions in maintaining wage differences between union and non-union members.

(Enquiry Skills, **8** marks)

[BLANK PAGE]

SYLLABUS AREA 2—CHANGING SOCIETY

QUESTION 2

(a)

> *Inequalities exist in both health and wealth amongst elderly people in the UK.*

Describe, **in detail**, the inequalities that exist in **both** health **and** wealth amongst elderly people in the UK.

(Knowledge and Understanding, **8** marks)

[Turn over

QUESTION 2 (CONTINUED)

(b)   Study the **Information about Dunelder and The Technology Park** below and **Sources 1 and 2** on *Page nine*, then answer the question which follows.

Information about Dunelder and The Technology Park

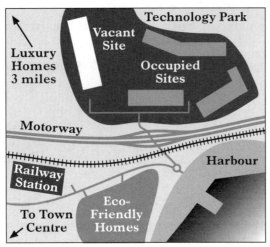

Dunelder is a town of 42,000 people in the South West of Scotland. Two years ago, Dunelder Council decided to build a technology park to attract new employment into the town. Only one site remains vacant, and to encourage businesses to consider setting-up there a package of financial help is available as follows:

Year 1 – £1·5 million
Year 2 – £1·0 million
Year 3 – £1·0 million
Year 4 – £0·5 million

- In recent years the town has suffered from high unemployment due to the closure of two large local factories. As a result, there are many people available for work, but they are mainly low-skilled.

- There are 3 companies already in the technology park. One is a computer firm specialising in producing software programmes. Of the remaining two, one produces solar heating panels and the other produces blades for wind turbines, both important types of renewable energy.

- There are 8 primary schools and 2 secondary schools in the town. The local council has spent a lot of money on these, and all now provide an excellent education. There is no university nearby, but the town does have a college which specialises in agriculture.

- Shopping and leisure facilities in the area are generally good. There are 3 supermarkets and the town centre has several traffic free shopping streets. There is a multi-screen cinema, several restaurants and 2 golf courses locally. A new development of luxury homes has recently been completed 3 miles outside of town. These are available at reduced prices due to the recent economic difficulties.

Selected health statistics	Dunelder	Scotland
People who smoke	27%	27%
People who exceed alcohol limits	11%	12%
Babies with low birth-weight	2·3%	2·6%
People who take no exercise	45%	38%

Survey of public opinion in Dunelder

Question: *How important do you think the following environmental actions are?*

Action	Unimportant	Not Very Important	Fairly Important	Very Important
More home insulation	12%	39%	34%	15%
More nuclear power	11%	27%	38%	24%
More renewable energy	15%	37%	35%	13%
Less air pollution	10%	25%	40%	25%

QUESTION 2 (b) (CONTINUED)

Two companies have applied for the last remaining site at the technology park. Sources 1 and 2 contain information about both companies.

SOURCE 1

Statements from the owner of Wave Power Systems

My company makes special equipment that produces electricity from the action of waves in the sea. Our factory will need access to the sea to allow us to test and transport our products.

The new factory will have a sport and fitness centre for employees. This will also be open to local residents, which will help improve the town's exercise levels.

Wave Power Systems is a world leader in the renewable energy field. Close links with a nearby university, to help our research, would be very important to our future success.

The factory in Dunelder would include a research centre. To achieve this we would need the cooperation of at least 2 other local companies involved in renewable energy.

The site should go to my company because people in the local area agree that renewable energy is the most important way of improving the environment.

SOURCE 2

Statements from the owner of Earth Save Insulation

My company will create 150 new jobs, most of which will be suitable for people with only basic skills. We will train them for the job we want them to do.

The factory will create a lot of excess heat. We will make this available to heat any new houses that are being built nearby. This will be good for the environment and local people.

To meet the costs of a new factory, my company would need at least £5 million in financial assistance within the first 5 years.

A management team will be moving into the Dunelder area to start up the factory. They will only move if the area has affordable good quality housing.

My company takes old plastic and re-cycles it to make insulation for houses. We should get the site as people in Dunelder agree that this is the most important way of helping the environment.

Use **only** the **Information about Dunelder and The Technology Park** on *Page eight* and **Sources 1 and 2** above.

(i) State **which company** you think would be the **more suitable** to build on the last remaining site at Dunelder Technology Park.

(ii) Give **three detailed reasons to support your choice.**

(iii) Give **two detailed reasons** why you have **rejected** the other option.

In your answer, you **must relate** "Information about Dunelder and the Technology Park" to the information about the **two** companies.

(Enquiry Skills, **10** marks)

[BLANK PAGE]

SYLLABUS AREA 3—IDEOLOGIES

QUESTION 3

Answer **one** section only: Section (A)—The USA on pages *eleven* to *fourteen*
          OR   Section (B)—China on pages *fifteen* to *eighteen*

(A) THE USA

(a) | *There are many ways in which Americans can **participate** in politics.*

Other than voting, describe **in detail**, the *ways in which Americans can participate in politics*.

In your answer, you **must** use American examples.

(Knowledge and Understanding, **8** marks)

[Turn over

QUESTION 3 (A) (CONTINUED)

You have been asked to carry out **two** investigations.

The first investigation is on the topic in the box below.

Employment in the USA

Now answer questions (*b*) and (*c*) which follow.

(*b*)   State a relevant **hypothesis** for your investigation.

(Enquiry Skills, **2** marks)

(*c*)   Give **two** relevant **aims** to help you prove or disprove your hypothesis.

(Enquiry Skills, **2** marks)

QUESTION 3 (A) (CONTINUED)

The second investigation is on the topic in the box below.

> **Health Care in the USA**

Now answer questions (*d*) and (*e*) which follow.

(*d*)   You decide to send a **questionnaire** to your relatives who live in Rockford City, California.

Here is a copy of the questionnaire you wish to send. **Read it carefully.**

HEALTH CARE IN THE USA

Where there is a choice please circle your answer.

Question 1
Which group do you belong to?

White   Black   Hispanic   Asian   Native American   Other

Question 2
How old are you?

Under 15   15–30   30–50   50–70   70 or older

Question 3
How satisfied are you with the health system in the USA?

Very Satisfied   Satisfied   Dissatisfied   Very Dissatisfied   Unsure

Question 4
Why do you think illegal immigrants should not get health cover?

_____

_____

_____

Question 5
If there was a new law requiring all Americans to have health insurance, would you support it?

Yes   No   Don't Know

After checking your questionnaire with your teacher, you are told that **two** of the questions are poorly expressed.

Identify the **two** questions that are **poorly expressed** and then explain, **in detail**, why each needs to be changed.

(Enquiry Skills, **4** marks)

QUESTION 3 (A) (CONTINUED)

(e) One of your relatives includes this table with your questionnaires when they send them back.

How concerned are you that current efforts to reform the health care system will . . .	very concerned %	somewhat concerned %	not too concerned %	not at all concerned %	unsure %
. . . reduce the quality of health care you receive?	57	23	10	9	1
. . . reduce your health insurance coverage?	55	26	9	9	1
. . . increase your health care costs?	62	22	9	7	0
. . . limit your choices of doctors or treatments?	56	23	12	8	1
Opinion Poll based on nationwide telephone interviews with 1000 adults, aged 18+, May 6th 2011 in USA Today					

Give **one** detailed reason why the above table is a **good source** for helping you with your investigation.

(Enquiry Skills, **2** marks)

NOW GO TO QUESTION 4 ON PAGE NINETEEN

QUESTION 3 (CONTINUED)

(B) **CHINA**

(a) | *There are a number of ways Chinese people can participate in politics.* |

Other than voting, describe **in detail**, the *ways in which Chinese people can participate in politics.*

In your answer, you **must** use Chinese examples.

(Knowledge and Understanding, **8** marks)

[Turn over

QUESTION 3 (B) (CONTINUED)

You have been asked to carry out **two** investigations.

The first investigation is on the topic in the box below.

Employment in China

Now answer questions (*b*) and (*c*) which follow.

(*b*)   State a relevant **hypothesis** for your investigation.

(Enquiry Skills, **2** marks)

(*c*)   Give **two** relevant **aims** to help you prove or disprove your hypothesis.

(Enquiry Skills, **2** marks)

QUESTION 3 (B) (CONTINUED)

The second investigation is on the topic in the box below.

Health Care in China

Now answer questions (*d*) and (*e*) which follow.

(*d*)   You decide to send a **questionnaire** to your relatives who live in Shanghai, China.

Here is a copy of the questionnaire you wish to send. **Read it carefully.**

HEALTH CARE IN CHINA

Where there is a choice please circle your answer.

Question 1
Which group do you belong to?

Han   Zhuang   Manchu   Hui   Uyghur   Other

Question 2
How old are you?

Under 15   15–30   30–50   50–70   70 or older

Question 3
How satisfied are you with the health system in China?

Very Satisfied   Satisfied   Dissatisfied   Very Dissatisfied   Unsure

Question 4
Why do you think illegal rural immigrants should not get health care in the cities?

_____

_____

_____

Question 5
If there was a new law requiring all Chinese people to pay for their own health insurance, would you support it?

Yes   No   Don't Know

After checking your questionnaire with your teacher, you are told that **two** of the questions are poorly expressed.

Identify the **two** questions that are **poorly expressed** and then explain, **in detail**, why each needs to be changed.

(Enquiry Skills, **4** marks)

QUESTION 3 (B) (CONTINUED)

(e)   One of your relatives includes this table with your questionnaires when they send them back.

How hopeful are you that in future the health care system will . . .	very hopeful %	somewhat hopeful %	not too hopeful %	not at all hopeful %	unsure %
. . . improve the quality of health care you receive?	57	23	10	9	1
. . . increase your life expectancy?	55	26	9	9	1
. . . standardise health care throughout China?	62	22	9	7	0
. . . increase your choices of doctors or treatments?	56	23	12	8	1
Opinion Poll based on nationwide telephone interviews with 1000 adults, aged 18+, May 6th 2011 in China Today					

Give **one** detailed reason why the above table is a **good source** for helping you with your investigation.

(Enquiry Skills, **2** marks)

NOW GO TO QUESTION 4 ON PAGE NINETEEN

SYLLABUS AREA 4—INTERNATIONAL RELATIONS

QUESTION 4

(a)   **European Union Policies**

Enlarged Membership	Common Fisheries Policy	Aid to the Regions	European Defence Force	Common Agricultural Policy	Single European Currency

Choose **two** of the policies shown above.

For **each** policy, describe, **in detail**, the ways in which it helps **meet the needs** of member states.

(Knowledge & Understanding, **8** marks)

[Turn over

QUESTION 4 (CONTINUED)

(b)   Study Sources 1 and 2 below, then answer the question which follows.

SOURCE 1

Libya's trading partners—top six importers of Libyan goods (%)

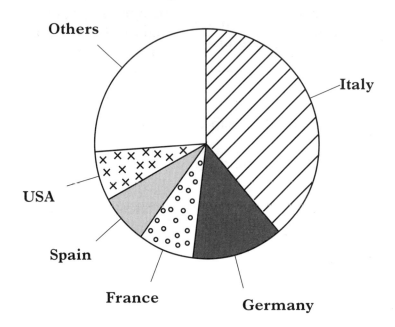

SOURCE 2

**Libya and its trading partners—
average income in US dollars**

Country	2000	2009
France	22,500	32,900
Germany	23,100	35,000
Italy	19,300	31,500
Spain	14,400	34,700
USA	34,600	47,100
Libya	6500	14,800

Of all Libya's trading partners, Spain has seen the largest increase in average income. Libya's biggest trading partner is also the country with the highest average income in both years.

View of Darren McCourt

Using **only** the information above, give **one** reason to **support** and **one** reason to **oppose** the view of Darren McCourt.

(Enquiry Skills, **4** marks)

[Turn over for Question 4(c) on *Pages twenty-two* and *twenty-three*

QUESTION 4 (CONTINUED)

(c)   Study Sources 1, 2 and 3 below and on the next page, then answer the question which follows.

SOURCE 1

Adults (15–49) living with HIV/Aids (%)		
African country	**2003**	**2008**
Botswana	23·6	23·9
Ethiopia	4·3	2·1
Lesotho	23·5	23·2
Swaziland	32·5	26·1
Zimbabwe	22·1	15·3

Population living in poverty (%)

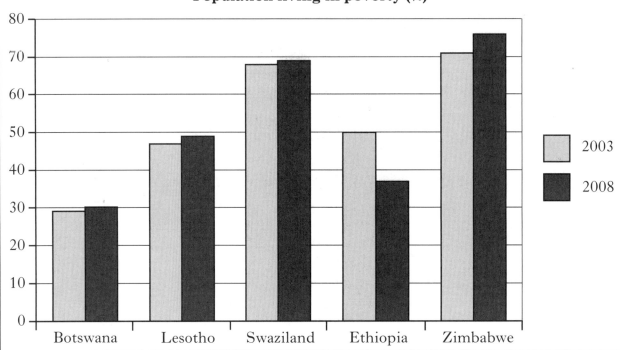

SOURCE 2

Education—How well is Africa shaping up?

UNESCO is promising to help African countries through its "Literacy Decade" campaign. However, it points out that Africa has a long way to go, as one fifth of African adults are illiterate.

The economic crisis in Zimbabwe has had an effect on the education budget in recent years. They cannot find enough qualified teachers to work in their schools.

The government of Lesotho has shown a commitment to education. They spent 13% of their GDP on schooling in 2008 whilst in 2003, it was 11%. This has had a positive effect on literacy rates.

In Botswana, literacy rates have changed from 80% to 84% since 2003. Every child in Botswana can expect to go to school for twelve years. Swaziland, a country badly affected by HIV/Aids, has seen literacy rates go from 74% in 2003 to 81% in 2008. The situation in Ethiopia mirrors much of Africa with literacy levels going up although they are still low when compared to developed countries.

QUESTION 4 (c) (CONTINUED)

SOURCE 3

Total Foreign Debt (Millions of US Dollars)		
African country	**2003**	**2008**
Botswana	392	422
Ethiopia	4400	3100
Lesotho	507	619
Swaziland	357	554
Zimbabwe	3400	5300

Total Aid received (Millions of US Dollars)

It is obvious that increasing aid always reduces poverty in African countries. It is also a fact that most countries with increasing debt are unable to reduce the problem of HIV/AIDS. However, despite these problems, education in the majority of African countries has improved.

View of Ruby McClay

Explain, **in detail**, **the extent to which** Ruby McClay could be accused of being **selective in the use of facts.**

Use **only** Sources 1, 2 and 3 above and opposite.

In your answer, you should:

* explain, **in detail**, why **each** of the statements made by Ruby McClay is either correct **or** incorrect;

* reach an **overall** conclusion **on the extent to which** Ruby McClay has been **selective in the use of facts**.

(Enquiry Skills, **8** marks)

[END OF QUESTION PAPER]

Acknowledgements

Permission has been sought from all relevant copyright holders and Bright Red Publishing is grateful for the use of the following:

The UNICEF flag © UNICEF (2007 General page 16);

A drawing containing The United Nations flag © The United Nations (2007 General page 16);

The SNP logo. Reproduced with permission (2008 General page 3);

The Conservative Party logo. Reproduced with permission (2008 General page 3);

The Labour Party logo. Reproduced with permission (2008 General page 3);

The Liberal Democrats logo. Reproduced with permission (2008 General page 3);

The logo for The Organisation of American States © The Organisation of American States (2009 General page 12);

Leaflets © Crown Copyright 2005. Reproduced under the terms of the Click-Use Licence (2010 General page 6);

A leaflet created by the British Medical Association. Reproduced with permission (2010 General page 6);

The Pizza Hut logo © Pizza Hut International LLC (2010 General page 16);

The NATO logo. Reproduced with permission (2010 General page 18);

A screenshot from www.focusonafrica.com. Reproduced with permission of David Anderson (2011 General page 21).

STANDARD GRADE | ANSWER SECTION

MODERN STUDIES GENERAL
2007

Syllabus Area 1 – Living In A Democracy

1. (a) The concept being assessed is Participation. Candidates are required to give detailed descriptions.
   Answers may include:
   - canvassing for support in the local area by going round all the houses in an area to speak to the public.
   - putting leaflets containing information about the candidate through peoples' doors.
   - phoning people at home to persuade them to support the candidate.
   - putting posters up on lamp posts and in shop windows to advertise their candidate.
   - mailing/posting campaign materials to voters in the area with information about the candidate.
   - going around the area in a van/car with a loudspeaker encouraging people to vote for the candidate.
   - using the electoral roll to check support for your candidate.
   - organise/provide transport to the polling station for the elderly/disabled.
   - any other valid point.

   (b) Candidates are required to make comparisons within a source and draw valid conclusions.
   The correct responses are:
   - in 2001, the most popular activity was contacting a local council official with 64%. In 2005 this changed to signing a petition which 60% of people did.
   - contacting your councillor has shown least change as it has fallen by only 3%.

   (c) The concept being assessed is Representation. Candidates are required to provide detailed descriptions.
   Answers may include:
   Problems:
   - no wage increase this year
   - health and safety concerns
   - canteen price rises
   - concerns over paying for the creche
   - any other valid point

   The shop steward could help by:
   - arranging a meeting/negotiating with the management to resolve the problem.
   - contacting full-time union officials to ask for their help and advice.
   - organise a ballot of members about industrial action.
   - organise appropriate industrial action such as work-to-rule, overtime ban or strike action if negotiations are not successful.
   - any other valid point

   (d) Candidates are required to provide evidence to support a given point of view.
   Answers may include:
   - Salma Khan says that workers benefit from being members of a trade union. This view is supported from Source 2 by the fact that workers in a trade union enjoyed a higher rate of pay of £11.38 per hour, compared to only £9.72 for workers not in a trade union.
   - Salma Khan also says that membership of trade unions continued to increase for some groups of workers. This is supported from Source 1 by the fact that the number of women members has increased from 3 210 000 in 2001 to 3 356 000 in 2005.

Syllabus Area 2 – Changing Society

2. (a) Candidates are required to express support for a personal point of view with valid reasons.
   For House A – Ground floor flat
   - A ground floor flat – Millie finds it more difficult to move about.
   - A 2 bedroom flat – Millie was finding her 4 bedroom house too big.
   - Elderly people live in the other 3 flats – Millie feels lonely.
   - All residents share a conservatory which looks onto a colourful garden – Millie enjoys her garden.

   For House B – Bungalow
   - A one-storey house – Millie finds it more difficult to move about.
   - A 2 bedroom house – Millie was finding her 4 bedroom house too big.
   - There is a very pleasant summer-house for sitting in – Millie enjoys her garden.
   - Fully double glazed throughout and with full gas central heating means the bungalow is cheap to heat in the winter – Millie is starting to feel the cold.

   (b) The concept being assessed is Equality.
   Candidates are required to provide detailed explanations.
   Answers may include:
   - some elderly people have more money than others and so can afford private medical care and have their health problems attended to more quickly.
   - some elderly people can afford adequate central heating in the winter whilst others have to choose between eating and heating.
   - some elderly people choose to take regular exercise and stay fit whilst other elderly people suffer from obesity and heart disease.
   - some elderly people take part in activities to stimulate their mind and so may enjoy better mental health than others.
   - some elderly people have a wide social circle of friends and family and so are less likely to suffer from depression and loneliness.
   - any other valid point

   (c) The concept being assessed is Ideology.
   Candidates are required to provide detailed descriptions.
   Answers may include:
   - provides state old age pension, winter fuel payments and income support to provide for the financial needs of the elderly.
   - provides free healthcare such as operations, GP consultations, eye examinations, prescriptions to meet the health needs of the elderly.
   - provides for some social needs such as free TV licence for the over 75s.
   - provides free personal care to meet the health needs.
   - provides free bus travel throughout Scotland.
   - any other valid point

(*d*) Candidates are required to detect exaggeration and provide explanations.

The correct responses are:

Statement 1

Sandy Brown said, 'Scottish men are the only men who work more than the EU weekly average.'

Reason 1

The statement is exaggerated because in Source 2 it shows that the EU Average is 41·3 hours, Scotland works 45·4 hours, Portugal 42·1 hours and Greece 41·7 hours per week'. They are all above the average.

Statement 2

Sandy Brown said, 'Very few Scottish workers fail to take all their annual holidays.'

Reason 2

The statement is exaggerated because in Source 1 it says 'About 73% of Scottish workers said they often failed to take all their annual holidays'. This is a lot, not very few.

Syllabus Area 3 –Ideologies

THE USA

3A. (*a*) The concept being assessed is Rights and Responsibilities. Candidates are required to provide detailed descriptions.

Answers may include:

Rights

- to stand for election in a Presidential or local election.
- to join a political party such as the Democrats or the Republicans.
- to vote for the candidate of their choice in election such as those for city mayor.
- to own a gun.
- to protest against a law passed by the Federal Government.
- to have free speech.
- to practise a religion of their choice.
- to have a fair trial.
- any other valid point

Responsibilities

- to use their vote in a considered way.
- to accept the result of the election.
- not to conceal their weapon or use it in an act of aggression.
- to accept the views of others.
- not to slander or libel someone.
- to tell the truth whilst under oath.
- any other valid point

(*b*) Candidates are required to support and oppose a given point of view.

Support the view:

Eva Kaye says 'It also showed greater participation in politics by voters in the USA'.

Evidence to support:

The percentage of voters turning out to vote was 49·0% in 1996 but had risen to 59·8% in 2004. This is greater participation in politics.

Oppose the view:

Eva Kaye says 'In the 2004 Presidential elections, the winner had a large majority'.

Evidence to oppose:

Bush only got 51% of the votes. This is not a large majority as he only won by 3% from Kerry.

(*c*) The concept being assessed is Ideology. Candidates are required to provide detailed explanations.

Answers may include:

- capitalism allows people to start up their own business such as Apple or Gap.
- the profit motive encourages people to work hard and to keep the profits from their business. Bill Gates of Microsoft is one example.
- competition between businesses such as Wal-mart and Target, keeps prices low and quality high.
- democracy allows American citizens to stand for election and challenge policies which they disagree with.
- affirmative action policies have helped many more women and ethnic minorities to become successful in education and employment.
- any other valid point

(*d*) Candidates are required to detect exaggeration and provide explanations.

The correct responses are:

Statement 1

Martin Baxter said 'The lowest level of support for President Bush has always been in his campaign against terrorism.'

Reason 1

The statement is exaggerated because in the table it shows that the level of support for his campaign against terrorism has always been the highest, in every year. This is not the lowest.

Statement 2

Martin Baxter said 'Support for his handling of the economy has steadily fallen each year.'

Reason 2

The statement is exaggerated because in the table it shows that his support for the economy actually increased by 4% between 2003 and 2004. This is not a fall.

RUSSIA

3B. (*a*) The concept being assessed is Rights and Responsibilities. Candidates are required to provide detailed descriptions.

Answers may include:

Rights

- to stand for election in a Presidential or local election.
- to join a political party such as United Russia, Yabloko or the Communist Party.
- to vote for the candidate of their choice in election such as those for the Duma.
- to own a gun.
- to protest against a law passed by the Government.
- to have free speech.
- to practise a religion of their choice.
- to have a fair trial.
- any other valid point

Responsibilities

- to use their vote in a considered way.
- to accept the result of the election.
- not to conceal their weapon or use it in an act of aggression.
- to accept the views of others.
- not to slander or libel someone.
- to tell the truth whilst under oath.
- any other valid point

(*b*) Candidates are required to support and oppose a given point of view.

Support the view:

Maria Chakvetadze says, 'In the 2004 Presidential election, the winner had a large majority.'

Evidence to support:

Putin won the election with 71% of the vote.

His nearest challenger only got 14% of the vote.

His winning margin was 57%, which is a large majority.

Oppose the view:
Maria Chakvetadze says, 'It also showed greater participation in politics by voters in Russia.'
Evidence to oppose:
Turnout at the election in 2004 was 64% which was 4% down on the turnout at the election in 2000 and 6% down on the election in 1996.

(c) The concept being assessed is Ideology. Candidates are required to provide detailed explanations.
Answers may include:
- the economic system in Russia allows people to start up their own business.
- the profit motive encourages people to work hard and to keep the profits from their business. Roman Abramovich is one example.
- competition between businesses can keep prices low and quality high.
- democracy allows Russian citizens to stand for election and challenge policies which they disagree with.
- any other valid point

(d) Candidates are required to detect exaggeration and provide explanations.
The correct responses are:
Statement 1
Alexia Gudrun said, 'More Russians thought Putin was 'doing a good job' in 2005 than in previous years.'
Reason 1
This statement is exaggerated because the table shows that 39% of the electorate thought he was doing a good job in 2005 but in 2003, the figure was higher at 42%.

Statement 2
Alexia Gudrun said, 'In 2003, most Russians thought Putin was 'doing a poor job'.'
Reason 2
This statement is exaggerated because the table shows that most Russians thought Putin was 'doing a good job' in 2003 with a 42% rating as opposed to 27% for 'doing a poor job'.

CHINA

3C. (a) The concept being assessed is Rights and Responsibilities. Candidates are required to provide detailed descriptions.
Answers may include:
- the right to elect village/local representatives/ deputies to Peoples' Congresses at city, provincial and national level. However, there is a responsibility for individuals themselves to take part in the running of villages, towns etc by voting or perhaps by becoming a candidate either for the Communist Party or for one of the approved opposition parties.
- the right to protest in pressure groups but the responsibility is to ensure that the authority of the Communist Party isn't challenged. Chinese people also have a responsibility to obey the law and to support the communist revolution by educating others and by reporting counter revolutionaries.
- the right to healthcare. Citizens often have to pay for treatments, drugs, etc.
- the right to an education. The responsibility is to send children to school in order to enhance the economy. Rural schools are often inadequate in terms of funding and staffing.
- the right to religion is written in to the Chinese constitution. Citizens can follow one of four recognized religions (Buddhism, Islam, Christianity and Taoism) but have the responsibility to only worship in 'patriotic' churches, temples, etc.

- the right to family life, within the limitations of the one child policy.
- any other valid point

(b) Candidates are required to support and oppose a given point of view.
Support the view:
Zi Yan says, 'It also showed greater participation in politics by voters in Duyun'.
Evidence to support:
This is true, as turnout figures have gone up from 85% in 1995 to 91% in 2005.

Oppose the view:
Zi Yan says, 'In the 2005 election, the winner had a large majority'.
Evidence to oppose:
This is not true as the winning candidate only had 46% of the vote ie less than half.
This is also not true as she only won by 6%.

(c) The concept being assessed is Ideology. Candidates are required to provide detailed explanations.
Answers may include:
- since the early eighties Chinese people have been allowed to start a business and keep the profit ie 'Socialist Market Economy'. Many millions of enterprises, of different sizes, are privately owned. Approximately 125 million Chinese work for small 'township enterprises'.
- many state owned enterprises have been forced to become more competitive, giving opportunities for bigger salaries in management etc. Some workers could buy shares in their factory etc.
- special Economic Zones have attracted a great deal of investment from foreign companies. Wages in these areas tend to be higher and unemployment lower. eg along the 'Coastal Strip'.
- China joined the World Trade Organisation, allowing greater freedom to business and hence greater affluence for some.
- Stock Market opened allowing individuals to invest in different companies. China now has many millionaires.
- Hong Kong returned to Chinese control bringing opportunities to Chinese citizens.
- agricultural reforms such as the responsibility system have brought wealth to some farmers.
- any other valid point

(d) Candidates are required to detect exaggeration and provide explanations.
The correct responses are:
Statement 1
Lye Zhang said 'The urban population of China will double between 1995 and 2010'.
Reason 1
This is exaggerated because the table shows that the urban population will increase from 30% to 44%. This is an increase of slightly less than 50%.
Statement 2
Lye Zhang said 'The biggest rise in the total population came between 2000 and 2005'.
Reason 2
This is exaggerated because the table shows that the increase between 2000 and 2005 was only 0·01 billion. The biggest increase was between 1995 and 2000 at 0·08 billion.

Syllabus Area 4 – International Relations

4. (a) The concept being assessed is Need. Candidates are required to provide detailed descriptions.
   Answers may include:
   - UN tries to meet needs in Africa via agencies. UNICEF gives aid to mothers and children, such as supporting breastfeeding.
   - countries can give bi-lateral aid eg Britain gave aid to Mozambique when a natural disaster occurred. The aid included tents, food and basic medicine.
   - Oxfam or other aid agencies, acting as managing agents for either individual governments or for a UN specialised agency, give small scale aid to local people eg helping young men to learn a trade.
   - any other valid point

   (b) Candidates are required to make comparisons within sources and draw valid conclusions.
   The correct responses are:
   Difference 1
   Source 1 says that 'They are being successful in making the lives of the people better' but
   Source 2 says that 'Afghanistan is now suffering from lawlessness, misery and starvation'.

   Difference 2
   Source 1 says that 'Some Afghans have had to flee from the fighting but they have been moved to clean, safe refugee camps' but Source 2 says that 'Many local people have been forced to flee to refugee camps where the conditions are dangerous and filthy'.

   (c) Candidates are required to give relevant aims for an investigative topic.
   The following receive no marks:
   - to find out when the EU was set up.
   - to find out who is in the EU.

   The following receive one mark:
   - to find out what Scotland gains from the EU.
   - to find out how many MEPs Scotland has.
   - any other valid aim

   (d) Candidates are required to state and justify an appropriate method of enquiry.
   Answers may include:
   - quick method of contacting a person.
   - people often respond quickly to an e-mail (compared to a letter).
   - easy to find the address (Google/EU page).
   - any other valid point

   (e) Candidates are required to state and justify an appropriate method of enquiry.
   The correct responses are:
   - Services: you could see if there were any relevant statistics or opinion polls to answer the aims.
   - 'In the Spotlight': the first topic, 'Crisis in Scotland', relates directly to Scotland and could have material for the investigation.
   - Search facility: could be used to find information not already identified.
   - Activities: 'What the EU does by subject'. 'Regional Policy' may have information about Scotland.
   - any other valid point

MODERN STUDIES CREDIT 2007

Syllabus Area 1 - Living In A Democracy

1. (a) The concept being assessed is Rights.
   Candidates are required to use understanding of the concept to provide detailed descriptions with relevant examples and appropriate generalisations.
   Answers may include:
   - to demonstrate/protest outside public/ government buildings. This may attract media attention and get their arguments over to a wider audience.
   - to lobby their MP at the House of Commons. Constituents have the right to visit parliament and ask to speak to their MP.
   - to send letters/e-mails of protest to their MP, Minister in charge, or Prime Minister.
   - to set up a petition, perhaps on the Internet, which allows the public to express their concerns as well.
   - any other valid point

   (b) The concept being assessed is Representation. Candidates are required to use understanding of the concept to provide detailed explanations with relevant examples and appropriate generalisations.
   Answers may include:
   Advantages of Single Transferable Vote:
   - no wasted votes. If a voter fails to get their first choice, it will be reallocated until it is counted.
   - smaller parties have a better chance of getting a candidate elected. This means that one party is less likely to dominate.
   - gives greater choice to voters as they could choose to vote for all the candidates in one party, or all women candidates, or all ethnic minority candidates. There are limitless variations as to how a particular person could vote.
   - coalitions between parties are much more likely. This will encourage parties to work together more, and better reflect the way people have voted.
   - any other valid point

   Advantages of Additional Member System:
   - the number of MSPs each party gains is much more proportional to the votes cast nationally. This better reflects the wishes of the people of Scotland.
   - smaller parties have a better chance of gaining seats. The parties that do well on the first vote are penalised on the second vote. This has allowed MSPs to be elected from the Green Party, Scottish Socialists, Solidarity, and other smaller parties.
   - fewer wasted votes, as in the second ballot, votes are redistributed. This gives a greater incentive to vote.
   - From 1999–2007, Scotland has had a coalition government. This reflected the way people in Scotland had voted. Where one party did not get an overall majority of the seats, they decided not to form a minority government but to seek a coalition partner.
   - any other valid point

   Advantages of First Past the Post:
   - it is fair as the candidate who gets most votes wins the constituency - more people voted for the winning party in a constituency.
   - it is a simple system which is easy for voters to understand. One cross is placed against the name of a candidate. It delivers a quick and readily understandable result.

- each constituency has a personal link with a single MP who can keep in close contact with the people in the area.
- it usually provides a clear winner nationally, allowing one party to form a strong government without the need to form a coalition.
- any other valid point

(c) Candidates are required to detect and explain examples of lack of objectivity in complex sources, giving developed argument when required.

Answers may include:

'The Conservative Party did badly in all areas of the country.'

From Source 1:

- in Scotland they did very badly with only 16% of the vote and 2% of the seats. They came fourth behind Labour, Liberal Democrats and the SNP.
- in Wales they also did badly with only 8% of the seats, well behind Labour and the Liberal Democrats.
- in the UK as a whole they did better, coming within 3% of Labour in terms of % vote, but still well behind in number of MPs.
- in England they did well and actually got more votes than Labour. However, they got far fewer MPs.

Karen Mitchell is being slightly selective, as it was only in England that they did well, and only in % of votes, not in the number of MPs.

'The Liberal Democrats, on the other hand, are the only party whose support increased amongst different age ranges ... compared with other parties, between 1997 and 2005.'

From Source 3:

- the Liberal Democrats increased their support in all 4 age ranges shown.
- support for the Labour party fell in all 4 of the age ranges.
- the Conservative party had a decrease in 2 of the age ranges, but did better in both the 35-64 and the 65+ age ranges.

Karen is being slightly selective. She is correct in what she says with the exception of two age groups for the Conservative Party.

'The Liberal Democrats, on the other hand, are the only party whose support increased amongst different social classes ... compared with other parties, between 1997 and 2005.'

From Source 2:

- support for the Lib Dems increased in all 3 social classes shown.
- support for the Labour party decreased from both the Working Class (Skilled) and the Working Class (Unskilled), but increased from the Middle Class.
- the Conservative Party got less support from the Middle Class, but increased support from both the Skilled and Unskilled Working Class.

Karen is being slightly/quite selective because although the Liberal Democrats increased their support within all social classes, it is also true that both the Labour and Conservative parties did see some increased support from certain social class groups. Overall, Karen is being slightly/quite selective in the use of facts, as there is evidence to show that the Conservatives did not do badly in all areas of the country, and that other parties apart from the Liberal Democrats did get increased support from different groups in society.

Syllabus Area 2 – Changing Society

2. (a) The concept being assessed is Need. Candidates are required to use understanding of the concept to provide detailed explanations with relevant examples and appropriate generalisations.

Answers may include:

- some families are unemployed and survive on a low income and therefore cannot financially afford to buy a nutritionally balanced diet.
- some families are single parents who go out to work for long hours and so the emotional needs of the children are not being met.
- some parents may have a disability which means that they cannot meet the physical needs of their children.
- some parents do not have access to their children which prevents them from meeting the emotional needs of their children.
- some parents cannot meet the developmental needs of their children due to a lack of education.
- any other valid point

(b) Candidates are required to provide evidence to support and oppose a given point of view.

The correct responses are:

View of Tom Hicks

'In 1995, unemployment was a bigger problem in the North than it was in the South.'

Reason to support:

All 7 regions in the 'North' had higher unemployment than 4 out of the 5 regions of the 'South'. Therefore, it was a bigger problem.

View of Tom Hicks

'Ten years on, the situation was the complete opposite.'

Reason to oppose:

As all 7 regions in the 'North' still have higher unemployment than 4 out of the 5 regions of the 'South' it was not the complete opposite. It was still the same.

(c) Candidates are required to make comparisons within and between complex sources and draw valid conclusions from them, with justification using developed argument when required.

Answers may include:

Changes in marriage and divorce in Britain:

- Between 1970 and 2005 **marriages have decreased** by more than 50% from 400 000 to under 200 000.
- **Divorces have nearly trebled** over the same time from about 60 000 to just under 200 000.

The link between changes in marriages and changes in the 'traditional' family

- The 'traditional' family has always been seen as a **couple with dependent children**. The % of the **'traditional' family has fallen** from 52% of households in 1971 to 37% in 2004.
- Between 1970 and 2005, **marriages have decreased** by more than 50%. **Therefore, as the % of marriages fell, the % of the 'traditional' family also fell.**

The difference between the percentages of lone parent families in Britain and Scotland's four main cities

- The % of lone parent families in Britain was 12% in 2004. The % of lone parent families in Scotland's four main cities was over 22-26%, with 3 of them between 27 - 48%. **Therefore, the % was much higher in Scotland's four main cities.**

The main difference between ethnic minority families and white families

- 62% of white families are married couples while all 4 ethnic minority families are over 75% married couples. **Therefore, ethnic minority families are more likely to be married couples**.
- 25% of white families are lone parent families while all 4 ethnic minority families are under 20% lone parent families. **Therefore, ethnic minority families are less likely to be lone parent families**.
- 13% of white families are cohabiting couples while all 4 ethnic minority families are under 5% cohabiting couples. **Therefore, ethnic minority families are less likely to be cohabiting couples.**

Syllabus Area 3 – Ideologies

THE USA

3A. (a) The concept being assessed is Participation. Candidates are required to use understanding of the concept to provide detailed explanations with relevant examples and appropriate generalisations.

Answers may include:

- increase in positive ethnic minority role models such as Condoleeza Rice, Colin Powell, Barack Obama and Ray Nagin.
- celebrity voting campaigns to encourage ethnic minorities to come out and vote. In 2004, P Diddy spearheaded the 'Vote or Die' campaign for the Presidential election.
- increase in the black middle class. More blacks are graduating college and are therefore more likely to register and vote in elections.
- concentration of ethnic minorities in a particular part of a city means that they are more likely to turn out to vote as they believe they have a better chance of getting an ethnic minority candidate elected.
- any other valid point

(b) Candidates are required to state a hypothesis relevant to the issue of 'Health care in the USA'

For example:

The following receive no marks:
- film stars get the most plastic surgery done in the USA.
- health care is important.

The following receive one mark:
- *ER* is a real picture of health care in the USA today.
- health care costs a lot in the USA.

The following receive two marks:
- all races in the USA get similar health care.
- only the really rich in the US get good health care.
- any other valid hypothesis

(c) Candidates are required to state aims relevant to the issue.

For example:

Hypothesis:
'All races in the USA get similar health care'

Possible aims:
- to find out if health care in the USA is good for some and bad for others.
- to find out if blacks have the worst health care in the USA.
- to find out the reasons for poor health care amongst different ethnic groups.
- any other valid aim.

(d) Candidates are required to justify the use of a given method of enquiry relevant to the issue of 'Education in the USA'.

The following good points receive one mark:
- The e-mail content explains who the pupil is and what they are trying to do.

- The e-mail content explains that the pupil has tried to find information first by looking at the school website.
- The e-mail thanks the head teacher for their time and any help they give.

The following bad points receive one mark:
- The e-mail expects the head teacher to print out the questionnaires, hand them out and send them back.
- The pupil wants things done as quickly as possible.
- The e-mail has no name or address to send the 50 copies of the questions back to.

(e) Candidates are required to explain why investigation questions are wrong.

The correct responses are:

Question 3
Are your school meals good and do students get them free?

Reason to change
This is a double-barrelled question but you can only give one answer. You may think that the school meals are good but that students do not get them for free. However, there is no way in which you can say this.

Question 4
Why do Blacks and Hispanics not do well at your school?

Reason to change
This question presumes an answer 'that Blacks and Hispanics do not do well', without getting the facts beforehand.

RUSSIA

3B. (a) The concept being assessed is Particpation. Candidates are required to use understanding of the concept to provide detailed explanations with relevant examples and appropriate generalisations.

Answers may include:
- it is the only way to peacefully change things within Russia.
- Russia has not been a democracy for very long so it is essential that people take part.
- the only way to get representatives from parties such as United Russia, Liberal Democratic Party of Russia or the Communist Party of Russia elected to the Duma is by voting for them or working on their behalf.
- any other valid point

(b) Candidates are required to state a hypothesis relevant to the issue of 'Health care in Russia'.

For example:

The following receive no marks:
- politicians get the most plastic surgery done in Russia.
- health care is important.

The following receive one mark:
- TV drama presents a real picture of health care in Russia today.
- health care costs a lot in Russia.

The following receive two marks:
- all nationalities in Russia get similar health care.
- only the really rich in Russia get good health care.
- any other valid hypothesis

(c) Candidates are required to state aims relevant to the issue.

For example:

Hypothesis:
'All nationalities in Russia get similar health care.'

Possible aims:
- to find out if health care in Russia is good for some and bad for others.
- to find out if Chechens have the worst health care in Russia.
- to find out the reasons for poor health care amongst different nationalities.
- any other valid aim

(d) Candidates are required to justify the use of a given method of enquiry relevant to the issue of 'Education in Russia'.
The following good points receive one mark:
- The e-mail content explains who the pupil is and what they are trying to do.
- The e-mail content explains that the pupil has tried to find information first by looking at the school website.
- The e-mail thanks the head teacher for their time and any help they give.

The following bad points receive one mark:
- The e-mail expects the head teacher to print out the questionnaires, hand them out and send them back.
- The pupil says they want things done as quickly as possible.
- The e-mail has no name or address to send the 50 copies of the questions back to.

(e) Candidates are required to explain why investigation questions are wrong.
The correct responses are:

Question 3
Are your school meals good and do students get them free?

Reason to change
This is a double-barrelled question but you can only give one answer. You may think that the school meals are good but that students do not get them for free. However, there is no way in which you can say this.

Question 4
Why is it that girls always do better than boys at your school?

Reason to change
This question presumes an answer 'that girls always do better than boys', without getting the facts beforehand.

CHINA

3C. (a) The concept being assessed is Participation. Candidates are required to use understanding of the concept to provide detailed explanations with relevant examples and appropriate generalisations.
Answers may include:
- **One-Party system:**
  Chinese Communist Party keeps strict control on politics at all levels and is given special protection by the constitution. Membership of the party is strictly controlled and is often essential for success in business.
- **Elections:**
  No free elections are held. Citizens can only vote at local level. Only candidates and parties sanctioned by the Communist Party are allowed to seek election. Eight other parties are legal but do not act as 'opposition' eg China Democratic League, Chinese Peasants' and Workers' Democratic Party.
- **Banned Opposition/dissent:**
  Several organisations that have opposed the Communist Party have been banned as dangerous and subversive, eg China Democracy Party, National Democratic Party of Tibet. Organisations like the Falun Gong and the independence movements for Taiwan and Tibet have also been banned and their members persecuted.
- **Arrest, imprisonment or exile:**
  The 'Laogai' system of 're-education through labour' still exists. Many dissidents have been in prison since Tiananmen Square and others have been exiled, eg Wei Jingshen.
- **Trade unions/pressure groups:**
  Independent trade unions are not permitted. The Federation of Trade Unions is linked to the Communist Party. Some pressure group activity is allowed but it cannot question the authority or legitimacy of the Communist Party. Environmental groups have grown in number, eg many campaigned against the building of the Three Gorges Dam.
- **Female Participation:**
  Discrimination stops many women taking part in politics. Attitudes have been slow to change and few women stand as candidates. The All-China Women's Federation (Linked to Communist Party) campaigns to promote equality.
- any other valid point

(b) Candidates are required to state a hypothesis relevant to the issue of 'Health care in China'.
For example:
The following receive no marks:
- politicians get the most plastic surgery done in China.
- health care is important.

The following receive one marks:
- TV drama presents a real picture of health care in China today.
- health care costs a lot in China.

The following receive two marks:
- all races in China get similar health care.
- only the really rich in China get good health care.
- any other valid hypothesis

(c) Candidates are required to state aims relevant to the issue.
For example:
Hypothesis:
'People living in cities in China have better health care than those living in the countryside.'
Possible aims:
- to find out if health care in China is good for some and bad for others.
- to find out if people living in Beijing have the best health care in China.
- to find out the reasons for the good health care they have.
- any other valid aim.

(d) Candidates are required to justify the use of a given method of enquiry relevant to the issue of 'Education in China.
The following good points receive one mark:
- The e-mail content explains who the pupil is and what they are trying to do.
- The e-mail content explains that the pupil has tried to find information first by looking at the school website.
- The e-mail thanks the head teacher for their time and any help they give.

The following bad points receive one mark:
- The e-mail expects the head teacher to print out the questionnaires, hand them out and send them back.
- The pupil says they want things done as quickly as possible.
- The e-mail has no name or address to send the 50 copies of the questions back to.

(e) Candidates are required to explain why investigation questions are wrong.
The correct responses are:

Question 3
Are your school meals good and do students get them free?

Reason to change
This is a double-barrelled question but you can only give one answer. You may think that the school meals are good but that students do not get them for free. However, there is no way in which you can say this.

Question 4
Why is it that children from rural areas always do worse at your school?

Reason to change

This question presumes an answer that 'children from rural areas always do worse' without getting the facts beforehand.

Syllabus Area 4 – International Relations

4. (*a*) The concept being assessed is Need.

Candidates are required to use their understanding of the concept to provide explanations in depth and detail.

Answers may include:

- **Euro**

  The policy on the Euro tries to meet the needs of Europeans by enabling businesses to deal with each other in the same currency. This saves time and money and encourages trade. Citizens are able to travel within the eurozone and not worry about changing money. A single currency makes Europe a strong partner to trade with and facilitates access to a genuine single market for foreign companies, who will benefit from lower costs of doing business in Europe.

- **Enlarged Membership**

  The policy on enlargement tries to meet the needs of Europeans by creating a larger market for products manufactured within the EU as there are few obstacles to trade. It allows workers to travel eg Polish workers to take up long-term vacancies in Scotland's less attractive jobs. All European citizens benefit from having neighbours that are stable democracies and prosperous market economies. Enlargement is a carefully managed process which helps the transformation of the countries involved, extending peace, stability, prosperity, democracy, human rights and the rule of law across Europe.

- **Common Fisheries Policy**

  The policy on fishing tries to meet the needs of Europeans by ensuring that there will be fish stocks in the future by using quotas and decommissioning vessels. This allows fish stocks to be conserved. This is important as many jobs in coastal areas of Europe are dependent on fishing and fish processing.

- **Aid to the regions**

  The policy on aid to the regions tries to meet the needs of Europeans by giving aid to poorer areas of the EU. The Highlands of Scotland have received money to improve transport links to try and improve employment in remote areas. This policy is now of great benefit to people in new EU countries which are poorer than older members.

- **European Defence Force**

  The policy on defence tries to meet the needs of Europeans by getting the members to work co-operatively to protect Europeans by providing manpower and equipment. In 2004 Eufor took over peace keeping in Bosnia-Herzegovina providing over 6 000 troops.

- **Common Agricultural Policy**

  The policy on agriculture tries to meet the needs of Europeans by supporting agriculture in the member states. It was reformed in 2004 as it was no longer meeting the needs of citizens as it was paying farmers to grow crops that weren't needed. Farmers mainly now receive money through The Single Farm Payment Scheme (SFPS). It also now tries to maintain the environment eg special payments for farmers who look after hedgerows etc.

- any other valid point on any of the policies

(*b*) Candidates are required to provide evidence to support and oppose a point of view.

Answers may include:

For Project One – Rose Energy

- Rose Energy want to develop large scale oil production and Focus on Chad supports this as many natural resources are underdeveloped.
- Rose Energy will build a city hospital near the oil development. This is needed as there is a lack of medical provision and health is the most important issue according to the pie chart at 27%.
- Drought is a problem and very little land is irrigated so building water pumps along the pipeline would be a positive development. This was a close third in the concerns with 23% and the introduction states 'lack of sanitation and clean water are major problems'.
- The project will raise much needed money for the government through tax which can be used to pay off some of the debt.

For Project Two – Helping Hands

- Chrissie is right, health care is the most important issue facing Chad (27%). Contraception is important as there's a much higher population growth than the UK and infant mortality is high at 94.
- Free health care is important as many live on a dollar or less a day and can't afford to pay doctors who need to be paid in advance. HIV/AIDS rate is high (5% compared to only 0·2% in UK).
- Chrissie says we must improve the income of farmers and 25% of people in Chad agreed that this was the most important issue. 80% of people rely on farming so this would improve the lives of many people.
- People have very few qualifications and are unable to get better paid jobs. Literacy is only 48% so community projects are needed to develop basic skills.

Against Project One – Rose Energy

- Only people in the south of the country will benefit from the oil development whereas Helping Hands will support people across the country.
- There has already been an oil development in the south of the country but people are still poor and the government is in debt.
- This is a company whose profits will go back to the parent company, not to the local community.

Against Project Two – Helping Hands

- People do not see education as a priority - only 15% see it as a concern compared to 27% for health.
- This project is only planning to invest $20 000 compared to Rose Energy's $1 billion.

MODERN STUDIES GENERAL 2008

Syllabus Area 1 – Living In A Democracy

1. (*a*) The concept being assessed is Rights and Responsibilities. Candidates are required to give detailed descriptions.
   Answers may include:
   Rights
   - to organise a petition in which supporters can sign their name to express support for your cause. This can be delivered to the authority that you are trying to influence.
   - to hold a protest march/demonstration in a busy public place. Supporters can carry banners and shout slogans to publicise your cause.
   - publicity stunts to attract the attention of the media will get your message across to millions of people across the country.
   - any other valid point.

   Responsibilities
   - to ensure that any protest/demonstration/stunt is peaceful and within the law.
   - to ensure that all signatures in a petition are genuine.
   - to support the group financially to help fund its activities.
   - to tell the truth and not slander or libel someone.
   - any other valid point.

   (*b*) Candidates are required to make comparisons within sources and draw valid conclusions.
   The correct responses are:
   Difference 1:
   Source 1 says 'We do not need special arrangements to attract more women into Parliament' but
   Source 2 says, 'We must find new ways to encourage more women to become MPs.'

   Difference 2:
   Source 1 says 'that women are now well represented in the UK' but
   Source 2 says 'women in the UK are still poorly represented when compared to other European countries.'

   (*c*) Candidates are required to give relevant aims for an investigative topic.
   The following receive one mark:
   - to find out the main methods used by political parties when campaigning.
   - to find out the laws/regulations that must be followed.
   - to find out which methods are most effective
   - any other valid aim.

   (*d*) Candidates are required to state and justify an appropriate method of enquiry.
   Answers may include:
   - write a letter as this would allow detailed questions/questionnaire to be included.
   - telephone them as this would be a very quick way of getting information.
   - visit the local office as this would allow face to face contact.
   - send an e-mail as this would allow detailed questions to be asked very quickly.
   - any other valid point.

   (*e*) Candidates are required to state and justify an appropriate method of enquiry.
   Answers may include:
   - lots of books, magazines and other publications which you can borrow and read to get information about your topic.
   - expert advice from librarians who are trained to help you find information.
   - most libraries offer free access to the Internet which you could use to search for information/ send e-mail.
   - any other valid point.

Syllabus Area 2 – Changing Society

2. (*a*) The concept being assessed is Ideology. Candidates are required to provide detailed descriptions.
   Answers may include:
   - Jobcentreplus displays vacancies and can help people find jobs.
   - computer courses and education for new skills.
   - Modern Apprenticeships to help young school leavers get skilled jobs eg electrician.
   - Government attracts foreign industry to Scotland with grants eg a Japanese computer factory.
   - sign up for New Deal.
   - getting a College course eg in plumbing skills.
   - any other valid point.

   (*b*) The concept being assessed is Need.
   Candidates are required to provide detailed explanations.
   Answers may include:
   - Broadband gives very easy Internet access and easy communication.
   - Web-cam means people can still communicate with their work.
   - many people do their work on a computer which can be used just as easily at home.
   - fax machine allows documents to be sent all over the world.
   - any other valid point.

   (*c*) Candidates are required to express support for a personal point of view with valid reasons.
   The correct responses are:
   For Scheme A – A Digital Community Centre
   - It aims to give local unemployed people basic to advanced ICT skills – young people need help to improve their ICT skills.
   - Help in completing application forms for anyone who feels that they need it – young people need help with completing job application forms.

   For Scheme B – Personal Advisors
   - It will concentrate on improving interview skills – young people need help to improve their interview skills.
   - It will give advice on filling in application forms for new jobs – young people need help with completing job application forms.

   (*d*) Candidates are required to disagree with a given point of view with valid reasons.
   The correct responses are:
   Disagree with the view:
   Abigail Smith says 'Self-employment amongst Whites and Bangladeshis has grown every year.'
   Evidence to prove:
   Bangladeshi self-employment between 2001 and 2003 fell from 12·3% to 9·9% – this is a drop.

   Disagree with the view:
   Abigail Smith says 'Pakistanis had the largest decrease in self-employment between 2003 and 2005.'

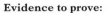

Evidence to prove:
Pakistani self-employment between 2003 and 2005 fell from 22·5% to 21·0%, a drop of 1·5%. However, Chinese self-employment fell from 18·3% to 16·0%, a drop of 2·3% which is a bigger drop, as is Black Caribbean at 1·7%.

Syllabus Area 3 – Ideologies

THE USA

3A. (*a*) The concept being assessed is Ideology. Candidates are required to provide detailed descriptions.
Answers may include:
- Americans can work in an area they have dreamed about, fulfilling the American Dream.
- motive to work hard and make business successful.
- successful business people can keep a share of the profits from their company.
- higher income allows Americans to enjoy a higher standard of living.
- any other valid point.

(*b*) Candidates are required to provide evidence to support and oppose a given point of view.
Answers may include:
Support the view:
Kelly Halcomb says, 'The USA enrolls less of its children in primary school than most other major countries.'
Evidence to support:
America enrolls 92% of its children whereas the UK and Japan enrol 100% and China enrolls 99%. Only Russia enrolls fewer children than the USA.

Oppose the view:
Kelly Halcomb says, 'People in the USA have both the highest average income and live the longest.'
Evidence to oppose:
Whilst the USA is the richest country as their average income is the highest at $41 400, they are not the healthiest as their life expectancy is 78 which is lower than the UK and Japan.

(*c*) The concept being assessed is Equality. Candidates are required to provide detailed descriptions.
Answers may include:
Education
- attend ghetto schools which receive less funding than suburban schools.
- fewer staff per pupil in ghetto schools.
- some recent immigrants may struggle with English as the main language in school.
- some schools may have a gang/violence problem which limits ability to learn in school.
- any other valid point.

Housing
- some Americans may be homeless.
- some minority groups may have no choice but to live in poor quality housing such as the projects. (Robert Taylor homes)
- recent immigrants may not be able to afford good quality housing and live in overcrowded/ sub-standard houses.
- racial segregation still exists between mainly vanilla suburbs and minority ghettoes.
- any other valid point.

Health
- some Americans cannot afford private insurance such as Blue Cross or Blue Shield.

- elderly may have to rely on Medicare and poor on Medicaid if they have no private insurance.
- any other valid point.

(*d*) Candidates are required to detect exaggeration and provide explanations.
The correct responses are:
Statement 1
'the government was well equipped to respond to the disaster.'
Reason 1
From Source 1: it says that 'Americans were upset at the size of the disaster and how poorly prepared all levels of government were to deal with the problem.' The President himself recognised the government's slow response.

Statement 2
'The majority of people agree that the government is doing a good re-building job.'
Reason 2
From Source 2: it shows that only 30% think the government is doing an excellent/good job, whereas a majority, about 65%, think the government is doing a not so good/poor job.

RUSSIA

3B. (*a*) The concept being assessed is Ideology. Candidates are required to provide detailed descriptions.
Answers may include:
- Russians can work in an area they have dreamed about which helps them fulfil their hopes.
- motive to work hard and make business successful.
- successful business people can keep a share of the profits from their company.
- higher income allows Russians to enjoy a higher standard of living.
- higher incomes have given many Russian people the opportunity to travel both within and outside Russia.
- any other valid point.

(*b*) Candidates are required to provide evidence to support and oppose a given point of view.
Answers may include:
Support the view:
Georgi Safin says, 'Russia enrolls less of its children in primary school than most other major countries.'
Evidence to support:
Russia enrolls 90% of its children whereas the UK and Japan enrol 100% and China enrolls 99% whilst the USA enrols 92%. Russia enrolls the fewest.

Oppose the view:
Georgi Safin says, 'People in Russia have both the lowest average income and shortest life expectancy.'
Evidence to oppose:
Whilst Russia has the lowest life expectancy at 65 years, it does not have the lowest average income. Average income in Russia is $3 410 whilst in China it is lower at $1 290.

(*c*) The concept being assessed is Equality.
Candidates are required to provide detailed descriptions.
Answers may include:
Education
- in Russia, education at all levels was free for anybody who could pass entrance exams.
- students were provided with small scholarships and free housing. This was considered crucial because it provided access to higher education to all skilled students, as opposed to only those who could afford it.

- expenditure on education has gone down over the years as the state could no longer afford it.
- schools and universities found themselves unable to provide adequate teachers' salaries, students' scholarships, and maintenance for their facilities.
- many private higher education institutions have now opened with students paying fees.
- latest figures show that 35% of students in Russia are now paying for their own education in state institutions and 20% are studying in private universities.
- any other valid point.

Housing

- under President Putin, affordable housing has been made one of Russia's four priority National Projects (along with healthcare, education and agriculture).
- the government is planning to invest on a large scale in upgrading Russia's run-down stock of municipal housing, while also promoting the growth of private housing.
- most Russians still live in apartment blocks which were built during the era of the Soviet Union. Many were poorly constructed.
- most Russians still rent their homes which are in poor condition.
- large private house-building projects have helped to provide more jobs in the construction industry.
- any other valid point.

Health

- basic medical care is available to most of the population free of cost, but its quality is extremely low by Western standards.
- significant increases in infant mortality and contagious diseases.
- the decline in health is due in part to environmental and social factors such as air and water pollution, contamination (largely from nuclear accidents or improper disposal of radioactive materials), overcrowded living conditions, inadequate nutrition, alcoholism and smoking.
- there is a lack of modern medical equipment and technology.
- any other valid point.

(d) Candidates are required to detect exaggeration and provide explanations.
The correct responses are:

Statement 1
'The majority of foreigners living in Moscow find the city expensive.'

Reason 1
Source 2 shows that only 15% of foreigners find the city very expensive whilst another 22% find it fairly expensive. Taken together, this is 37% which is not a majority.

Statement 2
'Shopping costs are similar both in the centre and in the outskirts of Moscow.'

Reason 2
Source 1 explains that shopping costs can be reduced by shopping in the outskirts of Moscow rather than in the city centre.

CHINA

3C. (a) The concept being assessed is Ideology. Candidates are required to provide detailed descriptions.
Answers may include:

- Chinese people are allowed to start a business and keep the profit ie 'Socialist Market Economy'. This has been especially common in the 'Special Economic Zones'.

- increased wealth can give access to better housing, education, health care etc. Many Chinese people now have access to consumer goods such as freezers, PCs etc. There has also been a boom in car ownership.
- small township enterprises have improved living conditions in rural areas.
- jobs are created by small businesses which spread wealth and create better living standards.
- higher incomes have given many Chinese people the opportunity to travel both within and outside China.
- any other valid point.

(b) Candidates are required to provide evidence to support and oppose a given point of view.
Answers may include:

Support the view:
An Qi says, 'China enrolls more of its children in primary school than most other major countries.'

Evidence to support:
This is true; Source 2 shows that only the UK enrolls more. China has a higher figure than India, Russia and the USA.

Oppose the view:
An Qi says, 'People in China also have both the second lowest average income and shortest life expectancy.'

Evidence to oppose:
This is not true; Source 1 shows that although China does have the second lowest average income, it does not have the shortest life expectancy. Both India and Russia have shorter life expectancies.

(c) The concept being assessed is Equality. Candidates are required to provide detailed explanations.
Answers may include:

Education

- cities and large towns have better quality schools, colleges and universities. Rural population has little choice and are often too poor to travel to towns for education. Rural lifestyle places low emphasis on formal education.
- many migrant workers who have gone from country to city have been denied access to education.
- some of the new business elite (of the cities) have access to foreign universities for their children.
- Communist party members still have greater choice and access to schools etc.

Housing

- rural housing is still very basic. Many still do not have running water and electricity. The major cities have a better choice of housing with access to electricity, running water etc. Many rural Chinese cannot afford such luxuries.
- migrant workers are often forced to live in very poor housing on the outskirts of the main towns. Conditions are as bad in some as the worst slums anywhere in the world.
- Communist party members tend to have better quality housing.
- although the one child policy was officially scrapped, some families are still disadvantaged.
- wages for skilled workers employed by foreign firms are higher than the average so better quality housing can be purchased.

Health

- towns and cities have more modern hospitals with more qualified doctors, nurses, specialist equipment etc. There is a shortage of medical staff in rural areas. People in these areas often rely on traditional methods.

- poor housing conditions and dangerous working conditions have damaged the health of many workers on the 'Coastal Strip' and in 'Special Economic Zones'. China is believed to have the world's worst figures for industrial injury and deaths. Official figures for this are impossible to find.
- air pollution in the largest cities is a serious problem. Rapid economic growth threatens air quality in many areas, including Beijing.
- levels of smoking have boomed in recent years. Experts from the WHO predict a crisis in future decades from cancer and other tobacco related illnesses.
- the new rich have more access to expensive treatments and to treatment abroad.
- any other valid point.

(d) Candidates are required to detect exaggeration and provide explanations.
The correct responses are:
Statement 1
'The majority of Chinese people are not pleased about the Olympics coming to their country.'
Reason 1
The statement is exaggerated because in Source 2 it shows that 20% are unhappy and 15% very unhappy. A total of only 35% which is not a majority.

Statement 2
'everyone in the country should benefit from the Games.'
Reason 2
The statement is exaggerated because in Source 1 it says that 'sixty-nine villages have been demolished to make way for the new Olympic facilities.' Clearly not 'everyone' is benefiting.

Syllabus Area 4 – International Relations

4. (a) The concept being assessed is Need. Candidates are required to provide detailed descriptions.
Answers may include:
- advice on farming methods.
- support to improve technology eg irrigation.
- campaign on children's rights.
- supporting mothers eg breastfeeding programmes.
- education – literacy programmes for adults and children.
- against child labour/child soldiers.
- immunisation programmes eg measles in Darfur/Sudan.
- training in basic medical skills – basic midwifery skills.
- any other valid point.

Good answers would identify specific agencies such as UNICEF, WHO, UNESCO, FAO. However, this is not essential for full credit.

(b) Candidates are required to make comparisons within a source and draw valid conclusions.
The correct responses are:
- the country with the biggest change in its armed forces is the USA. Its numbers fell by 689 000 compared to UK at only 92 000.
- as spending rises so does the size of a country's armed forces. Greece's armed forces went up by 8 000 and spending increased from $500 pp to $610 pp.

(c) The concept being assessed is Power. Candidates are required to provide detailed explanations.
Answers may include:
- cooperation between member states.
- regional aid eg Rosyth ferry.

- freedom of movement eg large numbers of Poles now working in UK.
- qualifications recognised so can work/study in 27 countries.
- larger market for products manufactured in their country ie improved trade.
- regional aid has raised living standards especially in poorer parts of Europe.
- opinion polls show that the majority of EU citizens are happy living in the EU.
- any other valid point.

(d) Candidates are required to detect exaggeration and provide explanations.
The correct responses are:
Statement 1
'No food aid was received by Niger.'
Reason 1
40 000 tonnes of energy biscuits received in August 2005.

Statement 2
'Debt is still a major problem.'
Reason 2
All debt cancelled at G8 summit in July 2005.

MODERN STUDIES CREDIT 2008

Syllabus Area 1 – Living In A Democracy

1. (a) The concept being assessed is Rights. Candidates are required to use understanding of the concept to provide detailed descriptions with relevant examples and appropriate generalisations.
   Answers may include:
   - to be represented by their shop steward or other union official who may try to negotiate a settlement to the dispute.
   - to take industrial action to try to force their employer to settle the dispute. This may include a work-to-rule, overtime ban or strike action.
   - to organise protest marches or demonstrations to gain publicity about the dispute, and try to gain the support of the public. This may attract the attention of the media and extend the coverage across the whole country.
   - to lobby local and national politicians to try to gain their support, and perhaps put pressure on the employer to settle the dispute.
   - any other valid point.

   (b) The concept being assessed is Representation. Candidates are required to use understanding of the concept to provide detailed explanations with relevant examples and appropriate generalisations.
   Answers may include:
   - a major aim of the Scottish Parliament was to get more people involved in decision making and its working practices were therefore designed to get all groups, including women more involved.
   - the working hours of the Scottish Parliament follow normal business hours, whereas Westminster works much later in the day, which may discourage women from taking part.
   - holidays in the Scottish Parliament tend to be at the same time as Scottish school holidays.
   - the Scottish Parliament has a creche to look after the young children of MSPs. This is not provided at Westminster.
   - the AMS voting system has resulted in more women being voted in as MSPs.
   - some political parties in Scotland have selected more women candidates to stand for election.
   - any other valid point.

   (c) Candidates are required to provide evidence to support and oppose a point of view. Answers must make explicit links between the background information about Gleninch Constituency **and** Sources 1 and 2.
   Answers may include:
   For Kirsty Reid
   - the statistical profile of Gleninch shows school leavers with Highers is 13% above the Scottish average. Kirsty says that she will work to ensure that the excellent education in the area continues.
   - she supports the new quarry because it will provide jobs to stop the decline of the local economy. The background information shows that 150 new jobs will be created in the quarry.
   - there are a number of transport problems in the area such as poor public transport and high petrol prices. Kirsty says that she will make it a priority to improve transport links.

Against Kirsty Reid
- she says the wind farm will provide many local jobs and help the local environment. However, the information says that it will create only a few temporary jobs, and will impact on the scenery of the area.
- she says that she should be selected because she is a woman and that this issue is a major priority for local party members. This is untrue, as the survey shows that the issue was considered least important with 67% of members considering it either unimportant or not very important.

For Robbie McKay
- he opposes the wind farm because it will be a blot on the landscape, and deter tourists. Tourism is very important to the area as it employs a lot of people in hotels and restaurants. There will also be a 15 mile power line which will spoil the scenery.
- local party members are concerned about the issue of health, with 88% considering it either fairly or very important. Robbie says this will be one of his main concerns too.
- he will do all that he can to make people in the area better-off. This is important because average income is 14% below the Scottish average, and Income Support claimants are 22% above average.

Against Robbie McKay
- he says that as crime is among the worst in Scotland he will campaign to improve policing. However, the statistics show that crime in the area is quite low, with housebreaking 93% lower than the Scottish average, and assaults 73% lower.
- he opposes the new quarry because the local party are more concerned about the environment than jobs. However, this is not true. The survey shows that 52% think that jobs are very important, compared to only 30% for the environment.

Syllabus Area 2 – Changing Society

2. (a) The concept being assessed is Need. Candidates are required to use understanding of the concept to provide detailed explanations with relevant examples and appropriate generalisations.
   Answers may include:
   Community Care within their own home
   - adaptations made to their own home to meet physical needs. For example stair lifts aid mobility and allow elderly people to move freely about their house.
   - Need for security is met by intercoms allowing elderly to feel safe at home.
   - Need for medical care can be addressed by personal care plans which build in visits from district nurses or GPs to take care of wound dressings, prescriptions etc.
   - meals on wheels can be provided to ensure elderly receive adequate nutrition to stay healthy.
   - the emotional needs of the elderly are met as the elderly continue to live in a familiar environment with their own possessions and family and friends nearby.
   - any other valid point.

   Sheltered Housing
   - this meets the elderly need for independence. Elderly still have their own flat and can take their own furniture and possessions with them providing a familiar environment.
   - a sense of security is provided as elderly know that there is a warden on call 24 hours a day in case of emergencies. This allows elderly to be independent, yet feel secure.

- the social needs of the elderly are met through the community which exists within the sheltered housing complex. They can meet with others in the communal lounge or else at one of the organised activities within the complex.
- the emotional needs of the elderly are met as the sheltered housing complex will often have rooms where relatives can come and stay for visits.
- any other valid point.

Residential Care Homes

- 24 hour trained nursing care can take care of physical needs of elderly such as assisting stroke victims with their personal care.
- meals are provided to ensure that elderly are receiving adequate nutrition, for example special meals can be prepared for diabetics.
- the social needs of the elderly are met via the common rooms in the nursing/residential homes allowing the elderly to have interaction with others.
- the homes are specially adapted with ramps to assist wheelchair users, bath hoists to assist stroke victims, etc.
- any other valid point.

(b) Candidates are required to state a hypothesis relevant to the issue of 'Help for families in the UK'.

For example:

The following receive one mark:
- the government gives a lot of help to families.
- different families get different help.

The following receive two marks:
- Child Care helps mothers get back to work.
- 'Child Benefit' should only be given to families in real need.
- any other valid hypothesis.

(c) Candidates are required to state aims relevant to their hypothesis.

For example:

Hypothesis:

'Child Benefit' should only be given to families in real need.

Potential aims:
- to find out if the value of Child Benefit has changed.
- to find out the ways in which Child Benefit helps different families.
- to find out if local people think that Child Benefit should be given to all families, no matter how well off they are.
- any other valid aim.

(d) Candidates are required to state relevant questions about the issue of 'Help for families in the UK'.

For example:

The following receive one mark:
- Do you help families?
- How much is Child Benefit today?

The following receive two marks:
- What kind of problems do families contact you with?
- What does Parliament do to help poor families throughout the UK?
- Do you think that the Child Support Agency does a good job?
- Any other valid question.

(e) Candidates are required to give a disadvantage and advantage of a method of enquiry.

Answers may include:

Disadvantage of buying from the website
- it costs £45 – this is very expensive for the school to buy for one investigation or pupil.

- it is out of stock – I need it right away so that I can finish my investigation on time.

Advantage of using Social Trends
- it is the 2008 edition – this is the latest edition which means that it will have very up to date statistics and tables.
- it is published by the Office for National Statistics using information from a range of government departments – so it will be very accurate and will be looking at statistics from all over the country.
- the data is presented in tables, figures and text – I can easily interpret them and use them in my investigation.
- any other valid point.

Syllabus Area 3 – Ideologies

THE USA

3A. (a) The concept being assessed is Participation. Candidates are required to use understanding of the concept to provide detailed descriptions with relevant examples and appropriate generalisations.

Answers may include:
- standing as a candidate in local, state or federal elections. For example McCain, Clinton and Obama in 2008 Presidential election state primaries and Hillary Clinton for Senate in 2006.
- joining a political party such as the Republicans and voting at the national party convention.
- fundraising for the political party of their choice. Holding a house party for the Republicans.
- register as a voter and turn out to support a candidate in 2006 mid-term elections.
- door-to-door canvassing for the Democratic party.
- write to the editor of the Washington Post to express your opinion on the federal government policy on the War on Terror.
- protest with a demonstration against a bill being passed in Congress.
- joining an interest group, such as the NRA or Emily's List, and lobbying Congress about a bill.
- any other valid point.

(b) Candidates are required to provide evidence to support and oppose a given point of view.

The correct responses are:

View of Wall Street Economist

'The biggest increase in personal income between 2003 and 2005 has been in Connecticut.'

Reason to support:

Between 2003 and 2005 Connecticut income increased by $5 500, which is more than any other state.

View of Wall Street Economist

'The richest states in the US are **all** to be found in the Mid East of the country.'

Reason to oppose:

Some of the top 10 richest states are to be found in the Southeast, Mid West, Rocky Mountains and New England.

(c) Candidates are required to detect and explain examples of lack of objectivity in complex sources, giving developed argument when required.

Answers may include:

'The Red Pines gated development will cause many problems for our health.'

From Source 1:
- Red Pines, at the moment, is used for walking and exercise.
- Doctor Joan Quincy thinks Rockford residents need more exercise.

- the health statistics show that Rockford residents are more overweight and take less exercise than the American people as a whole.

From Source 2:

- the opinion poll suggests that 70% of Rockford residents think that the Red Pines area is Important or Very Important for exercise.

Therefore, Findlay Smith is **correct** when he says that The Red Pines gated development will cause many problems for health in Rockford as it will reduce the chances for exercise.

'The Red Pines gated development will change the ethnic mix in Rockford.'

From Source 1:

- gated communities are mostly white developments with affluent blacks being less likely to choose to live there.

From Source 2:

- the 10 000 homes in Rockford are 32% White, 31% Black, 29% Hispanic and 8% other. Therefore, the main ethnic groups in Rockford are roughly the same.
- the opinion poll suggests that keeping the racial mix as it is today is important with 65% of Rockford residents believing it to be important or very important.

From Source 3:

- the 500 families wanting to move into Red Pines are 50% white, 24% Black, 25% Hispanic and 1% other.

Therefore, Findlay Smith is **correct** when he says that The Red Pines gated development will change the ethnic mix in Rockford as it will add more whites to the ethnic mix.

'(The Red Pines gated development) … will bring few benefits to the people of Rockford.'

From Source 1:

- a few short-term benefits but no long-term gain.
- building houses could cause problems for the residents of Rockford as it will lessen chances for exercise.

From Source 2:

- 60% of Rockford residents believe that jobs are a major issue. This is the majority of people in Rockford.

From Source 3:

- skilled workers needed in the building of the community.
- unskilled workers needed in the building of the community.
- unskilled jobs available later in servicing the community.
- more money spent in local shops providing more business from workers and then the residents.
- building companies increase trade.
- local shops can become suppliers.
- flood prevention measures will stop flooding.

Therefore, Findlay Smith is **wrong** when he says that The Red Pines gated development will bring few benefits as it will bring many benefits.

Overall conclusion on the extent of selectivity:

Findlay Smith is right in two statements and wrong in the other so he is slightly selective in the use of facts.

RUSSIA

3B. (*a*) The concept being assessed is Participation. Candidates are required to use understanding of the concept to provide detailed descriptions with relevant examples and appropriate generalisations.

Answers may include:

- standing as a candidate in local or national elections. Eg The Duma.
- fundraising for any of the national parties. Eg Yablonko.

- writing letters to local and national newspapers. Eg Pravda, Izvestia, Novosti Peterburga (St Petersburg) or the Moscow Times.
- many Russians use the Internet as a tool in the political process. It is here that many of the complaints about the clampdown on political expression are being made known.
- demonstrations are allowed but many are now more carefully controlled by the government.
- the Kremlin continues to separate Russia from Western democracies by tightening control over the media and harassing the already weak opposition. This has put a strain on people getting over their political point of view.
- any other valid point.

(*b*) Candidates are required to provide evidence to support and oppose a given point of view.

The correct responses are:

View of Russian Economist

'The amount spent on foodstuffs is the only one which has seen a rise between 2002 and 2005.'

Reason to support

Source 2 shows that although it dipped in 2003, foodstuffs overall have gone up by 3·5%. All the others have either stayed the same or gone down.

View of Russian Economist

'Both Industry and Agriculture have grown each year between 2002 and 2005.'

Reason to oppose

Source 1 shows that Industry has grown each year and whilst Agriculture has grown overall, in 2004, it went down from 309 to 302 before recovering to 625 in 2005. Therefore, both haven't grown each year.

(*c*) Candidates are required to detect and explain examples of lack of objectivity in complex sources, giving developed argument when required.

Answers may include:

'The Sosny Woods Gated Development will cause many problems for our health'

From Source 1:

- Sosny Woods, at the moment, is used for walking and exercise.
- Doctor Yuri Press thinks Vorkuta residents need more exercise.
- the health statistics show that Vorkuta residents are more overweight and take less exercise than the Russian people as a whole.

From Source 2:

- The opinion poll suggests that 70% of Vorkuta residents think that the Sosny Woods area is Important or Very Important for exercise.

Therefore, Dmitri Arshavin is **correct** when he says that The Sosny Woods Gated Development will cause many problems for health in Vorkuta as it will reduce the chances for exercise.

'The Sosny Woods Gated Development will allow outsiders to dominate Vorkuta.'

From Source 2:

- The opinion poll suggests that 65% of Vorkuta residents, which is the majority, believe that keeping in-comers to a minimum is important.

From Source 3:

- 90% of the new families coming into Vorkuta will be outsiders with 73% having no connection to the town whatsoever.
- however, the other 10% are already living in Vorkuta and as there will only be 500 new homes, this will cut the number of outsiders.

Therefore, Dmitri Arshavin is being **fairly selective** because the numbers involved do not mean that outsiders will dominate Vorkuta. They will change the balance somewhat but they will not be in the majority.

'It will bring few benefits to the people of Vorkuta.'
From Source 1:
- a few short-term benefits but no long-term gain.
- building houses could cause problems for the residents of Vorkuta as it will lessen chances for exercise.

From Source 2:
- 40% of Vorkuta residents believe that jobs are a major issue. This is a sizeable minority.

From Source 3:
- skilled workers needed in the building of the community.
- unskilled workers needed in the building of the community.
- unskilled jobs available later in servicing the community.
- more money spent in local shops providing more business from workers and then the residents.
- building companies increase trade.
- local shops can become suppliers.
- flood prevention measures will stop flooding.

Therefore, Dmitri Arshavin is **wrong** when he says that The Sosny Woods Gated Development will bring few benefits as it will bring a number of benefits. The jobs will be there for those who want or need them whilst the flood prevention measures will help the whole town.

Overall conclusion on the extent of selectivity:
Dmitri Arshavin is right in one statement and wrong in the other two so he is very selective in the use of facts.

CHINA

3C. (*a*) The concept being assessed is Participation. Candidates are required to use understanding of the concept to provide detailed descriptions with relevant examples and appropriate generalisations.
Answers may include:
Party Membership
Membership of the party is strictly controlled and is often essential for success in business. Ordinary citizens can be invited to join. Eight other parties are legal but do not act as 'opposition' eg China Democratic League, Chinese Peasants' and Workers' Democratic Party.

Elections
Elections are held regularly but are not 'free' in the western sense. Citizens can vote at local level for village congresses or councils. Only candidates and parties sanctioned by the Communist Party are allowed to seek election. Peoples' Congress elections are held at city, province and national levels.

Banned Opposition/dissent
Several banned organisations offer the chance to participate but these carry the risk of arrest and imprisonment. Eg China Democracy Party, National Democratic Party of Tibet. Independence movements for Taiwan and Tibet have been banned and their members persecuted.

Trade union/pressure groups
Independent trade unions are not permitted. The Federation of Trade Unions is linked to the Communist Party and offers some opportunities to participate. Some pressure group activity is allowed but it cannot question the authority or legitimacy of the Communist Party.

Environmental groups have grown in number eg many campaigned against the building of the Three Gorges Dam.

Peasants' revolts/demonstrations
In rural areas peasants have been involved in demonstrations against local party leaders. Many are being forced from their land to make way for factories. The government recorded 87 000 protests against forced relocation in 2005 alone. Some have been violent.

Female Participation
The All-China Women's Federation (linked to Communist Party) campaigns to promote equality. Small success in recent years – small increase in female candidates.

Any other valid point.

(*b*) Candidates are required to provide evidence to support and oppose a given point of view.
The correct responses are:
View of Chinese Economist
'The greatest increase in personal income has been experienced by those living in Shanghai.'
Reason to support
Source 1 shows that this is true, as Shanghai's average personal income has grown by 10 000 Yuan between 2003 and 2005. This is bigger than any other region.
View of Chinese Economist
'However, the wealthiest regions are evenly distributed throughout China.'
Reason to oppose
Source 2 shows that this is not the case. The ten wealthiest regions are concentrated on the eastern coast of the country.

(*c*) Candidates are required to detect and explain examples of lack of objectivity in complex sources, giving developed argument when required.
Answers may include:
Pu Wei – 'The Riverside Gated Development will improve the health of people living in Hankou.'
This is correct because:
- new sports facilities will be built (Source 1 column 1).
- sports facilities were very poor before (Source 1 'The Riverside area before').
- opinion of Doctor Pu Zihao – local residents aren't good at exercise and new facilities are needed to improve health.
- Doctor's opinion is backed by four statistics in Source 1 – ie Higher than national average overweight, fewer cyclists, fewer walkers, fewer golfers and tennis players.

Conclusion: In this part of the view, Pu Wei is not selective as all the evidence supports him.

Pu Wei – 'It will bring much needed benefits to the people of Hankou.'
This is correct because:
- the area is depressed. Wages are lower than the national average (Source 1) so new jobs are needed and many are low skilled. Source 3 highlights the impact that the development will have whilst Source 2 shows that jobs are important because according to it, 54% of people agree that this is very important (The sample for the survey was large at 8 900).
- 300 well paid jobs will be created. As well as improving average wages this will bring extra business to local shops.

- 81% in the survey say that attracting new business is either 'Important' or 'Very Important'. Source 1 states that many of the people attracted to the area will be business people and that new business will be set up. Source 2 states that existing businesses will become suppliers to the new restaurants.
- affordable sports facilities will be created which will benefit a lot of the people.

This is not entirely correct as:
- a few fishermen have lost their jobs including Li Jie and six others. However, 65% of those who responded in Source 2 didn't think this was important.
- according to Li Jie the benefits to the people of Hankou will not be that great as the residents will not shop in the town. They will stay in the complex or drive to the city.

Conclusion: in this part of the view, Pu Wei is being selective to a very small extent as jobs, wages, business and sports facilities will improve. The only opposition seems to come from one person ie Li Jie.

Pu Wei – 'Everyone living in Hankou is excited by the opening of Riverside Garden.'
This is not entirely correct as:
- Li Jie and his six friends who lost their jobs are not happy about it. He claims that all the fishermen are against the development. Although this is a small number out of a 50 000 population, it is clear that not 'everyone' is excited.
- 35% of people thought that protecting farmers and fishermen was important or very important. Although this isn't a majority there is some opposition to the plan.

Conclusion: in his third sentence, Pu Wei is being quite selective. Most people seem to favour the development, but it is not **all**.

Overall conclusion on the extent of selectivity
Overall, Pu Wei is being only **slightly** selective in his use of the facts.

Syllabus Area 4 – International Relations

4. (*a*) The concept being assessed is Need. Candidates are required to use their understanding of the concept to provide explanations in depth and detail.
Answers may include:
Civil War
Environment not safe for civilians, roads mined or prone to ambush. Money spent on arms not services (over $9 billion pa). Wars in Somalia and Angola worsening.

Trade
Terms of trade mean that cash crops don't generate sufficient income eg coffee/cotton/sugar.

HIV
Life expectancy decreasing after improvements in 1990s, working population becoming ill eg nearly 40% of pop in Swaziland HIV positive. Millions of AIDS orphans.

Any other valid point.

(*b*) The concept being assessed is Power. Candidates are required to use their understanding of the concept to provide explanations in depth and detail.
Answers may include:
- airport security – reduction in hand luggage, stricter security checks, armed police, new 'Borders Agency'.
- counter-terrorism Bill, length of detention.
- heightened security in UK generally eg Houses of Parliament.

- MI5 has doubled in size since 2000.
- removal of easy targets eg litter bins in tube stations.
- architects encouraged to think of security eg Emirates Stadium and Scottish Parliament building.
- any other valid point

(*c*) Candidates are expected to make comparisons within and between complex sources and draw valid conclusions from them with justification using developed argument when required.
Answers may include:
Progress towards MDG 1 – reduce child mortality
- Source 3 shows that there has not been an increase in child mortality for any of the countries shown. Burundi's rate has stayed the same but the others have all improved eg Malawi down by 41 to 175.
This shows progress.

Progress towards all of MDG 3 – remove extreme poverty and hunger
- According to Source 1, the third MDG is to eradicate extreme poverty and hunger. Source 3 shows that in the world's four poorest countries, Tanzania and Malawi have reduced the % of people who are undernourished. In Malawi, it is down from 50% in 1996 to 34% in 2006.
- Source 3 also shows that in the world's four poorest countries, Sierra Leone and Burundi have seen an increase in the % of people who are undernourished. In Sierra Leone, it has gone up by 6% whilst in Burundi, it has gone up by 4%
This would suggest some progress towards Goal 3 in some places but not in others.
- The bar graph in Source 1 shows how many people live on less than a dollar a day and **this shows a lack of progress** towards the MDG 3 as the figure has increased between 1995 and 2001 and it is over double the target figure or goal of 22%.

The commitment of More Developed Countries to meeting the UN aid recommendation
- Source 1 states that UN recommends 0·7% of GNI to be spent as aid. Source 2 shows that in 2004, only Portugal was close at 0·63%.
- By 2010, 3 out of the 4 countries shown were close eg UK at 0·59% but Portugal's aid has decreased and the USA still only gives 0·18%.
This shows a slight overall improvement but not a strong commitment to meeting the UN recommendations.

The commitment of Donor Countries to the world's four poorest nations
- Source 1 shows that the four poorest nations are Sierra Leone, Tanzania, Burundi and Malawi.
- Source 2 shows where the selected donor countries send their aid. Only Tanzania receives any aid ($265 million from UK).
This shows an almost complete lack of commitment to the world's four poorest nations.

MODERN STUDIES GENERAL 2009

Syllabus Area 1 – Living In A Democracy

1. (a) The concept being assessed is Representation. Candidates are required to provide detailed description.

   Answers may include:
   - an MSP represents his/her constituents by listening to what they say. They do this by having a surgery or reading letters sent to them. This means the MSP knows what people want
   - asking questions about the things that matter to local people. The MSP can do this at First Minister's questions on a Thursday or during a debate at the parliament. They could also raise local matters in committee
   - MSPs go on local visits eg to schools and factories. This allows them to discuss local issues with people and might highlight things they weren't aware of. They can decide how to use this information
   - MSPs can represent constituents by writing letters/talking to other representatives eg councillors as MSPs are more influential than individuals.

   (b) Candidates are required to both support and oppose a point of view with evidence.

   Two pieces of evidence are required for full marks.

   Support the view
   - Holly Kerr says, "Edinburgh and Glasgow have the highest percentage of spoilt ballot papers".
   Evidence for this:
   - This is correct as both Glasgow and Edinburgh are in the two regions with the highest numbers of spoilt papers.
   Oppose the view
   - Holly Kerr says, "The number of spoilt ballot papers did not affect the result in any of the selected constituencies".
   Evidence for this:
   - This statement is incorrect as in one of the constituencies the spoilt papers is greater than the majority so this could have affected the result. Airdrie and Shotts were affected in this way.

   (c) The concept being assessed is Rights and Responsibilities. Candidates are required to provide detailed descriptions.

   Answers may include:
   - a right TU members have is to be safe at their work
   - they might work with dangerous machinery so the boss needs to give them goggles and a hard hat
   - another right TU members have is to get the right pay
   - the union might help them get pay when they are pregnant or off sick
   - members of a trade union have the right to elect a representative/shop steward
   - this person will take their views to management during a dispute eg local council workers
   - trade union members have the right to take industrial action
   - if they feel their rights are being ignored eg postal workers went on a go slow and then on strike over pay and conditions.

   (d) Candidates are required to make comparisons between sources and draw conclusions.

   Answers may include:
   - the main cause for industrial disputes in 2006 was Pay. It was 73%, with the next biggest being Redundancy at only 22%

   - the year which was the furthest from the average for working days lost was 2002. It was approximately 0·7 or 700000 away from the average, with the next closest being 2004 at approximately 0·4 or 400000.

Syllabus Area 2 – Changing Society

2. (a) The concept is Need. Candidates are required to provide detailed descriptions.

   Two ways are required for full marks.

   Answers may include:
   - a Warden to look out for any problems will make them feel secure
   - a communal lounge area to meet friends to stop them feeling lonely
   - a spare room for family to stay when visiting allows them to keep in touch
   - ramped access to make moving about easy for those in wheelchairs
   - a garden where they can enjoy good weather and mix with others.

   (b) Candidates are required to detect exaggeration and provide explanations.

   The correct responses are:

   Statement 1
   "The percentage of male workers has increased much more than the percentage of female workers."

   Reason 1
   Source 1 shows that the increase of male workers was only 5·6% compared to 11·2% for women.

   Statement 2
   "Total unemployment has fallen every year since 2000."

   Reason 2
   Source 2 shows that in 2006 total unemployment rose from 3·2% to 3·3%.

   (c) The concept is Equality. Candidates are required to provide detailed explanations.

   Answers may include:
   - some may have private or occupational pensions as well as a state pension
   - some may not get the state pension and depend on other benefits
   - some may have had a good job and have savings, but others may have been unemployed
   - financial help from family members for some but not for others.

   (d) Candidates are required to make comparisons within sources and draw valid conclusions.

   Two differences are required for full marks.

   The correct responses are:

   Difference 1
   Source 1 says that JSA is just enough to meet the needs of the unemployed, but Source 2 says it is not enough for them to live on.

   Difference 2
   Source 1 says that JSA aims to get unemployed people into a job that best suits their qualifications, but Source 2 says that it pushes them into any low paid job that is available.

Syllabus Area 3 – Ideologies

THE USA

3A. (*a*) The concept being assessed is Participation. Candidates are required to provide detailed descriptions.

Two ways are required for full marks.

Answers may include:
- Americans can register to vote in elections
- They can then use their vote in elections, eg greater numbers of Black Americans voting for Barack Obama for President in 2008
- Americans can stand for election eg to be Mayor of Rockford City or President
- Americans can join an Interest Group eg The American Association of Retired Persons or Rock the Vote.

(*b*) Candidates are required to provide evidence to support and oppose a given point of view.

Two pieces of evidence are required for full marks.

Answers may include:

Support the view
Ann Struther says, "The group with the lowest unemployment in 2006 has seen the greatest increase in home ownership".

Evidence to support
From Source 1 the group with the lowest unemployment in 2006 was Asian at 3·0%.

From Source 2 Asians had the biggest increase in home ownership at 8%, much greater than any other group.

Oppose the view
Ann Struther says, "In 2006, unemployment was at its lowest for all ethnic minority groups".

Evidence to oppose
Source 1 shows that 2000 was the lowest unemployment for blacks at 7·6%, not 2006.

(*c*) Candidates are required to give **relevant** aims for an investigative topic.

Two aims must be given for full marks.
- to find out if blacks commit more crime than whites
- to find out if crime rates are the same all over US
- to find out about the Death Penalty
- any other valid aim.

(*d*) Candidates are required to state and justify an appropriate method of enquiry.

Two methods must be addressed for full marks.

Answers may include:
- can plan questions in advance
- should be knowledgeable about situation in their own city
- can ask supplementary questions
- relaxed, informal interview with someone you know
- first hand information
- can record answers and refer to them later.

(*e*) Candidates are required to state and justify an appropriate method of enquiry.

Two methods must be addressed for full marks.

Answers may include:
- can use the statistics which give 'Violent crime figures'
- these show how states differ and will make a good graph to use in the investigation
- can read and use the 'Crime in the USA – Special Report' on pages 10 and 11

- might have more statistics, information and figures for the investigation
- can sign up for a weekly e-mail on youth crime
- will be kept up to date and get very recent figures to use in the investigation.

CHINA

3B. (*a*) The concept being assessed is Participation. Candidates are required to provide detailed descriptions.

Two ways are required for full marks.

Answers may include:
- polling clerk helping to count vote in village/township elections
- becoming a member of the Communist Party
- voting at the Communist Party Congress
- taking part in a protest march/demonstration, eg residents of the eastern Chinese city of Xiamen have blocked construction of a chemical plant with a text message campaign.

(*b*) Candidates are required to provide evidence to support and oppose a given point of view.

Two pieces of evidence are required for full marks.

Answers may include:

Support the view
- Kathy Lou says, "Unemployment has increased in all selected regions".

Evidence to support
- Unemployment in Beijing has increased from 0·8% to 2·5%, in Guangdong from 3·0% to 3·7% and in Henan from 3·0% to 4·8%.

Oppose the view
- Kathy Lou says, "The region with lowest rate of unemployment in 2006 has the highest average monthly income".

Evidence to oppose
- Beijing has lowest unemployment with 2·5% yet Guangdong's average wage is $11 higher.

(*c*) Candidates are required to give relevant aims for the investigative topic.

Two aims must be given for full marks.
- to find out if the crime rates are the same in all regions of China
- to find out whether youth crime is a problem in China
- to find out what types of crime are most common in China
- to find out about the Death Penalty
- any other valid aim.

(*d*) Candidates are required to state and justify an appropriate method of enquiry.

Two advantages must be given for full marks.

Answers may include:
- can plan questions in advance
- should be knowledgeable about situation in their own city
- can ask supplementary questions
- relaxed, informal interview with someone you know
- first hand information
- can record answers and refer to them later.

(*e*) Candidates are required to state and justify an appropriate method of enquiry.

Two methods must be addressed for full marks.

Answers may include:
- can use the statistics which give 'Violent crime figures'
- these show how parts of China differ and will make a good graph to use in the investigation
- can read and use the 'Crime in China' – special report on pages 10 and 11
- might have more statistics, information and figures for the investigation
- can sign up for weekly e-mail on youth crime
- will be kept up-to-date and get very recent figures to use in the investigation.

Syllabus Area 4 – International Relations

4. (*a*) The concept being assessed is Need. Candidates are required to provide detailed descriptions.

Answers may include:

War/Conflict
- Health care unable to cope with casualties/civilian casualties
- Increased numbers of orphaned children
- No foreign investment
- No agricultural produce
- Refugees

Debt
- Unable to invest in schools, hospitals etc
- Obligation to richer countries
- Dependency on Aid

HIV/AIDS
- Strain on health services
- Orphans
- Falling population affects economy

Unsafe water
- Disease
- Strain on medical services
- Low incomes.

(*b*) Candidates are required to detect exaggeration and provide explanations.

The correct responses are:

Statement 1
"A large percentage of the UK's population are undecided about the Treaty."

Reason 1
It is not a 'large' percentage. 'Don't know' is not only the smallest of the three responses to Question 1 in Source 2, but it is only 9%

Statement 2
"Most people agree with the UK government about a referendum on the Treaty."

Reason 2
In Source 1 it states the government doesn't think a referendum is necessary but the majority appear to disagree in Source 2, Question 2. Almost 75% answered 'Yes'.

(*c*) The concept being assessed is Power. Candidates are required to provide detailed explanations.

Answers may include:
- co-operation between member states eg 2008 banking crisis
- Regional Aid bringing investment and jobs eg Rosyth ferry, infrastructure in the Highlands and Islands
- freedom of movement eg large numbers of Poles now working in UK to fill the 'skills gap'

- qualifications recognised so can work/study in 27 countries
- larger market for products manufactured in their country ie improved trade
- Regional Aid has raised living standards especially in poorer parts of Europe
- opinion polls show that the majority of EU citizens are happy living in the EU.

(*d*) Candidates are required to express support for a personal point of view with valid reasons.

Two pieces of evidence are required for full marks.

The correct responses are:

For Project A – New Factories
- Wages are $1000 for permanent workers which is twice the town's average income.
- Jobs are low skilled and require little education, which is good as only 58% of the town is literate.
- Wages are $1000 for permanent workers whilst at the moment, half of the people in the town live on less than $1 per day.

For Project B – Schools
- 2000 children will get the chance to go to school; this is good as only 58% are literate.
- 100 teachers will earn $1200, which is more than double the town's average.
- 100 teachers will earn $1200, whilst, at the moment, half of the people in the town live on less than $1 per day.

MODERN STUDIES CREDIT 2009

Syllabus Area 1 – Living In A Democracy

1. (a) The concept being assessed is Participation. Candidates are required to use their understanding of the concept to provide explanations in depth and detail.

    Answers may include:
    - joining a political party eg Liberal Democrats and actively supporting them
    - attending political meetings
    - watching Party Election Broadcasts, reading election literature
    - helping a candidate during the campaign eg putting up posters, handing out leaflets
    - canvassing with a candidate in the local area
    - contributing financially to an election campaign.

    (b) The concept being assessed is Responsibilities. Candidates are required to use their understanding of the concept to provide explanations in depth and detail.

    Answers may include:
    - inform the police before a demonstration
        - enables the police to plan and have enough officers available, close routes
        - people might get hurt, chaos can ensue if police not informed
    - keep protests within the law
        - the law is designed to protect citizens
        - group might lose respect or political support
    - represent members' views
        - people joined in good faith, let down if their views are ignored
        - membership would fall if group seen as irresponsible
    - only use accurate information during campaigns
        - group could be prosecuted if they make false claims.

    (c) Candidates are required to detect and explain examples of lack of objectivity in complex sources, giving developed argument when required.

    For full marks, all three sources must be used.

    Answers may include:

    In 2007 there were more MSPs in favour of independence then ever before.

    Source 1

    The SNP and the Green Party are in favour of independence. The overall numbers in favour of independence increased from 34 out of 129 MSPs in 2003 to 49 MSPs in 2007. This shows that Callum is correct.

    The West of Scotland Region had the largest increase in voter turnout.
    Source 2
    The turnout did increase in the West (by 3·2%). However, in Lothian Region it increased by 3·5%. Therefore, Callum is incorrect.

    ...since the establishment of the Scottish Parliament people feel more Scottish.
    Source 3
    In 1999 25% of people said they felt more Scottish than British. This increased to 32% in 2006. Therefore, Callum is correct.
    Overall, Callum was correct in two statements and incorrect in one.

The conclusion as to the degree of selectivity is that overall, he was being **slightly** selective.

Syllabus Area 2 – Changing Society

2. (a) The concept being assessed is Ideology. Candidates are required to use understanding of the concept to provide detailed descriptions with relevant examples and appropriate generalisations.

    Candidates are required to describe two policies.

    Answers may include:

    Educational Maintenance Allowance
    - A weekly payment of between £10 – 30 paid directly to young people from low-income families who continue to attend full time education in school or college.
    - This may then improve their qualifications and therefore job prospects when they eventually leave.
    - Bonuses are awarded if attendance and attainment targets are achieved, thus motivating pupils from poorer families.

    New Deal
    - Helps unemployed people to find a job as part of the governments "Welfare to Work" strategy.
    - Gives the unemployed new opportunities to gain new skills and work experience, and makes them more employable. A personal adviser will provide support until they are ready for work.
    - Gives subsidies and training grants to employers to take on unemployed people. The unemployed can claim benefits and help with transport costs.

    Child Benefit
    - A regular payment for each child under the age of 16, or up to 19 if in full time education or training.
    - It is not means tested and is available to all parents to help pay the cost of bringing up children.
    - In 2009, parents received £20 per week for the eldest child and £13·10 for each additional child.

    Child Tax Credits
    - A regular payment from the government to help with the everyday cost of caring for children.
    - It is means tested, but 9 out of 10 families with children get it. The amount received varies depending on income, so poor families get more.
    - It is paid directly to the main carer to make sure it is more likely to benefit the children.

    Sure Start
    - A government initiative to provide the best start in life for every child, especially in the early years (0-3).
    - It encourages close cooperation between education, social work, health services and voluntary groups to meet the needs of families with young children.
    - Help is to be targeted to the poorest and most deprived areas of the country.

    Child Trust Fund
    - A tax-free savings account set up by the government for each child born on or after 1 September 2002. Any money put into this cannot be taken out until the child reaches 18.
    - The government puts £250 into the account to start it off, with a further £250 on each child's seventh birthday. Children from poorer families receive more than this.
    - Parents and family can put money into this account for the children as well.

    (b) Candidates are required to provide evidence to support and oppose a given point of view.

The correct responses are:

View of Asif Iqbal
"Pakistani households have had a bigger fall in poverty than all other ethnic groups."

Reason to support:
Source 1 shows that they have fallen by 15% from 70% in 2000 to 55% in 2005. All other groups fell less than this, with Bangladeshis being closest at 13%.

View of Asif Iqbal
"The group with the smallest increase in hourly pay had the smallest drop in poverty."

Reason to oppose:
Source 2 shows that Blacks had the lowest pay increase of only £0·29 and Source 1 shows that White households had the smallest fall in poverty from 22% down to 18% – a fall of only 4% compared to a fall of 7% for the black group.

(c) Candidates are expected to make comparisons within and between complex sources and draw valid conclusions from them with justification using developed argument when required.

The correct answers are:

The relationship between education and unemployment.
Using Source 3 and Source 4, it is clear that those boroughs with the best education tend to have lower unemployment. For example, Sutton has the highest % of pupils with 5 or more exam passes (70·8%) and it also has the lowest unemployment rate (4·9%)

The relationship between total crime and income.
Using Source 2 and Source 4, it is clear that the boroughs with the lowest income tend to have higher total crime. For example, Newham, Brent and Barking and Dagenham had the highest total crime. They are also the 3 with the lowest income.

The borough whose ethnic mix is most like that of London as a whole.
Using "Focus on London" and Source 1, it is clear that Kensington and Chelsea is most like London as a whole. It is closest to the London % for 4 groups (White, Black, Bangladeshi and Chinese), second closest for 2 others (Pakistani and Others), and third closest for Indian.

The borough that would be the most desirable to live in.
Sutton would be most desirable because it has the highest % of pupils attaining 5 or more exam passes, the lowest crime rate, the lowest unemployment rate and the second highest average income.
OR
Kensington and Chelsea would be most desirable as Source 4 shows that it has by far the highest weekly income of £818·40 which is £312 higher than Sutton.

Syllabus Area 3 – Ideologies

THE USA
3A. (a) The concept being assessed is Equality. Candidates are required to use understanding of the concept to provide detailed descriptions followed by detailed explanations with relevant examples and appropriate generalisations.

Answers that do not mention detailed American examples should be awarded a maximum of 5 marks.

Answers may include:

Education
- The inequality is that lower attainment leads to poor employment prospects for some groups.
- Some Americans attend and stay on at excellent schools, others do not and may drop out early.
- Asians and Whites are most likely to complete education, followed by Black Americans with Hispanics the least likely.

Health
- The inequality is that there is poorer health for some minority groups.
- Black Americans having the highest death rates.
- Some Americans can afford private health, others may have to rely on Medicare and Medicaid.
- Whites are most likely and Hispanics least likely to have private health insurance.
- Asians/Hispanics can have much lower death rates.

Employment/Unemployment
- The inequality is that some groups have poorer incomes.
- Most Americans are in work but some cannot find work due to poorer qualifications.
- Asians/Whites are the ethnic groups most likely to be employed, Blacks/Hispanics the least.
- The recent economic changes have hit some groups more than others.

Wealth/Poverty
- Asians/Whites are the ethnic groups with the highest incomes followed by Hispanics and Black Americans.
- Many Americans have a wealthy lifestyle due to a good job and pay – The American Dream.
- Some Americans have a very low income due to unemployment or low pay.
- American government welfare payments are low.
- This leads to poverty for some groups.

Prejudice and Discrimination
- Inequality in all of the above can be the result of discrimination on the basis of race, gender, religion and nationality.

(b) Candidates are required to provide evidence to support and oppose a point of view.

Answers must make explicit links between the background information about The Illegal Immigration Debate and Sources 1 and 2.

Answers may include:

For Corrine Padilla
- Corrine says, "I, like many Californians, feel that illegal immigrants in California are exploited. My first priority will be to improve their pay and working conditions." This is **true** as 'Many Californians are concerned that illegal immigrants often live and work as 'modern-day slaves' because they work for low wages.
- Corrine says, "… many Californians are not in favour of a high-tech fence". This is **true** as the statistics show that 59% of Californians say no to a high-tech fence', which is many.
- Corrine says, 'California needs workers to come and help our farmers pick their crops'. This is **true** as 53% of farming workers and 90% of crop pickers in California are illegal immigrants.

Against Corrine Padilla
- Corrine says, "I am not concerned about illegal immigration as the numbers entering the US are not rising steeply". This is **wrong** as the USA Illegal Immigration graph shows they are rising steeply, from 0·1 million in 1990 to 0·9 million in 2005.

- Corrine says, "We do not need to increase the number of Border guards and most Californians agree with me". This is **wrong** as the statistics show that 71% of Californians say yes to increasing the number of border guards.

For Peter Head

- Peter says, "Illegal immigrants already in California cost a lot of money. Because of this they should become legal citizens so that they pay their taxes". This is **true** as illegal immigrants cost $650 million healthcare, $2·2 billion education and $5 billion overall which is a lot of money.
- Peter says, "The high-tech fence should not be built as it will not protect all of the California/Mexico border". This is **true** as the map shows the border is 140 miles long and the high-tech fence is in two parts only 67 miles long.
- Peter says, "The money saved by not having the high-tech fence would be better spent on more guards patrolling the border, which is what Californians want." This is **true** as the statistics show that 71% of Californians say yes to more border guards.

Against Peter Head

- Peter says, "California only has a very small percentage of all US illegal immigrants." This is **wrong** as California has one-third of the US total, which is 33% and so not a very small %.
- Peter says, "I, like most Californians, believe that illegal immigrants take the jobs that Californians want". This is **wrong** as 70% of Californians think that illegal immigrants are doing jobs that others do not want.

CHINA

3B. (a) The concept being assessed is Equality. Candidates are required to use understanding of the concept to provide detailed descriptions followed by detailed explanations with relevant examples and appropriate generalisations.

Candidates must link the description of the inequality which exists with the reasons why it exists.

Answers may include:

Rural/Urban

- Economic inequalities exist between rural and urban Chinese. Chinese in urban areas earn up to 3 times that of rural Chinese. Lack of industry and a reliance on farming mean income is low in the countryside.
- Those Chinese who live in "Special Economic Zones" are allowed to start up their own business and keep the profit through the "Socialist Market Economy". These Chinese are wealthier than others living outwith these zones.
- Increased wealth has given some Chinese access to better housing, education and the opportunity to buy consumer goods. Many more Chinese in urban areas now own freezers, PC's, televisions and cars compared to those in rural areas.

Housing/Education

- Within the urban areas, inequality exists between rich and poor. Migrant workers live in slum conditions on the outskirts of cities whereas those skilled workers who are employed by foreign companies based in China earn higher wages and can afford better quality housing.
- Members of the Communist party have access to better housing and education than those who are not members of the party.
- Poor levels of education in the countryside mean that many Chinese are only educated to primary level and therefore have to rely on low paid jobs. Few make it to university from the countryside.

Gender

- There continues to be gender inequality within the Communist Party. Although there has been some success in recent years there are still fewer women candidates than men.

Health

- The standard of healthcare is lower in the countryside than in urban areas as there are fewer hospitals and a shortage of medical staff; people in these areas rely on traditional Chinese medicine.
- The new rich in China may also be able to afford to travel abroad to access medical treatments there.

(b) Candidates are required to provide evidence to support and oppose a point of view.

Answers must make explicit links between the background information about the Migration Debate and Sources 1 and 2.

Answers may include:

For Liu Wang

- Liu says, "I want to see temporary migrant workers being made permanent residents to stop them being exploited". It is **true** that many are exploited as they often have their wages withheld by their employer and many (74%) Beijing residents agree with Liu and would like them to become permanent.
- President Hu Jintao has promised greater spending on health and education in rural areas to reduce the differences which exist between there and the cities. Liu believes that something must be done to raise the standard of living in the countryside. Therefore, the evidence supports Liu Wang.
- 62% say 'No' to additional taxes being imposed on people moving to the city. This is **true** as it agrees with Liu's opinion when he says that it is no good punishing workers who move to the city with additional taxes and that most people agree with him.

Against Liu Wang

- Liu says many migrants are college educated or better. This is **wrong** as in the information it shows us the educational background and only a very small % are college/university educated, most are educated to junior high school level or less.
- Liu Wang believes that Chinese citizens think they should look after themselves. This is **wrong** because over half of Beijing residents believe that foreign firms ought to invest in rural development when they locate in China.

For Cho Yuen

- Cho believes that the income which migrant workers send home to the countryside is vital to the rural economy and that it should continue. This is **true** as urban workers can earn three times that of rural workers and the money they send home helps to look after aging parents and pay for siblings to study.
- China has become the 'workshop of the world' and Cho says that she is not alone in thinking that foreign firms should invest in rural China. This is **true** as 52% of Beijing residents believe that foreign firms ought to invest in rural China's development.
- Until education in the countryside improves, Cho wants to work to allow migrants to come to Beijing to gain basic schooling. This is a reason to **support** Cho as few (1%) have college/university education, only 4% have completed high school and 2% have no education. This accentuates the wealth gap.

Against Cho Yuen

- Cho thinks that the numbers moving to the cities are small and are not rising steeply. This is **wrong**. Between 1990 and 2005, the urban population will have increased by 200 million and by 2020, 60% of China's population will live in towns and cities.
- Cho's first priority is to encourage further migration as migrants fit in well and make Beijing a better place to live. **This is not a priority that people would support** as many feel that the cities cannot cope with the growing number of migrants as there is a shortage of housing, hospitals, power and transport. It is also claimed that migrants are responsible for 70% of crime.

Syllabus Area 4 – International Relations

4. (*a*) The concept being assessed is Power. Candidates are required to use their understanding of the concept to provide descriptions in depth and detail.

Answers may include:

Threats – International Terrorism

- 9/11 attacks, London underground bombings, Madrid bombings, Bali bombings, Glasgow airport attack.

Responses

- Airport security – reduction in hand luggage, stricter security checks, armed police, increased use of 'Sky marshals' by some airlines, new 'Borders Agency'.
- Counter-terrorism Bill, length of detention.
- Heightened security in UK generally eg Houses of Parliament.
- MI5 has doubled in size since 2000.
- Removal of easy targets eg litter bins in tube stations.
- Architects encouraged to think of security eg Emirates Stadium and Scottish Parliament building.
- Introduction of ID cards.
- Invasion of Afghanistan and Iraq as part of the 'War on Terror'.

Threats – Nuclear proliferation

- Attempts by some countries to build nuclear weapons eg, North Korea, Iran.

Responses

- Sanctions placed on trade etc through the UN Security Council.
- Diplomatic discussions.
- Aid used as bargaining tool.
- US missile defence system built across Europe.

Threats – Russian Aggression

- Russian aircraft straying into foreign airspace eg UK, Georgia, Ukraine.
- Russian military action against neighbours eg in Georgia.
- Use of Oil reserves to force cooperation from the west and some neighbours, eg Ukraine.
- Alexander Litvinenko affair.

Responses

- UK aircraft scrambled to intercept Russian planes.
- Protests to UN and direct to Russian government.
- Georgian army opposed Russian invasion but to little effect.
- 'Tit for tat' diplomatic expulsions between UK and Russia.
- US missile defence system and willingness of states like Georgia to join NATO.

(*b*) Candidates are required to state a hypothesis relevant to the issue of 'HIV/Aids in Africa'.

The following receive 1 mark:

- HIV/Aids causes serious problems in Africa.
- A lot of aid is given to help with HIV/Aids in Africa.

The following receive 2 marks

- Better education would help with the problems caused by HIV/Aids in Africa.
- Botswana cannot afford to feed and educate the numbers of 'Aids orphans' it has.

(*c*) Candidates are required to state aims relevant to their hypothesis.

For example:

Hypothesis: "Botswana cannot afford to feed and educate the numbers of 'Aids orphans' it has."

- To find out what has happened to the numbers of orphans in recent years.
- To find out the specific health problems facing orphans.
- To find out how UK aid is helping in Botswana.
- To find out what action Botswana's government is taking to tackle the problems.

(*d*) Candidates are required to describe the factors which determine the validity of a method of enquiry.

Answers may include:

- sample size, eg 10 – 1000. It makes a difference
- type of sample eg random or stratified
- type of questions eg open or closed
- phone, postal, face to face
- time of day
- location.

(*e*) Candidates are required to demonstrate an awareness of the benefits or limitations of a method for the collection of information relevant to a topic.

The correct answer is:

- "EU expansion or EU growth – The benefits explained" This is the only result that deals with "benefits" and it is the most up to date result. (ie 9/5/2009)

MODERN STUDIES GENERAL 2010

Syllabus Area 1 – Living in a Democracy

1. (a) The concept being assessed is Representation. Candidates are required to provide detailed descriptions.

   Answers may include:

   Give two ways councillors find out about a local problem
   - Reading local newspapers.
   - Attend local meetings.
   - Local councillors hold surgeries.
   - Some constituents will write to the councillor.
   - Any other valid point.

   Describe one action councillors could take to help solve the problem
   - Raise the matter with the wider council.
   - Attend the relevant committee.
   - If not a council problem then take it to the correct representative eg MSP.
   - Any other valid point.

   (b) Candidates are required to provide evidence to oppose a given point of view.

   Two pieces of evidence are required for full marks. Both sentences in the view must be dealt with for full marks.

   The correct responses are:
   - Iain McEwan says "In Glasgow East, the support for all political parties decreased between 2005 and 2008".

   Evidence to oppose this:
   This is incorrect as Source 1 shows that although support for most parties went down, support for the SNP increased by 6,009.
   - Iain McEwan says "Labour continues to be the largest party in the Scottish Parliament".

   Evidence to oppose this:
   This statement is incorrect as Source 2 shows that although Labour was the largest party in 1999, they were forced into second place in 2007 by the SNP. This proves that they are not the largest party.

   (c) The concept being assessed is Rights and Responsibilities. Candidates are required to provide detailed descriptions.

   Answers may include:

   Rights
   - To form a group eg Fathers 4 Justice (disbanded 2008 but always popular).
   - Free speech eg giving interviews to the media.
   - To protest eg Stop the War mass marches.

   Responsibilities
   - Not to coerce people into joining.
   - Not to slander or libel others to try and strengthen your argument.
   - Inform the police prior to any marches or rallies.
   - Any other valid point

   (d) Candidates are required to detect exaggeration and provide explanations.

   The correct responses are:

   Statement 1
   The SNP and the Conservative Party agreed on all policies during the year.

Reason 1
From Source 1, it says that "In February 2008 the SNP MSPs voted to scrap the one-off student fee which students must pay when they graduate. Labour and Conservative MSPs voted against it." This shows that the SNP and Conservatives did not co-operate.

Statement 2
The SNP is likely to get most votes in a UK Parliament Election.

Reason 2
From Source 2, it shows that only 30% of Scots would vote for the SNP in a UK election compared to 34% for Labour.

Syllabus Area 2 – Changing Society

2. (a) The concept being assessed is Need. Candidates are required to provide detailed explanations.

   Answers may include:
   - As people get older, they are much more likely to suffer from poor health and so they may need to visit their GP more often than younger people.
   - The NHS invites the elderly to visit their GP regularly for check-ups and to get vaccinated against the flu.
   - There are many illnesses linked to old age such as Alzheimer's Disease, dementia and arthritis, which require treatment using drugs prescribed by the NHS.
   - Many old people have falls leading to broken limbs which must be treated at hospital.
   - Any other valid point.

   (b) Candidates are required to make comparisons within sources and draw valid conclusions.

   Two differences are required for full marks.

   The correct responses are:

   Difference 1
   - Source 1 says "Huge rises in gas and electricity bills are the main causes of this increase in fuel poverty" but Source 2 says "The main cause of fuel poverty is poor insulation in many houses allowing heat to escape through walls, windows and roof".

   Difference 2
   - Source 1 says "The best way to solve fuel poverty is to increase State benefits to vulnerable groups such as the elderly and families with children" but Source 2 says "The Government should provide better insulation for homes to help reduce fuel poverty".

   (c) Candidates are required to give relevant aims for an investigative topic.

   Two aims must be given for full marks.

   The following receive 1 mark:
   - To find out the problems faced by families with young children.
   - To find out the help available to families.
   - To find out the views of parents with young children about the help they get.

   (d) Candidates are required to describe in detail an appropriate method of enquiry.

   Two descriptions are required for full marks.

   Answers may include:
   - Contact the nursery to arrange a date and time.
   - Prepare relevant questions that you are going to ask.
   - Consider how to record the answers for future use.
   - Find out the location of the meeting, and make travel arrangements.
   - Any other relevant point.

(e) Candidates are required to state and justify an appropriate method of enquiry.

The correct answer is:

Q2 – What do you think about the level of Child Benefit?

Explanation
- All parents with young children get Child Benefit, and so will be able to answer it.
- You can make conclusions about the opinions of the people who have replied.
- Any other valid answer.

Syllabus Area 3 – Ideologies

THE USA

3A (a) The concept being assessed is Participation. Candidates are required to provide detailed descriptions.

Two ways are required for full marks.

Answers may include:
- Americans can write to their Congressman/woman or Senator. They can also send e-mails. If enough people contact them, then they may alter their point of view.
- They can directly lobby their Congressman/woman or Senator in Washington DC.
- Write to newspapers such as the New York Times, Washington Post or the San Francisco Examiner. This can get the issue out in the open for debate by others.
- Take part in a protest.
- Join an Interest group which has a particular issue at its heart.
- Americans can register to vote and vote for candidates who might support their point of view.
- Any other valid point.

(b) Candidates are required to detect exaggeration and provide explanations.

The correct responses are:

Statement 1
"Few Americans watched the TV debates between Obama and McCain."

Reason 1
The timeline shows that in October 2008 'The TV debates were watched by many Americans'.

Statement 2
"Unfortunately the President was elected with less than half the popular vote."

Reason 2
The timeline shows that in November 2008 'The winner was Barack Obama with 52.5% of the popular vote'.

(c) The concept being assessed is Ideology. Candidates are required to provide detailed descriptions.

Two ways are required for full marks.

Answers may include:
- Capitalism encourages Americans to start businesses and try to make profits.
- Americans who start off in a poorly paid job, like cleaning, but work hard, can get better jobs and pay.
- Americans who do well at school, get good grades and go to college, get better jobs and pay.
- Americans who work hard in an area they have dreamed about, can fulfil the American Dream.
- Americans who own their own business can make it a successful international company and earn lots of money eg Bill Gates and Microsoft or Google's founders Larry Page and Sergey Brin.
- Any other valid point.

(d) Candidates are required to provide evidence to support and oppose a given point of view.

Two pieces of evidence are required for full marks. Both sentences in the view must be dealt with for full marks.

Answers may include:

Support the view
Emma Steele says, "In recent years, there has been a continuous increase in the average income of people in the USA".

Evidence to support
The 'Average income per person' graph shows income was $35,000 in 2002 and increased each year to 2008 when it was $45,000.

Oppose the view
Emma Steele says, "The USA has the lowest percentage of its population living below the poverty line".

Evidence to oppose
The 'Percentage living below the poverty line' graph shows China at 10% was lower than the USA at 13%.

CHINA

3B (a) The concept being assessed is Equality. Candidates are required to provide detailed explanations.

Two ways are required for full marks.

Crime
- Migration to the cities has caused the family to break down, this has led to youth crime increasing and the development of gangs.
- One child policy has put children under greater pressure and this has resulted in more crimes taking place.
- People in the countryside are facing greater levels of crime than ever before. Capitalism is blamed for this problem.
- Those who commit crimes against foreigners in China are punished more severely than those committing crimes against Chinese citizens.
- Migrant workers in the cities are blamed for the greater levels of crime there.

Housing
- Rural housing is still very basic. Many still do not have running water and electricity. The major cities have a better choice of housing with access to electricity, running water etc. Many rural Chinese cannot afford such luxuries.
- Migrant workers are often forced to live in very poor housing on the outskirts of the main towns. Conditions are as bad in some as the worst slums anywhere in the world.
- Communist party members tend to have better quality housing.
- Although the one child policy was officially scrapped, some families are still disadvantaged.
- Wages for skilled workers employed by foreign firms are higher than the average so better quality housing can be purchased.

Health
- Towns and cities have more modern hospitals with more qualified doctors, nurses, specialist equipment etc. There is a shortage of medical staff in rural areas. People in these areas often rely on traditional methods.
- Poor housing conditions and dangerous working conditions have damaged the health of many workers on the "Coastal Strip" and in "Special Economic Zones".

China is believed to have the world's worst figures for industrial injury and deaths. Official figures for this are impossible to find.

- Air pollution in the largest cities is a serious problem. Rapid economic growth threatens air quality in many areas, including Beijing.
- Levels of smoking have boomed in recent years. Experts from the WHO predict a crisis in future decades from cancer and other tobacco related illnesses.
- The new rich have more access to expensive treatments and to treatment abroad.
- HIV and the spread of the disease in rural areas.
- Any other valid point.

(b) Candidates are required to detect exaggeration and provide explanations.

The correct responses are:

Statement 1
"Protests about human rights only took place in London."

Reason 1
This statement is exaggerated because April 2008 tells us that protests also took place in San Francisco, New Delhi and Canberra.

Statement 2
"Reporters were given greater freedom during the Olympics."

Reason 2
This statement is exaggerated because in August 2008 the source tells us that many Internet sites were blocked to reporters.

(c) The concept being assessed is Ideology. Candidates are required to provide detailed descriptions.

Two ways are required for full marks.

Answers may include:
- Those working for foreign companies will have higher incomes and be able to enjoy access to better housing, education, health care etc. Many Chinese people now have access to consumer goods such as PCs, mobile phones, cars etc.
- Chinese people are allowed to start a business and keep the profit ie 'Socialist Market Economy'. This has been especially common in the 'Special Economic Zones'.
- Small township enterprises have improved living conditions in rural areas.
- Many companies producing manufactured goods for export have expanded rapidly. China is known as the 'workshop of the world'.
- Any other valid point.

(d) Candidates are required to provide evidence to support and oppose a given point of view.

Two pieces of evidence are required for full marks. Both sentences in the view must be dealt with for full marks.

Answers may include:

Support the view
Li Yifan says "China has the lowest percentage of its population living below the poverty line".

Evidence to support
This is true as China Today shows that China has only 10% living below the poverty line compared to 12% in USA and 25% in India.

Oppose the view
Li Yifan says, "there has been a continuous increase in the average income of people in China".

Evidence to oppose
Average income increased from just over $4000 in 2002 to over $6000 in 2006 however it then fell to around $5000 in 2008. The increase was not continuous.

Syllabus Area 4 – International Relations

4. (a) The concept being assessed is Need. Candidates are required to provide detailed reasons

Answers may include:
- The idea of collective security.
- Sharing research and development costs of new weapons etc eg Euro-fighter or missile defence.
- Protection from terrorism.
- Protection from growing Russian aggression.
- Any other valid point.

(b) Candidates are required to express support for a personal point of view with valid reasons.

Two pieces of evidence are required for full marks.

The correct responses are:

For Project A – School bus in Chomba
- Fifty extra children could go to school, thus improving education for young people.
- Medical supplies could be brought in from the city, helping to improve basic health care.

For Project B – Community Centre in Soppo
- The new nursery would help improve childcare in Cameroon.
- The ten wind-up laptops will help improve education for young people.

(c) The concept being assessed is Power. Candidates are required to provide descriptions.

Answers may include:
- Rich countries can be selective about which poor countries they give aid to, depending on the natural resources they expect to receive in return.
- Poor countries encouraged to grow cash crops that the rich world needs.
- Poor countries are still in debt to rich countries and may feel under an obligation.
- The price of basic agricultural produce is largely determined by the rich world.
- Poor countries may feel pressurised to support aid donors in forums such as the UN.
- Military aid can be used as a lever for economic or political support and cooperation.
- Any other valid point.

(d) Candidates are required to make comparisons within a source and draw valid conclusions.

The correct responses are:
- The UK has had the biggest change in oil production increasing by 270 000 barrels per day between 2005 and 2008.
- As oil production has risen, a country's oil imports have fallen. This is true for three of the four countries eg UK Germany and Poland. Production and imports in France have remained the same.

MODERN STUDIES CREDIT 2010

Syllabus Area 1 – Living in a Democracy

1. (a) The concept being assessed is Representation. Candidates are required to use their understanding of the concept to provide explanations in depth and detail.

   Up to 3 marks will be awarded for each point, depending on the quality of the description, relevance and accuracy.

   Answers may include:
   - MSPs can attend debates within the Parliament which are relevant to the local area and ensure that they get to speak, making local issues a national concern eg threats to local industry, proposed school closures etc.
   - An MSP could raise a motion ie start a debate.
   - An MSP could ask a question at First Minister's Questions on a Thursday lunchtime.
   - MSPs can also join a variety of Committees. These may discuss matters which affect local people and so the MSP could represent their views.
   - An MSP not on Government benches can introduce a Members' Bill (like a Private Member's Bill in Westminster). This could reflect local issues.
   - Members' Business is when MSPs can raise local matters in the Parliament which would not otherwise be discussed.
   - Any other valid point.

   (b) The concept being assessed is Participation. Candidates are required to use their understanding of the concept to provide explanations in depth and detail.

   Up to 3 marks will be awarded for each point, depending on the quality of the explanation, relevance and accuracy.

   Answers may include:
   - Participating in a TU protects the worker's rights eg if there is a problem with pay and conditions, health and safety etc they can ask the shop steward to speak to management on their behalf.
   - Being part of a union protects the worker eg insurance against injury.
   - By joining a union the worker will be able to protest more effectively eg thousands of local council workers got a better pay deal by going on strike. One worker striking would not make any difference.
   - Any other valid point.

   (c) Candidates are required to state a hypothesis relevant to the issue of 'Representation in the House of Commons'.

   Up to 2 marks will be awarded for a hypothesis depending on the level of insight displayed.

   The following receive 1 mark:
   - Minorities are represented in the House of Commons.

   The following receive 2 marks:
   - Women are not proportionally represented in the House of Commons.
   - British Asians are not well represented in the House of Commons.
   - Any other valid hypothesis.

   (d) Candidates are required to state aims relevant to their hypothesis.

   1 mark will be awarded for each aim depending on its relevance to the hypothesis.

The following receive 1 mark:
- To find out how many MPs are from minority ethnic groups.
- To find out if minority groups are represented on Committees in the House of Commons.
- Any other valid aim.

(e) Candidates are required to describe in detail, factors to be taken into account when setting up a video conference.

Up to 2 marks will be awarded for each problem, depending on the quality of the description, relevance and accuracy.

Answers may include:
- Time zones – it might be difficult to find a suitable time due to time differences.
- Language – Scottish pupils may not speak a second language.
- Finding a school with the appropriate technology.
- Technical difficulties with the technology.
- Willingness to participate.
- Any other valid point.

(f) Candidates are required to describe the advantages of video conferencing.

Up to 2 marks will be awarded for a description depending on the quality of the description, its relevance and accuracy.

Answers may include:
- Can ask direct questions and get an immediate response.
- Follow up on answers which are not detailed enough or miss the point.
- Primary research can be more relevant than written sources.
- Far more of a personal experience.
- Any other valid point.

Syllabus Area 2 – Changing Society

2. (a) The concept being assessed is Equality. Candidates are required to use understanding of the concept to provide detailed explanations with relevant examples and appropriate generalisations.

   Up to 3 marks will be awarded for an explanation depending on quality, relevance, accuracy and level of detail.

   Candidates are required to consider two groups. Answers that fail to do this will be awarded a maximum of 5 marks.

   Answers may include:

   Parents with young children
   - The cost of childcare such as a nursery or a child minder may make it uneconomic to work in low paid jobs.
   - There may be a lack of childcare facilities in the local neighbourhood or the work place, which makes employment difficult.
   - The need to care for young children may mean that parents are less flexible, and are not able to do shifts and weekend work.
   - Prejudice from employers who may feel that a parent may take frequent time off to look after children if unwell.
   - Any other valid point.

   People with disabilities
   - Unable to do some jobs due to their disability, and this reduces the pool of jobs they can apply for.
   - Employers may be unwilling to spend money to modify the workplace and so do not hire disabled workers.

- Disabled people may have had interruptions to their education and may have lower qualifications as a result.
- Prejudice from employers who may feel that disabled people may have lots of time off.
- There may be transport difficulties in getting to work, which may put disabled people off from travelling from the local area.
- Any other valid point.

Older people
- Older workers may have outdated skills and have not yet retrained to acquire more modern skills, which would help them compete with younger workers.
- Prejudice from employers who may feel that older workers may be absent more due to ill health, or might not have as much energy as others.
- Lack of confidence to try something new after many years in the same job.
- Any other valid point.

Minority Ethnic Groups
- Language difficulties for those for whom English is not their first language will result in not doing well in job interviews or in jobs that involve dealing with the public.
- Prejudice from employers who may be reluctant to give jobs to ethnic minority applicants.
- Lower educational qualifications are more likely with some ethnic groups, which means that others are chosen before them.
- Any other valid point.

(b) Candidates are required to provide evidence to support and oppose a given point of view.

Up to 2 marks will be awarded for a reason depending on the relevance and development of the evidence.

Candidates who do not make an explicit link between the view and the sources will be awarded a maximum of 2 marks.

The correct responses are:

View of Fiona Clark
"Spending an additional £4 billion would help more children than current government spending plans."

Reason to support
From Source 2, it is clear that by spending an extra £4 billion, the percentage of children in poverty will be lower for every group in comparison to what would happen based on current spending. Also the change in thousands would also be much higher, ranging from 240,000 to 320,000 less for each group.

View of Fiona Clark
"Two European countries have shown a continuous decline in child poverty rates."

Reason to oppose
From Source 1, it is clear that only one country has shown a continuous decline. France has fallen from 17% in 1999 to 15% in 2003 and finally to 13% in 2006.

(c) Candidates are required to detect and explain examples of lack of objectivity in complex sources, giving developed argument when required.

Up to 2 marks will be awarded for an example of selectivity or otherwise, depending on the quality of explanation.

A maximum of 2 marks will be awarded for each part of the view, and a maximum of 2 marks will be awarded for an overall conclusion as to the extent of selectivity.

Answers which do not make an explicit link between the view and the sources, will be awarded a maximum of 4 marks.

The correct responses are:

"The number of people receiving free personal care at home and in care homes have both risen."

From Source 1
The number of people receiving free personal care at home has increased from 33,030 in 2004 to 42,400 in 2008. In care homes, the number of people receiving free personal care also increased from 8340 to 9600. Therefore, Cameron Petrie's statement is **correct**.

"All local authorities that spent more in 2007 than 2003 on care homes have seen an increase in the places available between these years."

From Source 2
All local authorities spent more between 2003 and 2007. However, they did not all have an increase in places available in care homes; one authority, South Lanarkshire, had a reduction in places from 2926 in 2003 to 2796 in 2007. Therefore, Cameron Petrie's statement is **wrong**.

"Older females, for every reason, make more use of day care services than every other group."

From Source 3
There are two areas or reasons where elderly females do not make the greatest use of day care services. For Drug/Alcohol problems, males under 65 make the greatest use and elderly females use them least. Also for Learning Disabilities it is females under 65 who make most use of day care services with a figure of 3842, which is over ten times higher than the figure of 349 for elderly females. Therefore, Cameron Petrie's statement is **wrong**.

Overall conclusion on the extent of selectivity
Cameron Petrie is right in one statement and wrong in the other two, so he is mainly selective or selective to a large extent in his use of facts.

Syllabus Area 3 – Ideologies

THE USA

3A (a) The concept being assessed is Rights and Responsibilities. Candidates are required to use understanding of the concept to provide detailed descriptions with relevant examples and appropriate generalisations.

Up to 3 marks will be awarded for a description depending on the quality of description, relevance, accuracy and level of detail.

Answers that do not mention detailed American examples will be awarded a maximum of 5 marks. Candidates who fail to deal with both Rights and Responsibilities will be awarded a maximum of 4 marks.

Answers may include:
- The right to vote in city, local, state and federal elections for a large variety of elected posts.
- The right to freedom of speech means that Americans can express their opinions at meetings and through the media.
- The right to protest and demonstrate to gain attention for your views. For example, a march outside the White House or the Capitol building in Washington DC.
- The right to join a political party or an interest group with other people who have similar opinions. For example, the Republican and Democratic Parties and/or an interest group such as the National Rifle Association.

- The responsibility to register for elections, use your vote, and to do so in a considered way.
- The responsibility to respect the views of others and not tell lies – America has powerful laws against libel and slander.
- The responsibility to demonstrate peacefully, to stay within the law and to follow a pre-arranged route.
- Any other valid points.

(b) Candidates are expected to make comparisons within and between complex sources and draw valid conclusions from them with justification using developed argument when required.

1 mark will be awarded for a correct conclusion and 1 mark will be awarded for the evidence to prove the conclusion.

The correct responses are:

The relationship between the **total population** of these states and **violent crime**.

- As the population of a State increases, the amount of violent crime increases.
  Vermont with only 624,827 of a population has a violent crime rate of 137 per 100,000 population while New York with a huge population of 19,300,000 has a higher violent crime rate of 435 per 100,000 population.

The relationship between the **type of population** of these states and **income**.

- As the population of a State becomes more urban, the annual income of people increases. Vermont with a 28% urban population has an average annual income of about $34,000 while New York with a 91% urban population has a higher average annual income of approx $52,000.

The relationship between **the percentage of the population with no health insurance** in each of these states and **infant deaths**.

- As the percentage of a State's population with no health insurance increases, the number of infant deaths increases. Minnesota has 8.6% of its population with no health insurance and 4.8 infant deaths per 1,000 births while New York has 13.5% of its population with no health insurance and a higher rate of 6.0 infant deaths per 1,000 births.

The state which is **most like the USA** as a whole.

- The average annual income of the USA is $40,800, which is most like Minnesota.
  22% of children under 18 live in poverty in the USA, which is most like New York.
  The USA teen birth rate is 39.9 per 1,000, which is most like New York.
  The USA murder rate is 5.7 per 100,000, which is most like New York.

The conclusion is 'New York' state is most like the USA as a whole.

CHINA

3B (a) The concept being assessed is Rights and Responsibilities. Candidates are required to use understanding of the concept to provide detailed descriptions with relevant examples and appropriate generalisations.

Up to 3 marks will be awarded for a description depending on the quality of description, relevance, accuracy and level of detail.

Answers that do not mention detailed Chinese examples will be awarded a maximum of 5 marks. Candidates who fail to deal with both Rights and Responsibilities will be awarded a maximum of 4 marks. No credit will be given to points that refer to non-political rights such as religion.

Answers may include:

- The right to vote in local and national elections.
- The right of all regional and ethnic groups to be entitled to equal representation at all levels of government.
- The right to access many Internet sites, but not all, and to read the views of others.
- The right to protest about the actions of the government. For example, protests during the Beijing Olympics in 2008.

- The responsibility to turn out and use the vote at local village elections.
- The responsibility to listen to the views of others and consider who they vote for.
- The responsibility to avoid sites which are blocked by the Great Firewall.
- The responsibility to ensure that protests are authorised.
- Any other valid points.

(b) Candidates are expected to make comparisons within and between complex sources and draw valid conclusions from them with justification using developed argument when required.

1 mark will be awarded for a correct conclusion and 1 mark for evidence to prove the conclusion.

Answers may include:

The relationship between the **literacy rate** of the provinces and **percentage of children under 18 living in poverty**.

- The province with the lowest level of literacy has the greatest number of children under 18 living in poverty. In Henan literacy is at its lowest at 86% whilst child poverty is at its highest at 11%. The reverse is also true in Jiangsu where literacy levels are highest at 93% and child poverty is lowest at about 1%.

The relationship between the **type of population** of the provinces and **income**.

- Income levels are higher in the more urban provinces. Jiangsu has over double the size of urban population at 53% than both Gansu and Henan. Jiangsu has also over double the income of the other provinces with $4430.

The relationship between **doctors per 100,000** and **infant mortality**.

- Infant mortality is highest where there are fewest doctors. In Gansu, there are only 1.2 doctors per 100,000 and infant mortality is highest at 21. The reverse is true of Jiangsu where there are 3.4 doctors per 100, 000 and only 8 child deaths per 1000 births.

The province which is **most like China** as a whole.

- Jiangsu is the province most like China as a whole as it has the most similar income, only $1000 difference. It showed the most similarity in urban population with 53% compared to 42% in China, life expectancy is 70 years compared to China's 73 and there is only 1% difference in level of literacy.

Syllabus Area 4 – International Relations

4. (a) The concept being assessed is Need. Candidates are required to use their understanding of the concept to provide descriptions in depth and detail.

Up to 3 marks will be awarded for each point, depending on the quality of the description, relevance and accuracy. Candidates are required to consider two groups. Answers that fail to do this will be awarded a maximum of 5 marks.

Answers may include:

UNICEF
- Agency involved in helping meet the specific needs of children.
- Oral Rehydration Therapy across Africa.
- Campaign in Southern Africa to prevent AIDS transmission from mothers to children – Setting up clinics, school visits and poster/TV campaigns.
- Campaign to help child soldiers in Sudan – 'de-mob' camps.

WHO
- Agency involved in helping meet African health needs.
- Research into Africa's killer diseases such as Aids and malaria.
- Building and equipping of clinics across Africa such as recently in Congo.
- Campaign to increase the number of blood donors in Ethiopia. This also includes training and education programmes.
- Ongoing vaccination programmes against Polio across Sub-Saharan Africa.
- Donation of ICT equipment to African health ministries to help coordinate healthcare and use of health resources.
- Supporting charity campaigns to donate old spectacles to Africa.

UNESCO
- Agency involved in helping meet African education, cultural and science needs.
- Setting up world heritage sites to protect African heritage.
- Teacher training in Sub-Saharan Africa (TTISSA) campaign.
- The LIFE campaign – Literacy Initiative for Empowerment.
- The school in a suitcase campaign. All the equipment to run a classroom anywhere, in one bag.
- EDUCAIDS – campaign to improve AIDS education across Africa.
- Education for all by 2015. UNESCO's major campaign to try to meet the Millennium Development goals.

FAO
- Agency mainly concerned with the production of food in Africa and in helping develop agricultural efficiency.
- Recent campaign against high food prices.
- Help for small farmers to increase production eg Emergency rice programme in West Africa.
- Campaigns to protect vulnerable crops against virus and disease eg cassava.
- Campaigns to educate farmers on the use of fertilizers and farm machinery.
- Funding of research into GM seeds and other 'bio-agriculture'.

WFP
- Prepare reports which help National Governments and NGOs understand more clearly what the problems are with food security, nutrition, health and education within a country.
- Reduce hunger and under-nutrition everywhere.
- Save lives and protect livelihoods in emergencies by getting food to where it is most needed and quickly. The WFP does this by launching appeals to the international community for funds and food aid.
- The WFP relies entirely on voluntary contributions to finance its operations.
- Restore and rebuild lives after emergencies.
- Any other valid point.

(b) Candidates are required to provide evidence to support and oppose a point of view.

Up to 2 marks will be awarded for a reason depending on relevance and development of the evidence.

Answers must make explicit links between the information contained in the European Union Factfile and Sources 1 and 2. Answers that do not make explicit links will be awarded 0 marks. Candidates who fail to explain why they rejected the other candidate country will be awarded a maximum of 6 marks.

The correct responses are:

For Country A
- Country A's police have done well in clamping down on drug trafficking. According to the EU opinion survey, 88% of Europeans saw this as fairly important or very important.
- 88% of respondents in the survey also saw a good human rights record as fairly or very important. Country A would meet the criteria for the ECHR.
- University entrants in Country A have been growing in number and are getting close to the EU average of 51%. The EU's economy needs more university graduates.

Against Country A
- Several member states have become concerned about the number of poor countries who are applying to join the EU. Country A's average income (11,200) is less than half of the EU average (23,100).
- The EU takes good care of vulnerable groups, like children. Country A would struggle to meet these standards as shown in a recent UNICEF investigation, which criticized it for "terrible conditions".

For Country B
- Country B is self-sufficient in oil and is already producing 19 million barrels per day more than it uses. EU dependence on Russia would be reduced. This would be good as many would like to admit countries with oil reserves.
- 100% in the survey said that low unemployment was fairly important or very important. The graph shows that Country B's unemployment rate is consistently less than the EU average.
- Country B has been praised for reducing illiteracy rates to below 10%. This is coming close to the levels achieved by schools in the EU.

Against Country B
- Country B has a huge agricultural industry. Over one third are employed in this sector. This would make it difficult to reduce the EU's agriculture budget, which the member states see as necessary.
- Country B has poor health care. Life expectancy is twenty years below the EU average and infant mortality rate is more than double.

MODERN STUDIES GENERAL 2011

Syllabus Area 1 – Living in a Democracy

1. (a) The concept being assessed is Participation. Candidates are required to provide detailed description.

    Answers may include:
    - Creating and distributing election materials about their candidates and party eg leaflets, posters and rosettes.
    - Canvassing in the local area to persuade people to turn out and vote for their party eg the Greens.
    - Organising and attending speeches.
    - Volunteering eg stuffing envelopes with political materials.
    - Talking to the media about issues from the manifesto.
    - Any other valid point.

   (b) Candidates are required to make comparisons between sources and draw conclusions.
    - The age most people think Scots should be allowed to vote – conclusion is that most people think it should be 16. Evidence from Source 1 is 72% believe this.
    - Link between minimum voting age and turnout – lower voting age means a greater turnout. Evidence from Source 2 – Austria is 16 and 79% whereas the USA is 18 and 57%.

   (c) The concept being assessed is Rights and Responsibilities. Candidates are required to provide detailed descriptions.

    Answers may include:
    Rights
    - A right TU members have is to be safe at their work. They might work with dangerous machinery so the boss needs to ensure the employee has a hard hat etc.
    - Another right TU members have is to get the correct pay. The union might help them get pay when they are pregnant, off sick or paid incorrectly.
    - Members of a trade union have the right to elect a representative/shop steward. This person will take their views to management during a dispute eg local council workers or fire fighters.
    - Trade union members have the right to take industrial action if they feel their rights are being ignored eg postal workers have been on a go slow and then on strike.

    Responsibilities
    - Union members are required to pay their union fees (also subs or dues).
    - Not to carry out industrial action without a secret ballot.
    - To behave within the law if carrying out industrial action.
    - Any other valid point.

   (d) Candidates are required to detect exaggeration and provide explanations.

    The correct responses are:

    Statement 1
    MPs' pay is similar to the average pay in the UK.

    Reason 1
    They are paid much more than the average person by about £40,000.

    Statement 2
    All MPs' claims for expenses were shown to be within the rules.

    Reason 2
    Two MPs claimed for houses they no longer owned so the claim was not within the rules.

Syllabus Area 2 – Changing Society

2. (a) The concept being assessed is Need. Candidates are required to provide detailed descriptions.

    Two descriptions are required for full marks.

    Answers may include:
    - Unemployed people need an income. As they don't have a job, they will not be getting a wage, making it difficult to pay for the things they need to buy such as food, housing and energy costs.
    - Unemployed people need training. They may have no job because they lack certain skills required by employers. Learning these skills will improve their chance of finding employment.
    - Unemployed people need advice and information. They need to know about what jobs are available in their local area. Also, they need advice about what benefits and training schemes are available for them.
    - Any other valid point.

   (b) Candidates are required to express support for a personal point of view with valid reasons.

    Two reasons are required for full marks.
    Answers that do not make an explicit link between the map and the information about Bill Laird and his needs will be awarded a maximum of 2 marks.

    The correct responses are:

    For House A
    - Bill needs to visit the Post Office to deal with his pension and pay bills. House A is just across the road from the Post Office. A pedestrian crossing is conveniently placed.
    - Bill is frightened that his house may be broken into again. House A is two streets away from the police station.
    - Bill needs to visit the community nurse. The Community Health Centre is a short walk away.

    For House B
    - Bill needs regular check-ups from the community nurse. The Community Health Centre is just at the end of the street that House B is in.
    - Bill meets friends regularly for lunch. House B would be best because there is a Church Lunch Club nearby where they could go.
    - Bill needs to feel safe. The police station is nearby.

   (c) The concept being assessed is Ideology. Candidates are required to give detailed explanations.

    Answers may include:
    - Free nursery school places for 3 and 4 year olds. This gives all children a good start to their education, and allows parents to return to work and earn more money.
    - Childcare Voucher Schemes. These are provided jointly between an employer and the government, allowing parents to get tax relief on childcare costs up to £55 per week per parent.
    - Education Maintenance Allowance, which provides money to enable 16 and 17 year olds to stay on at school. This improves their educational qualifications and may improve their chances of getting a job.

- Benefits such a Child Tax Credit and Child Benefit. These provide money to help parents pay for the cost of bringing up children. This helps to reduce Child Poverty and gives families a better standard of living.
- Any other valid point.

(d) Candidates are required to provide evidence to both support and oppose a given point of view.

Two pieces of evidence are required for full marks. Both sentences in the view must be dealt with for full marks.

Answers which do not make an explicit link between the view and the sources, will be awarded a maximum of 2 marks.

Support the view
Asif Khan says, "Whites have fewer people on low pay than any other ethnic group."

Evidence for this:
This is correct as in Source 1 it says that the figure for whites is 20%. The second lowest figure is for Indians at 28%, with all other groups above this.

Oppose the view
Asif Khan says, "The biggest rise in unemployment between 2007 and 2009 was amongst people from the Pakistani community."

Evidence for this:
This is incorrect as in Source 2 it shows that unemployment for Pakistanis increased by only 0.3%. The biggest rise was 3% for the Black Caribbean group.

Syllabus Area 3 – Ideologies

THE USA

3A (a) The concept being assessed is Equality. Candidates are required to provide detailed explanations.

Two ways are required for full marks. 1 mark will be awarded for each correct way identified.

Answers may include:
- Some Americans may be poor and others rich.
- Some Americans may have good health and others poor health.
- Some Americans may get a good education and others a poor education.
- Some Americans may be homeless or in poor quality housing and others live in huge houses.
- Any other valid way.

Explain why not all American citizens are equal

Up to 2 marks will be awarded for an explanation.

Answers may include:
Some Americans may be poor and others rich
- Some may have a poorly paid job like cleaning while others who own their own business may be well off.

Some Americans may have good health and others poor health
- Some may have private insurance such as Blue Cross while some elderly may have to rely on Medicare and those in poverty on Medicaid.

Some Americans may get a good education and others a poor education
- Some may go to good private schools and get good grades and go to college while others may go to ghetto schools where there are gang problems and the quality of the education not as good.

Some Americans may be homeless and others live in huge houses
- Some may be poorly paid and only able to live in poor quality housing while others may have well paid jobs and be able to afford expensive housing.
- Any other valid point.

(b) Candidates are expected to detect exaggeration and provide evidence.

The correct responses are:

Statement 1
The majority of people agree that President Obama is doing a good job with the economy.

Reason 1
In Source 2, the graph shows that 10% think President Obama has made the economy 'Much Better' and 15% 'Better'. This is only 25% which is not the majority of people thinking that President Obama is doing a good job with the economy. Also, a majority of people, 54%, thought Obama's policies have had no effect.

Statement 2
"The American Recovery and Reinvestment Act" has not helped the economy.

Reason 2
In Source 1, the information says, 'The government believes that these measures have already helped the economy to improve as the number of companies closing down has fallen'.

(c) The concept being assessed is Participation. Candidates are required to provide detailed descriptions.

Two ways are required for full marks.

Answers may include:
- Americans can demonstrate against a decision and get themselves on to TV, to show the government that lots of people disagree with their decisions.
- Americans can express their opinions at meetings and get them printed in national newspapers to try to change government decisions.
- Americans can write letters to national newspapers, such as the *New York Times*, to complain and gather support about an issue such as illegal immigration and hope to change government decisions.
- Americans can take part in radio station 'phone-ins' to criticise a decision taken by the Government.
- Americans can use the Internet to set up a website to get their point across and start an e-mail campaign to change a government decision.
- Any other valid point.

(d) Candidates are required to provide evidence to support and oppose a given point of view.

Two pieces of evidence are required for full marks. Both sentences in the view must be dealt with for full marks.

Answers which do not make an explicit link between the view and the sources will be awarded a maximum of 2 marks.

Answers may include:
Support the view
Drew Laburn says, 'California and Florida are the two states with the lowest percentages of people in poverty'.

Evidence to support

Source 2 shows that Florida (12.1%) and California (12.3%) are the two States with the lowest percentages of people in poverty. All other states have higher figures eg New York (13.9%). This supports the view of Drew Laburn.

Oppose the view

Drew Laburn says, 'California has the highest percentage of Hispanic owned businesses'.

Evidence to oppose

Source 1 shows that Florida, at 17.3%, has the highest percentage of Hispanic owned businesses. California has only 14.7%, which opposes the view of Drew Laburn.

CHINA

3B (a) The concept being assessed is Equality. Candidates are required to provide detailed explanations.
1 mark will be awarded for each correct way identified. Up to 2 marks will be awarded for an explanation. Two ways are required for full marks.

Income

- Some Chinese people work for foreign or Chinese multi-national companies like Chelan and their salaries are higher.
- Some rural Chinese people work on farms and produce only enough food to eat. They have no income.
- Some Chinese people have started up their own business and earn a higher income.
- Some Chinese people work for very little money in a sweatshop in Guangzhou or the SEZ.
- Some state-owned enterprises (SOEs) have become profit making businesses.

Health

- Towns and cities have more modern hospitals with more qualified doctors, nurses, specialist equipment etc. There is a shortage of medical staff in rural areas. People in these areas often rely on traditional methods.
- Rich Chinese people can afford treatment in modern hospitals in cities like Beijing.
- The spread of HIV and the limited treatment available for it is a big problem in the Chinese countryside.

Education

- A growing number of Chinese students, especially in the cities, are staying on longer at school and are attending college/university eg Peking University and Tsinghua University.
- Many in the countryside have no access to this level of education or are unable to afford it.
- Some choose to go to vocational schools where they can learn skills useful for getting them a job.
- Literacy rates are increasing but they are increasing faster in urban areas compared to rural areas.
- Any other valid point.

(b) Candidates are required to detect exaggeration and provide evidence.

The correct responses are:

Statement 1

Few rural migrants are returning home to the countryside to work.

Reason 1

According to Source 1, 20 million rural migrants have returned home. This is not a few.

Statement 2

The majority of people surveyed are not satisfied with their income.

Reason 2

According to the opinion poll in Source 2, only 15% are not satisfied. This is not a majority.

(c) The concept being assessed is Participation. Candidates are required to provide detailed descriptions.

Two ways are required for full marks.

Answers may include:

- Chinese people may find themselves sent to a labour camp to be re-educated if they protest against the Government without permission.
- People who use the Internet to blog or post information/create new sites criticising the Government may face detention by the police such as those who are members of Students for a Free Tibet.
- The death penalty is the ultimate punishment handed out by the Government.
- Internet control can be tightened and video and social networking sites such as Youku and Fanfou as well as YouTube and Facebook can be blocked.
- The army can be called in to enforce calm and quash any protest such as that which happened in Xinjiang in 2009.
- Any other valid point.

(d) Candidates are required to provide evidence to support and oppose a given point of view.

Two pieces of evidence are required for full marks.
Both sentences in the view must be dealt with for full marks.
Answers which do not make an explicit link between the view and the sources will be awarded a maximum of 2 marks.

Answers may include:

Support the view of Jinqu Zou

The province with the greatest level of foreign trade also has the highest average income and the highest percentage of pupils completing junior secondary school.

Evidence to support

Zhejiang has greatest level of foreign trade at $6.68 billion and their average income is higher than all the rest at 42,000 Yuan, and 93% complete junior secondary which is higher than all other provinces.

Oppose the view of Jinqu Zou

Gansu and Sichuan have the biggest percentage of people living in poverty.

Evidence to oppose

Gansu has 10% which is the highest but Qinghai comes next with 8%, Sichuan is lower that this at 7%.

Syllabus Area 4 – International Relations

4. (a) The concept being assessed is Need. Candidates are required to provide detailed descriptions.

Answers may include:

- Emergency Aid – areas suffering natural disasters have received large quantities of water, food, blankets, tents, medicines etc. Several UN agencies were involved such as the WFP, UNICEF and WHO.

- Medical Aid – many Africans have been helped by the World Health Organisation. They have carried out research into Africa's killer diseases such as AIDS and malaria. They have built and equipped many clinics across Africa. They have worked hard to increase the number of blood donors in Ethiopia. For many years they have funded vaccination programmes against polio and many other killer diseases across Sub-Saharan Africa.
- Several UN campaigns have been on-going in order to help African communities access clean water supplies. UNICEF has been heavily involved in this. Many wells have been dug, pumping equipment supplied and pipes provided to transport the water itself eg UNICEF's Play Pump initiative.
- Many African people have suffered because of war in their country. The UN has supplied several peacekeeping forces to different parts of Africa to bring peace. These have, for example, helped improve security, education, health and farming. Current peacekeeping missions include those in Sudan (Darfur), Liberia, Cote d'Ivoire and the DR Congo.
- Any other valid point.

(b) Candidates are required to make comparisons within sources and draw valid conclusions.

Two differences are required for full marks.

The correct responses are:

Difference 1
Source 2 says that only a few countries have sent troops, but Source 1 says that 42 different countries have sent troops.

Difference 2
Source 2 says that NATO hasn't stopped the civil war against the Afghan government, but Source 1 says that NATO has brought peace and stability to Afghanistan's government.

(c) Candidates are required to give relevant aims for an investigative topic.

Two aims must be given for full marks.

The following receive 0 marks:
- To find out about war in Africa.
- To find out about guns.

The following receive 1 mark:
- To find out which countries in Africa are at war.
- To find out how war affects life expectancy in Africa.
- To find out the main causes of war in Africa.
- Any other valid aim

(d) Candidates are required to state and justify an appropriate method of enquiry.

Two advantages must be addressed for full marks.

Answers may include:
- Can plan questions in advance.
- May be able to record interview and refer to answers later.
- Can ask supplementary questions.
- Relaxed, informal interview with someone you know.
- First-hand information.
- Any other valid point.

(e) Candidates are required to demonstrate the use of an appropriate method of enquiry.

Answers may include:
- Can use the figures for "War refugees" from "Statistics of the week" – these are up to date. These show how states differ and will make a good graph to use in the investigation.
- Can click on the link to "Child soldiers" in the "This week's issues" section. This could provide more recent information on a relevant issue.
- Can sign up for a monthly e-mail on news ie "War in Congo". These are kept up to date and get very recent figures on a country still suffering from war.

MODERN STUDIES CREDIT 2011

Syllabus Area 1 – Living in a Democracy

1. (*a*) The concept being assessed is Representation. Candidates are required to use their understanding of the concept to provide explanations in depth and detail.

Up to 3 marks will be awarded for each point, depending on the quality of the description, relevance and accuracy

Candidates are required to consider both advantages and disadvantages of the chosen electoral system. Answers that fail to do this will be awarded a maximum of 5 marks.

Answers may include:

System	Advantages	Disadvantages
STV	• Ranks candidates so more choice for voters • Benefits marginalised groups • No votes are wasted	• Some may be confused by the system • Longer to get results • Multi-member representation eg 3 or 4 councillors
AMS	• More proportional • Retains elements of FPTP so some direct representation • Smaller parties can be successful eg Greens in Scottish Parliament	• Too many representatives • Representatives to parliament elected under two different systems • System more complex than FPTP
First Past the Post	• Straightforward system means voters not confused • Directly elected representative – one per constituency • Usually a quick result	• Not proportional so many votes are wasted • Encourages electorate to vote tactically • Emphasis on marginal constituencies
List	• Most proportional of all systems • Straightforward for the electorate	• Party decides ranking on the list • No direct representation

• Any other valid point.

(*b*) Candidates are expected to make comparisons within and between complex sources and draw valid conclusions from them with justification using developed argument when required.

Up to 2 marks will be awarded for a conclusion and justification depending on the quality of explanation given and accurate use of evidence.

The correct responses are:

The change in union membership within "Traditional Industries"

• The traditional industries are mining, quarrying and the utilities. Union membership in these industries has decreased. This decrease is greater than in any other

employment sector. There has been a decline of 14.6% for utilities and 10.4% for mining and quarrying.

The link between gender and trade union membership across all ethnic groups

• Union membership is higher for females in all ethnic groups. For example, within the Black ethnic group 34% of females are TU members compared to only 26% of men.

The link between regional unemployment and regional trade union membership

• The areas of Great Britain with the highest unemployment also have the highest rates of union membership. The North East and Wales have the highest union membership at over 35% whilst unemployment is over 8% which is the highest category. The reverse is also true. The areas of Great Britain with the lowest unemployment also have the lowest rates of union membership.

The success of trade unions in maintaining wage differences between union and non-union members

• Trade Unions want to maintain the difference in wages for members. They have not been successful in doing this as the difference has decreased from over 25% in 1995 to 12% by 2008.

Syllabus Area 2 – Changing Society

2. (*a*) The concept being assessed is Equality. Candidates are required to use understanding of the concept to provide detailed descriptions with relevant examples and appropriate generalisations.

Up to 3 marks will be awarded for a description depending on quality, relevance, accuracy and level of detail.

Candidates are required to consider both health and wealth inequalities. Answers that fail to do this should be awarded a maximum of 5 marks.

Answers may include:
Health Inequalities

• Some elderly people experience great health problems which make their daily life very difficult. For example, they may suffer from Dementia, Alzheimer's Disease, Arthritis, Parkinson's Disease and many other illnesses which become increasingly common in old age.
• Other elderly people have no serious health concerns, and enjoy an active life often participating in activities such as sport, leisure and travel.
• Some elderly people enjoy the benefits of private health care, allowing them to see a doctor and receive treatment quickly and conveniently.
• Other elderly people have no access to private health care, relying only on the NHS. This often means delays in receiving treatment.
• Any other valid point.

Wealth Inequalities

• Elderly people who depend only on welfare benefits from the government have a low standard of living. This is because the state retirement pension and pension credit are thought to be the minimum amount needed to provide for the basic necessities of life. There is little left for luxuries such as holidays, leisure and running a car.
• Housing is a very big expense, and poor elderly people may find it difficult to run, modernise and repair their house. As a result, many old people live in houses that are cold, damp and in a poor state of repair.

- Those elderly people who have additional sources of income such as savings, private and/or occupational pensions can afford a much better lifestyle. This often includes frequent holidays, membership of golf and leisure facilities, dining out with friends, and car ownership.
- Any other valid point.

(b) Candidates are required to provide evidence to support and oppose a given point of view.

Up to 2 marks will be awarded for a reason, depending on the relevance and development of the evidence.

Answers must make explicit links between the Information about Dunelder and The Technology Park and Sources 1 and 2. Answers that do not make explicit links will be awarded 0 marks.

Candidates who fail to explain why they rejected the other company will be awarded a maximum of 6 marks.

Answers may include:
For Wave Power Systems
- The company needs access to the sea to allow them to test and transport their products. According to the map, there is a harbour in the town with a road running from it to the technology park.
- There will be a health and fitness centre at the new factory for both employees and local residents. This will be good, as 45% of people in Dunelder take no exercise – well above the Scottish average of 38%.
- The research centre will need the cooperation of at least 2 other companies involved in renewable energy. The technology park would provide this as there are already factories producing solar heating panels and blades for wind turbines.

Against Wave Power Systems
- Close links with a nearby university are very important to Wave Power Systems, but the information says that there is no university nearby – only an agricultural college.
- The owner of Wave Power Systems says that local people agree with him that renewable energy is the most important way of improving the environment. However, the survey shows that people in Dunelder think that both "Less air pollution" (25%) and "More nuclear power" (24%) are more important to them than "More renewable energy" (13%).

For Earth Save Insulation
- 150 jobs will be created, suitable for people with only basic skills. Dunelder has many people available for work, and they are mainly low-skilled.
- The factory will create a lot of excess heat, which will be made available to heat houses that are nearby. The map shows that there are eco-friendly homes next to the technology park, which would benefit from this.
- The management team that will be moving into the area need affordable good quality housing. A new development of luxury homes has recently been completed just outside Dunelder, and these are available at reduced prices.

Against Earth Save Insulation
- The company would need at least £5 million in financial assistance within the first 5 years. The information makes it clear that there is only £4 million available, and that is over 4 years.
- The owner of Earth Save Insulation says that his company should get the site because the people in Dunelder think that house insulation is the most important way of helping the environment. This is not

the case, as "Less air pollution" (25%) and "More nuclear power" (24%) are both more important than "More home insulation" (15%).

Syllabus Area 3 – Ideologies

THE USA

3A (a) The concept being assessed is Participation. Candidates are required to use their understanding of the concept to provide descriptions in depth and detail.
Up to 3 marks will be awarded for a description depending on the quality of description, relevance, accuracy and level of detail.

Answers that do not mention detailed American examples will be awarded a maximum of 5 marks.

Answers may include:
- Joining a political party, such as the Democrats or Republicans, and voting at the national party convention.
- Standing as a candidate in local, state or federal elections. For example, McCain, Clinton and Obama in the 2008 Presidential election state primaries and Hilary Clinton for Senate in 2006.
- Fundraising for the political party of their choice.
- Forming a new political party or movement such as the 'Tea Party'.
- Door-to-door canvassing for the political party of their choice.
- Write to the editor of a local or national newspaper to express your opinion on government policy towards a political issue. For example, writing to the Washington Post with your opinions on the War on Terror.
- Protest with a demonstration against a bill being passed in Congress.
- Join an interest group, such as the NRA or Emily's List, and lobbying Congress about a bill.
- Any other valid point.

(b) Candidates are required to state a hypothesis relevant to the issue of '**Employment in the USA**'.

Up to 2 marks will be awarded for a hypothesis depending on the level of insight displayed.

For example:
The following receive 0 marks
- Lots of people are employed in the USA.
- Having employment is important in the USA.

The following receive 1 mark
- Hispanics are employed most in the USA.
- Help for the unemployed costs a lot in the USA.

The following receive 2 marks
- The credit crunch is causing employment problems for all Americans.
- The unemployed in the USA do not get enough government help to live on.
- Any other valid hypothesis.

(c) Candidates are required to state aims relevant to their hypothesis.

1 mark for will be each aim depending on its relevance to the hypothesis.

For example:
Hypothesis: 'The credit crunch is causing employment problems for all Americans.'

The following receive 0 marks
- To find out about employment.
- To find out about the car industry.

The following receive 1 mark

- To find out how the credit crunch can affect families in the USA.
- To find out if blacks have the worst employment problems.
- To find out the reasons for different employment rates among ethnic groups.
- Any other valid aim.

(d) Candidates are required to identify questions which are poorly expressed and to explain why.

1 mark will be awarded for correctly identifying each poorly expressed question.

1 mark will be awarded for each correct reason.

(e) Candidates are required to demonstrate an awareness of the benefits of the source provided.

Up to 2 marks will be awarded for a reason depending upon the quality, relevance and accuracy of the reason provided.

The following reasons receive 1 mark

- The poll was conducted countrywide.
- The poll shows the answers from a lot of people.
- The poll has been carried out by USA Today.
- The poll was done recently.
- The poll has a wide range of questions.

The following reasons receive 2 marks

- The survey has a wide range of ages so that it compares what people of different ages think.
- The poll shows the answer from 1,000 people over 18, which is a very large amount and much larger than I could ask.
- The poll has been conducted by USA Today and so will be trustworthy information from an important US newspaper.
- It was conducted on May 6th 2011 which is very recent so the information is very up-to-date.
- The poll has a wide range of questions and answers that can be turned into graphs or tables.
- Any other valid reason.

CHINA

3B (a) The concept being assessed is Participation. Candidates are required to use understanding of the concept to provide detailed descriptions with relevant examples and appropriate generalisations.
Up to 3 marks will be awarded for a description depending upon the quality of description, relevance and accuracy. Credit highly those candidates who provide detailed exemplification in their answer.

Answers that do not mention detailed Chinese examples will be awarded a maximum of 5 marks.

Answers may include:
Join a political party
- Membership of the party is strictly controlled and is often essential for success in business. Ordinary citizens can be invited to join. Eight other parties are legal but do not act as "opposition" eg China Democratic League, Chinese Peasants' and Workers' Democratic Party.

Banned opposition/dissent
- Several banned organisations offer the chance to participate but these carry the risk of arrest and imprisonment eg Falun Gong. Independence movements for Taiwan and Tibet have been banned and their members persecuted.

Pressure groups
- 2010 saw large scale protests in China over several issues like the farmers in Jiangsu province protesting about land relocation or those in Yunan province who have protested about state land acquisition.

Public Opinion System
- More than 70% of the county-level governments have established a Public Opinion System. They hold public hearings, meetings and discussions to find out public opinion on new laws.

Female Participation
- The All-China Women's Federation (linked to Communist Party) campaigns to promote equality. Small success in recent years – small increase in female candidates.

- Any other valid point.

(b) Candidates are required to state a hypothesis relevant to the issue of 'Employment in China'.

Up to 2 marks will be awarded for a hypothesis depending on the level of insight displayed.

For example:
The following receive 0 marks:
- Lots of people are employed in China.
- Having employment is important in China.

The following receive 1 mark:
- Many people are unemployed in China.
- It is easy to find a job in China.

The following receive 2 marks:
- Manufacturing is the most common type of work in China.
- Foreign companies will only locate in Special Economic Zones in China.
- Any other valid hypothesis.

(c) Candidates are required to state aims relevant to their hypothesis.

1 mark will be awarded for each aim depending on the relevance to the hypothesis.

For example:
Hypothesis: 'Foreign companies will only locate in Special Economic Zones in China.'

The following receive 0 marks
- To find out about employment.
- To find out about industry in China.

The following receive 1 mark
- To find out where foreign companies are located in Special Economic Zones.
- To find out why foreign companies will only locate in Special Economic Zones.
- To find out why foreign firms will not locate in rural China.
- Any other valid aim.

(d) Candidates are required to identify questions which are poorly expressed and to explain why.

1 mark will be awarded for correctly identifying each poorly expressed question.

1 mark will be awarded for each correct reason.

The correct responses are:

Question 2

How old are you?

Under 15   15-30   30-50   50-70   70 or older

Reason poorly worded

Some of the ages (15, 30, 50, 70) appear in 2 categories which would lead to confusion.

Question 4

Why do you think illegal rural immigrants should not get health care in the cities?

Reason poorly worded

It is a leading question and assumes that all people think illegal rural immigrants should not get health care.

(e) Candidates are required to demonstrate an awareness of the benefits of the source provided.

Up to 2 marks will be awarded for a reason depending upon the quality, relevance and accuracy of the reason provided.

The following reasons receive 1 mark

- The poll was conducted countrywide.
- The poll shows the answers from a lot of people.
- The poll has been carried out by China Today.
- The poll was done recently.
- The poll has a wide range of questions.

The following reasons receive 2 marks

- The survey has a wide range of ages so that it compares what people of different ages think.
- The poll shows the answer from 1,000 people over 18, which is a very large amount and much larger than I could ask.
- The poll has been conducted by China Today and so will be trustworthy information from an important Chinese newspaper.
- It was conducted on May 6th 2011 which is very recent so the information is very up-to-date.
- The poll has a wide range of questions and answers that can be turned into graphs or tables.

Syllabus Area 4 – International Relations

4. (a) The concept being assessed is Need. Candidates are required to use their understanding of the concept to provide explanations in depth and detail.

Up to 3 marks will be awarded for a description depending on quality, relevance, accuracy and level of detail.

A maximum of 5 marks will be awarded to an answer which only refers to 1 policy

Answers may include:

Enlarged Membership

- Enlargement tries to meet the needs of EU member states by creating a larger market for products manufactured within the EU as there are few obstacles to trade.
- It allows workers to travel eg UK citizens working in holiday resorts on the Mediterranean.
- All European citizens benefit from having neighbours that are stable democracies and prosperous market economies.
- Enlargement is a carefully managed process which helps the transformation of the countries involved, extending peace, stability, prosperity, democracy, human rights and the rule of law across Europe.

Common Fisheries Policy

- The CFP tries to meet the needs of EU member states by ensuring that there will be fish stocks in the future by setting quotas and facilitating the decommissioning of vessels.
- This allows fish stocks to be conserved. This is important as many jobs in coastal areas of Europe (including Scotland) are dependent on fishing and fish processing.

Aid to the Regions

- Aid to the regions tries to meet the needs of EU member states by giving aid to poorer regions of the EU. For example, the Highlands and Islands of Scotland have received money to improve transport links to try and improve employment in remote areas.
- Several of the new member states such as the Baltic States (Estonia, Latvia, and Lithuania) are benefitting from this policy.

European Defence Force

- The policy on defence tries to meet the needs of Europeans by getting the members to work co-operatively to protect Europeans by providing manpower and equipment. In 2004, Eufor took over peace keeping in Bosnia-Herzegovina providing over 6 000 troops.
- The EDF has also been involved in the Democratic Republic of Congo, Georgia, Indonesia, Sudan and Palestine.

Common Agricultural Policy

- The CAP tries to meet the needs of EU member states by supporting agriculture.
- It was reformed in 2004 as it was no longer meeting the needs of citizens as it was paying farmers to grow crops that were not needed.
- Farmers mainly now receive money through the Single Farm Payment Scheme (SFPS).
- It also now tries to maintain the environment eg special payments for farmers who look after hedgerows etc.

Single European Currency

- The Euro tries to meet the needs of EU member states by enabling businesses to deal with each other in the same currency. This saves time, reduces conversion charges and encourages trade.
- Citizens are able to travel within the "eurozone" and not worry about changing money, thus increasing convenience for tourists.
- A single currency makes Europe a strong partner to trade with and facilitates access to a genuine single market for foreign companies, who will benefit from lower costs of doing business in Europe.
- Any other valid point on these policies.

(b) Candidates are required to provide evidence to support and oppose a given point of view.

Up to 2 marks will be awarded for a reason depending on the relevance and development of the evidence.

Candidates who do not make an explicit link between the view and the sources will be awarded a maximum of 2 marks.

The correct responses are:

View of Darren McCourt:

"Of all Libya's trading partners, Spain has seen the biggest increase in average income."

Reason to support:
Source 2 supports this part of the view. Spain's average income has grown by $20,300 in the period shown. This is more than any other country.

View of Darren McCourt:
"Libya's biggest trading partner is also the country with the highest average income in both years."

Reason to oppose:
Sources 1 and 2 oppose this part of the view. Libya's biggest trading partner is Italy. However, the country with the highest average income in 2000 and in 2009 was the USA.

(*c*) Candidates are required to detect and explain examples of lack of objectivity in complex sources, giving developed argument when required.

Up to 2 marks will be awarded for an example of selectivity or otherwise, depending on the quality of explanation.

A maximum of 2 marks will be awarded for each part of the view, and a maximum of 2 marks for an overall conclusion as to the extent of selectivity.

Answers which do not make an explicit link between the view and the sources, will be awarded a maximum of 4 marks.

The correct responses are:

"It is obvious that increasing aid always reduces poverty in African countries."

From Sources 1 and 3
In all the countries shown there has been an increase in the amount of aid given between 2003 and 2008 (Source 3). However, this has not created a reduction in poverty in four out of the five. Ethiopia is the only country to have experienced a fall in poverty during this period (Source 1). **This shows that Ruby is incorrect.**

"It is also a fact that most countries with increasing debt are unable to reduce the problem of HIV/AIDS."

From Sources 1 and 3
Source 3 shows that debt is increasing in Botswana, Lesotho, Swaziland and Zimbabwe. However, only Botswana has shown an increase in the percentage of adults living with HIV/AIDS (Source 1). The other three have all seen a decrease in the percentage of adults living with HIV/AIDS. **This shows that Ruby is incorrect.**

"However, despite these problems, education in the majority of African countries has improved."

From Source 2
Source 2 shows that there have been improvements in education in Lesotho (increasing spending to 13% of GDP); in Botswana where literacy rates have increased from 80% to 84% and in Swaziland where literacy rates have also increased (74% to 81%). Only Zimbabwe has not shown an improvement in education. Therefore, education has improved in most countries. **This shows that Ruby is correct.**

Overall, Ruby was correct in one statement and incorrect in the other two. Therefore, she was being very selective in her use of the facts.

Hey! I've done it